Transformative Research and Higher Education

Transformative Research and Higher Education

EDITED BY

AZRIL BACAL ROIJ

Uppasala University, Sweden

United Kingdom – North America – Japan – India – Malaysia – China

Emerald Publishing Limited
Howard House, Wagon Lane, Bingley BD16 1WA, UK

First edition 2022

Reprints and permissions service
Contact: permissions@emeraldinsight.com

British Library Cataloguing in Publication Data
A catalogue record for this book is available from the British Library

ISBN: 978-1-80117-695-8 (Print)
ISBN: 978-1-80117-694-1 (Online)
ISBN: 978-1-80117-696-5 (Epub)

Printed and bound by CPI Group (UK) Ltd, Croydon, CR0 4YY

ISOQAR certified
Management System,
awarded to Emerald
for adherence to
Environmental
standard
ISO 14001:2004.

Certificate Number 1985
ISO 14001

INVESTOR IN PEOPLE

Table of Contents

About the Editor

Azril Bacal Roij has a PhD in Sociology from Uppsala University. He is currently CEMUS affiliate at Uppsala University and Swedish Agricultural University (SLU) and Professor on Peace Education at CIPAE-Puebla, Mexico (2005–2021); a Guest lecturer in Participatory Action-Research at Mälardalen University-Eskilstuna (2017–2021), Sweden (R); Senior Lecturer in Sociology and Cultural Studies (1993–2006); Visiting Lecturer in Urban Planning at UCLA (1996); and has been part of Rural Development team at the University of Córdoba (2001–2003). He was also an Endowment Humanities Scholar, at Otterbein College (1995); University Teacher and Researcher ('Prototype of Integrated Farming') at Colegio de Postgraduados, Mexico (1981–1987); Associate Professor of Human Sciences at UNALM, Perú (1967–1980, 2011–2015); Guest lecturer at the Anthropology Department, Uppsala University; Advisor to the Minister of Agriculture (Agrarian Reform, Rural Development, Peasant Training, Peasant Radio-Forum program), Perú; Academic Coordinator for the Latin American Master Program in Communication (1967–1969); Chairman of Anthropology and Sociology at UDLAP-Puebla, México (1983–1985); Consultant at UNESCO-OREALC (Teacher-Training in Rural and Areas of Marginal Latin America 1981–1982) and at IIIA ('Rural Development in Indigenous Areas of Latin America'); and Academic Coordinator of the workshops 'Conflict Prevention and Management', PCRI-Uppsala University-UNALM, Perú (2013–2017). His research includes Ethnicity; Ethno-Politics; Ethnic Discrimination; Participatory Experiential Action-Research; White Nationalist-Populism; Rural Development; Self-Management; Higher Education; Quality of Working Life and Democratization – in Latin America, SIDA (1989–1991); ethnic identity of elder Latinas, Research Program on Ethnic Aging, Research & Development, Social Services and Ethnology Department, Stockholm (1993–1997). He is a member of 'Red Universidad y Compromiso Social', Seville, Red Paulo Freire, Swedish PAR Association (SPARC); board member of research committees 10, 05, 26, International Sociological Association; IRIPAZ; former member at Paulo Freire Institute. He is a popular educator and cultural worker at the film and poetry forum: 'equal value of all human beings', cultural division, Uppsala Municipal Council. He has published poems in Spanish, Swedish and English. He is an engaged scholar in social movements for environmental, climate justice and peace.

About the Contributors

Dr John Andersen is Professor in Sociology and Planning at Roskilde University, Denmark. He worked as research and development consultant in the third European Anti-poverty Programme, and was a Councilor in the City of Copenhagen (2014–2017). His research is rooted in action research and case study traditions and is focused on peoples' empowerment and capacity building in urban and rural communities.

Dr Umut Erel is Professor of Sociology at the Open University, UK. She has widely published on the intersections of migration, ethnicity, citizenship, racism, gender and class. Her methodological interests are in creative and participatory methods for research and engagement. For recent publications, see http://www.open.ac.uk/people/ue27.

Dr John Foran is Distinguished Professor of Sociology at UC Santa Barbara, California. His teaching centres on confronting the climate crisis through social movements and systemic alternatives beyond capitalism. He is Co-director of NXTerra (https://www.nxterra.orfaleacenter.ucsb.edu/), a platform for teachers and students of the climate crisis, climate justice and critical sustainability. He participates in the Eco Vista project (www.ecovistacommunity.com), Transition US (https://www.transitionus.org/), and the Global Tapestry of Alternatives (https://globaltapestryofalternatives.org/).

Dr Martin Severin Frandsen is Associate Professor of Urban Planning at Roskilde University, Denmark. His research revolves around questions of participation, segregation, disadvantaged urban areas and sustainability. Methodologically, he combines the historical study of the emergence and transformation of problems with action research and experimental engagement in working out solutions to these problems. https://forskning.ruc.dk/en/persons/martinfr.

Erene Kaptani is a participatory performance artist, social scientist, drama therapist and PhD candidate in Sociology and Theatre at the University of Greenwich. She employs narrative and movement-based methods of improvisation, Physical and Forum Theatre for social research, community development and public impact. She has produced and performed plays at Studio Upstairs Arts Community at Playback South Theatre Company. She published academic papers, storytelling for displacement and spoken word in journals and media. https://erenekaptani.wordpress.com/.

Dr Frans Lenglet has a PhD in Education from Stanford University, and works as an independent researcher in the domain of education and sustainability. He was Director of the Swedish International Centre of Education for Sustainable Development at Uppsala University, Sweden. He is a member of a number of international networks supporting individuals and collectivities in making decisions and acting on choices about just cultural, social, economic and bio-physical conditions affecting their livelihoods and well-being, as well as those of other people and future generations.

Dr Erik Lindhult is a Senior Lecturer, Innovation, Management & Entrepreneurship at Mälardalen University, Sweden. His main area of research is participatory, collaborative and democratic innovation and action research, as well as entrepreneurship for a sustainable development of society. He is board member of Swedish Participatory Action Research Society (SPARC), Swedish Interactive Research Association (SIRA), and associate board member of ISA's Research Committee 10 Participation, Organizational Democracy and Self-management.

Dr Vicente Manzano-Arrondo is Professor of Behavioral Research at University of Seville, Spain. He has a PhD in Psychology, Education and Economics, with postgraduate studies in inter-linguistics (focused on Esperanto). Once acknowledged as best psychology teacher in Spain, his research explores ways to overcome oppression in the realms of academics and linguistics. As an engaged researcher, he builds collaborative channels between the university and social movements, to place the university at the service of people systematically neglected in most societies.

Dr Christina Marouli studied Biochemistry, Urban and Environmental Policy, and Sociology. She is an Associate Professor at the Environmental Studies program of DEREE – the American College of Greece, where she founded and directed the Center of Excellence for Sustainability. She is an experienced consultant on environmental issues and women's and children's issues. She won a Fulbright Award for research on multicultural environmental education. Her research interests include sustainable cities, education for sustainability and social change, and food waste.

Dr Maggie O'Neill is Professor in Sociology at University College Cork, Head of the Department of Sociology & Criminology and member of the Centre for the Study of the Moral Foundations of Economy and Society. Maggie does participatory research on asylum, migration and gender, using biographical and arts-based methods, collaborating with artists and communities. Her concept of 'ethno-mimesis' articulates ethnographic and arts-based (walking) research. She has researched and published on critical theory, PAR, sex work and migration, asylum and borders.

Dr Tracey Reynolds is Professor of Social Sciences and Director of the Centre for Applied Sociology Research at the University of Greenwich. Tracey's teaching and research areas include an interest in Black and racialised migrant mothering, families and communities. Tracey's most recent projects deal with neighbourhood organizations, using creative, participatory and co-produced projects to explore migrant families' community resilience, and the impact of the United Kingdom's hostile environment policies during the COVID-19 pandemic.

Acknowledgements

Warm thanks are due to Kimberley Chadwick, at Emerald Publishers (UK), Rasoul Nejadmehr at FID, Gothenburg (Sweden), and Annette Bilfeldt and John Andersen at Aalborg Universitetsforlag (Denmark), the kind publishers who granted the green light to draw excerpts from my recent publications, respectively, The Legacy of Dorothy Lee and Paulo Freire to Active Learning in Higher Education (Bacal, 2018): *The Contributions of Paulo Freire to Intercultural Dialogue* (Bacal, 2018) and *The Promise and Challenges of Transformative Participatory Action-Research in the 21st Century: The Legacy of Paulo Freire and Orlando Fals-Borda* (Bacal, 2018). I am deeply indebted to Frans Lenglet and Christina Marouli, for their careful reading and constructive suggestions which considerably contributed to improve on the coherence and legibility of this text.

Introduction

Azril Bacal Roij

Summary

The aim in this book is to contribute to the contemporary efforts to replace the hegemonic neoliberal university with an alternative collaborative academic system. This alternative approach to university life and knowledge democracy is already under construction. The authors of this anthology join in this respect an emerging global network of concerned scholars, who are currently engaged in dialogue with civil society and social movements. In arguing for the transformation of research and education, this book provides concrete examples of creativity, innovativeness and knowledge democracy in this endeavour. This paradigmatic shift is called for against the backdrop of a generalized global crisis. The authors seek in this context to enhance the agenda, curricula and debate on how a transformed university might help in the construction of another possible post-pandemic world built on premises of justice and peace. This book shares pertinent insights from classical authors like Dorothy Lee, Paulo Freire and Orlando Fals-Borda, with up-to-date innovative practices in research and higher education.

Context

When approaching this academic venture, we are painfully aware that the situation of the world has dramatically changed in the past years due to the COVID-19 pandemic and climate change. This global emergency confronts humanity and universities with severe problems, challenges and new possibilities. The features of this crisis come in the guise of environmental and tropical forest devastation, zoonotic diseases, humanitarian refugee catastrophe, growing militarism, neo-liberalization of research and education and the return of far-right social movements to the international political arena. These features unveil nonetheless how global inequalities correlate with zoonotic diseases and global warming. While not dwelling in depth with these issues, the authors highlight the pervasive lack of vision and democratic governance in the world system of research and higher education.

This generalized neglect reflects the spell of the neoliberal agenda, associated with ideological premises of market fundamentalism and privatization of the fruits of public research and education via patents and the like. The authors

Transformative Research and Higher Education, 1–10
Copyright © 2022 Azril Bacal Roij
Published under exclusive licence by Emerald Publishing Limited
doi:10.1108/978-1-80117-694-120221001

contend that after the pandemic is over, there is no going back to the situation of 'business as usual'. The present venture is an attempt made by a small collective of critical scholars to examine and respond to various problematic features of this global crisis, thereby proposing viable changes in the institutional frameworks of research and education. Historically, most of the production and transfer of knowledge take place in elitist and increasingly privatized spaces of research and education. At the same time, transformative research and education are emancipatory tools available in the university world. This anthology weaves together theoretical insights and practical guidelines on how to surpass conventional ways of designing and conducting research and education. These reflections are here with shared with colleagues and students immersed in the realms of research and learning. Thereby the authors seek to include them in the crucial collaborative task of surmounting together the threatening clouds looming on the world horizon.

Perspective

What then is the role of the new paradigm and praxis of research and higher education envisaged by the authors? The vision in this book entails the need to scrutinize the ways in which the organizational design, curricula and institutional operation of schools and universities might be functionally irrelevant at best. The authors propose concrete ways to replace obsolete features previously mentioned. The pedagogical legacy of Paulo Freire is a common thread of inspiration in the chapters in this book. While not completely new for readers familiar with his work, this book appeals to a younger generation of scholars, teachers and students, unaware of his seminal contributions. This book highlights the seminal contributions of Paulo Freire to awareness-raising pedagogics via critical teaching and learning, participatory action-research, cultural dialogue and hope. In this light, the reader is better able to understand the consequences from the educational counter-reforms by military regimes in Latin America (for example, in the mid-sixties in Brazil and 1973 in Chile). This authoritarian wave hit the world at large after the fall of the Berlin Wall in 1989, resulting in the hegemony of the neoliberal doctrine of instructional education.

In the light of the international celebration of Freire's 100th birthday anniversary, Vicente Manzano-Arrondo examines in Chapter 8 of this anthology the dual role of universities. On the one hand, helping to reproduce societal conditions of vertical hierarchy and conformity.

On the other hand, helping the human potential and creativity of researchers, teachers and students presently engaged in the production, diffusion, dialogue and access to useful knowledge by people who need it the most. A common bond shared by the authors is the belief that it is possible and desirable to make timely changes in universities, aligned with the ongoing efforts by civil society to change the world. This viewpoint is arguably one strategic mission of a post-neoliberal university adopted by the authors, who both examine and respond to the reductionist policies and privatization mantra pushed by the neoliberal agenda of research and the banking approach to education. To counteract the damage, this book presents a wide variety of approaches, definitions and case studies. The prefix transformative points to a paradigmatic shift from the production of knowledge that in the past benefited the privileged few to a new paradigm endorsed in this book. This new paradigm seeks to ensure that the fruits of research and education directly benefit the common good, as proposed by the university reform movements in the past. Given the existing limitations of time and space, this volume does not cover all possible regions and ethno-cultural diversity of the world. It is nonetheless an attempt to respond to the challenges of the contemporary world situation, where the authors raise and seek answers to questions about contemporary research and higher education, in timely and significant ways.

Freire as Inspiration

The common theme that frames and weaves together the various chapters in this book lies in the pedagogical pertinence of Paulo Freire, seeking to link his insights with contemporary research findings. The enclosed chapters provide the reader with concrete examples of viable changes in research and education. Transformative education alludes to personal and organizational changes in teachers, students, curricula, school organization and decision-making process. In this regard, learning is a life-long process, as suggested by UNESCO. It also pays attention to often neglected formative values of students that support their autonomy, critical thinking, awareness and engagement in society as concerned citizens. As proposed by Freire, education is either oppressive and alienating or liberating and emancipatory.

In a similar way, transformative research refers to changing the conventional ways of doing research, by making it more participatory by empowering researched communities and enhancing their role as citizens in society. Culture dialogue entails ways to address and respectfully deal and overcome ethnocentric bias in research and higher education. Participatory action-research is one way to bridge the realms of research and higher education, by making research an integral part of the educational process and education more research-oriented. Looking at the two-faced academic *Janus*, the authors contend that the modus operandi of universities makes them an integral part of the problems in question.[1] At the same time, this book shows that universities are privileged social spaces where social knowledge is available for the common good.[2] This anthology collects and shares the actual experience and reflections from a small network of engaged scholars who dwell in various disciplines and different corners of the Western world. While some chapters are more theoretical in character, the book provides useful examples and practical resources, available for those interested in transforming university research and education to overcome world problems and challenges. The authors argue in this light for the need to change the university as an integral part of social transformation.

Study Problems

The key study problems and issues addressed in this book read as follows: (1) In current education, too much emphasis is placed on learning instruction and student motivational techniques, while critical thinking and formative values receive insufficient attention. (2) The academic division of labour that divorces teaching/learning activities from research. (3) The perils to democracy from cultural intolerance, racism and neo-fascism. (4) The threats to the planet and civilization from environmental and social devastation in the Anthropocene. (5) The many structural and cultural barriers that block the way of social change and university transformation. (6) The severity of climate change turned into a climate emergency. (7) Due to restrictive migratory policies, migrant families confront increasing 'hostile environments' in the rich world. (8) Top-down urban planning and unsustainable city growth are narrowing the options for humane and sustainable spatial conditions. (9) Technocratic and undemocratic tendencies characterize conventional science and modes of enquiry. (10) The complexity of 'Wicked' problems and dilemmas demand innovative and interdisciplinary practices in research and education. (11) The mounting costs and negative consequences for society from the operation of absurd and dysfunctional universities.

Some of the corresponding research questions were, for example, how to align theory, methodology and social practice with ethical, philosophical and democratic values? What changes in research and educational institutions are necessary? What are the resources needed to surmount the challenges and obstacles lying ahead in our path to transform research and teaching/learning? What is the intended audience of readers we want to reach with this publication? A particular contribution of this book lies in the historical, geographical, positional and situated diversity of the authors' backgrounds.

Brief Synopsis of the Chapters

In Chapter 1: 'Active Learning, Participatory Action-Research and Intercultural Dialogue' regarded as three windows to look at transformative research and higher education. Azril Bacal at the Sociology Department, Uppsala University and CIPAE-Puebla, México, introduces significant contributions made by Dorothy Lee, Paulo Freire and Orlando Fals-Borda to these study fields, from a perspective of dialogue, hope, autonomy, self-determination, democracy, justice and peace. These value premises provide the theoretical and normative threads weaving together the research and reflections by Bacal on these subjects. The author also borrowed selected insights from Martin Buber, Dag Hammarskjöld and Federico Mayor Zaragoza, concerned with the role of dialogue in building community, democracy, diplomacy and sustainable peace. The aims in this study are to help raise the awareness and behaviour of our fellow colleagues, young scholars and concerned citizens and to help them bridge the realms of theory, research, social knowledge and innovations, to guide our transformative praxis. The illustrations and included vignettes mirror the life-long experience and reflections of the author. In the end, the author contends in this chapter that the living legacy of the alluded authors defies the passage of time, in an era that prizes absurdity and the latest academic fad.

In Chapter 2 on 'Critical Pedagogy for Environmental and Social Change: How? What Helps? What Obstructs? Theory and Practice in Dialogue', Christina Marouli, currently an Associate Professor in Environmental Studies at Deree American College of Greece, invites the reader to acknowledge the fact that contemporary societies face serious environmental and social challenges that require decisive action.

In 1970, Environmental Education (EE) was first introduced as a method to raise awareness about environmental problems and also to bring about needed changes in social practices that can lead to environmental protection, and more recently sustainable development (transforming EE – to Education for Sustainability (EfS)). In the context of EE and EfS and aiming to change behaviour, a task akin to critical pedagogics intended to encourage and empower citizens to solve the alluded social problems, the author raises the following questions: What pedagogical approaches and educational methods are more effective in bringing about changes in attitudes and social practices? Which are the keys of instructional design and practice that facilitate such transformation? What are the challenges? These questions trouble environmental educators and are worth reflecting on, in the present context of knowledge societies and of higher education significantly impacted by a neoliberal ideology. This chapter contributes to the ongoing discussion on these questions, through dialogue between theory and practice. Framed by critical theory and pedagogics, both EE and EfS unveil many theoretical insights based in the author's more than 30-years teaching experience (primarily in Greece). A discussion of the instructor's key pedagogical influences and the evolution of her instructional practices follows, to identify instructional practices that have a transformative potential, within the context of the challenges and facilitating parameters of contemporary societies and educational contexts. The author's self-reflections as an instructor in addition to the analysis of the students' qualitative comments in course evaluations and other informal evaluative situations enhance a self-study research approach. The author ends this chapter with the parable of Plato's cave, aiming to highlight the key elements of transformative educational praxis such as: The freeing of the body to involve the whole learner (body, mind, spirit) in the learning process; to create supportive and loving learning environments that incite wonder, imagination and hope; to democratize learning environments and thereby help students to connect with their wondering selves and critical consciousness; and to connect educational contexts with the local community and nature, thereby fostering relevant learning and wonder-creating learning settings.

In Chapter 3: 'Transforming the University to Confront the Climate Crisis', John Foran, a university professor of sociology and environmental studies at the University of California, Santa Barbara, draws from his teaching about movements for radical social change for many years.

For the last decade, the author has dedicated his attention to questions of how to transform the university to confront the climate crisis. His chapter explores the crisis of higher education with respect to the most pressing existential challenge of the twenty first century and proposes various approaches, actions, activities and projects for both classroom teachers and networks of educators. There is a long list of innovative experiences in higher education developed by the author, among which stand out the UC-CSU NXTerra Knowledge Action Network, the University of California at Santa Barbara (UCSB) developed a nearly carbon neutral conference, and the students engaged in the design and implementation of systemic alternatives outside the classroom and in their own communities. One such student research and social change project is Eco Vista, with the 23,000-member mixture of students and the more permanent inhabitants of Isla Vista, a neighbourhood adjacent to UCSB, presented as just one example among others. The UC-CSU NXTerra Knowledge Action Network is another example of collaboration of 15 faculties from the University of California and California State University systems that produces teaching resources on the climate crisis, climate justice and critical sustainability for university (and high school) teachers and their students. This happens across all disciplines, thereby establishing a bridge of the humanities with the social and natural sciences. Currently comprising 17 'topics', these scholars invite new topics through a network strategy of connection with fellow teachers who might add to and/or deepen the range and scope of pedagogies with which the climate crisis is addressed. The essay ends with a vision of new type of university, exemplified in the world spanning Ecoversities Alliance and dreamed of in 'Transition U and Eco Vista U', two prototypes of participatory action-research and active higher education currently being co-created by students, staff, faculty and community members in Santa Barbara, California, and in the Transition US movement.

Chapter 4 presents the main features of a study entitled: 'PAR: Resistance to Racist Migration Policies in the UK', by Umut Erel, Erene Kaptani, Maggie O'Neill and Tracey Reynolds, at the School of Social Sciences and Global Studies, Faculty of Arts and Social Sciences, The Open University, United K. The authors share their research findings from the collaborative research project 'PASAR: Participatory Arts and Social Action in Research' in (http://fass.open.ac.uk/research/projects/pasar).

It combines the participatory action-research methods of participatory theatre and walking methods in order to understand the way in which racialized migrant women challenge their exclusion and subjugation in the context of the United Kingdom. The problematic situation of migrant families in the United Kingdom points to the 'hostile environment' and migratory policy. This policy 'is a sprawling web of immigration controls embedded in the heart of our public services and communities'. The government requires employers, landlords, private sector workers, NHS staff and other public servants to check a person's immigration status before they can offer them a job, housing, healthcare or other support. Migrant families are casted as outsiders to citizenship, challenging the social and cultural cohesion of the nation. Indeed, UK immigration policies render it difficult for migrant families to secure their social and economic reproduction. Against this backdrop, the researchers explore how racialized migrant families develop their subjugated knowledge to claim belonging and participate in the society they live in. The authors share their the key methodological findings, challenges and benefits of working with a PAR approach for co-producing knowledge with a potential of fostering transformation, together with migrant families and advocacy organizations. The authors reflect on the potential for transformation of these methods for research purposes and additionally show the use of these methods to develop a kind of citizenship practice of transformation together with research participants.

In Chapter 5: Action Research in Planning Education: The Legacy of Paulo Freire at Roskilde University, John Andersen and Martin Severin Frandsen, at Roskilde University, Denmark, tell us that Roskilde University came into being in 1972, as a result from the 1968 student revolt. Established as a critical reform university, it adopted the principle of interdisciplinarity, with the vision to be participant problem-oriented and project learning process (PPL). The university launched a new master's programme in Urban Planning in the year 2009. This chapter presents the experiences from student projects working with action research in facilitating citizen-driven urban development, taking into account the following considerations: In the first place, students outline the key theoretical foundations of the Planning Studies programme: planning as social learning, empowerment and social mobilization. Secondly, the principles of Roskilde University pedagogical model (PPL) are rooted in the tradition of experiential and critical pedagogy of Oskar Negt, John Dewey, Paulo Freire and others.

The chapter presents two concrete cases of problem-oriented projects working with action research in bottom-up urban planning and sustainable transition in Copenhagen, the capital of Denmark. The first case concerns the empowerment of young residents in the redesign of a public square through a series of aesthetic experiments. The second case concerns an experiment with alternative transport solutions and sustainable ways of street redesign through the reduction of private car use and the creation of new public spaces on former parking lots. The article concludes with the authors contending that action research in problem-oriented project work is a promising way of involving students in community empowerment processes. Doing participatory action-research strengthens the student's ability to comprehend 'the logic of practice' and their ability to master practical and ethical judgements, in the context of complex real-world empowerment and learning processes. This prepares them for professional practice and provides an embodied and pragmatically empowered understanding of how transformations towards a more sustainable and just society can be brought about.

In Chapter 6: 'The Movement towards Knowledge Democracy in Participatory and Action Research', Erik Lindhult, at the University of Mälardalen, Eskilstuna, Sweden, tells us that one common feature of different variants of participatory and action research is a rejection of technocratic, undemocratic tendencies in science and enquiry. Their purpose is to break the dominance of traditional academic views of science, while opening it up for broader participation of people and emancipating knowledge creation that can produce actionable knowledge with transformative potentials. The purpose of this contribution is to recognize and clarify a striving for 'knowledge democracy', a recent concept still in the process of initial formulation. In this early stage, knowledge democracy denotes a global mobilizing and unifying thinking, to articulate scattered networks and movements in the world, engaged in participatory-oriented research. This vision is rooted in the First Global Assembly for Knowledge Democracy in June 2017, Cartagena, Colombia. Based on his experiences, discussions and mutual reflection in and on this movement in thinking and practice, the author clarifies the emerging meaning and significance of knowledge democracy in a practical, political and at the same time utopian context of engagement and struggle of people engaged in alternative approaches to enquiry and transformation.

In Chapter 7: Frans Lenglet, an independent educational researcher in Uppsala, examines the evolution of 'transformative education', against the background of the world's existential and wicked problems that are posing formidable challenges to mainstream education and learning approaches. This chapter examines the evolution and intellectual sources of theories of education and learning that explicitly focus on transforming the learners' self-understanding as well as the structures, arrangements and formations in which these and their educational and learning processes are embedded. These theories spanning over the last 50 years go beyond the functionalist understanding of education and learning are meant to socialize learners, within existing or dominant cultural and societal structures and/or in function of the transmission of knowledge, skills and attitudes from generation to generation. The ideas of transformative learning or learning for transformation are examined borrowing insights from Freire, Habermas, Mezirow and other. The later discussion continues with an examination of the concepts of collaborative learning, social learning and deliberative social learning, as these evolve into transformative and transgressive learning, by i.a. Wals and Lotz-Sisitka. In the process, a colourful tapestry of transformative education and learning emerges. As shown over time, the pertinence of transformative learning has not diminished but only increased. The evolution of transformative learning presents itself as a virtual cycle, starting from marginalized and 'excluded' people and communities via persons (individuals) engaged in adult education and environmental education, to (groups of) people participating in collaborative and transgressive social learning, thereby becoming capable and empowered actors in processes of change and transformation.

In Chapter 8: 'Finding Hope in the Midst of an Absurd University', Professor Vicente Manzano-Arrondo at Universidad de Sevilla, Spain, confides that it is unfortunately too easy to find examples of absurd functioning in the university. It has never been a perfect institution because that is an impossibility. One observes in recent years that the chronic problems afflicting universities have not disappeared. In the face of a steamroller working at the planetary level, the university has plunged into an even greater absurdity. Paradoxically, we observe that the institution created to be free and work for human emancipation through the expansion of knowledge has chosen to submit itself as a slave to the dynamics of the current global model of society. In doing so, it further fosters slavery by strengthening this global hegemony. Three examples of absurd modus operandi of universities follow next. The first example alludes to the recruitment and shaping of obedient teachers.

The university is not an exception to the banking educational system, as originally described by Freire. Outdated universities raise the production of individual conformity, adaptation and obedience to its maximum exponential. The second example refers to the renunciation of the social usefulness of the knowledge produced at the university. This happens when adopting operational models from the production of commodities, for example, quality measurement, which undermines the institutional mission of universities. The third absurdity alludes to the destruction of thought and language diversity, viewed as two sides of the same coin. While the aforementioned processes are noticeably fast and transcendent, there are better alternatives of higher education underway, which entail encouraging projects and realities under construction. The author mentions other examples of alternative university projects under construction, organically linked with grassroots university movements and, additionally, other socio-educational projects framed by hope. This work highlights the complexity of language pointing to its relative neglect, thereby looking at the dimensions of absurdity and hope in university life.

Concluding Remarks

The reader finds in this book a wide range of useful knowledge and practical resources to change the university and thereby contribute to solving or mitigation of the critical problems today confronted by humanity. The emphasis on transformation points to another kind of research and higher education, based on critical pedagogics, participatory action-research and cultural dialogue. This new paradigm challenges the existing vertical division of academic labour, replaced by a collaborative organization. Useful knowledge is co-produced, framed by a new division of scientific labour, which combines the efforts of the affected population with those of a community of engaged researchers. The readers find in this book various concrete ways to produce, democratize and facilitate accessibility to useful scientific knowledge produced in universities. The prefix transformative points to a paradigmatic shift from the production of knowledge in the worlds of research, and teaching/learning in the world of education, that in the past benefited the privileged few to a new paradigm, in which the fruits of research and education directly benefit the common good. Transformative education points to changes needed in teachers, students, curricula, school organization and decision-making process.

The changes alluded above entail paying attention to the neglected formative values of students in the teaching/learning process, supporting their autonomy, critical thinking and thereby raising their awareness and engagement as responsible 'Citizens for the Future'. In a similar vein, transformative research seeks to make the university more participatory and thereby empowering researched communities and enhancing their role in society. Cultural dialogue alludes to the way to address and transcend the barriers of ethnocentrism in research and higher education. Participatory action-research is one way to bridge the realms of research and higher education. Research is an integral part of the educational process. Given the existing limitations of time and space, this volume does not include all possible regions and ethno-cultural diversity of the world. It represents nonetheless an attempt to respond to the challenges of the contemporary world situation, where the authors raise and seek answers to questions about contemporary research and higher education, in timely and significant ways. Being aware of how Eurocentrism pervades our academic formation, the authors would love to encourage and support the valuable wok of colleagues in the Global South, to similarly collect their experiences and reflections, as they also confront similar problems and challenges of the neo-liberalization of university management, research and education, often with lesser resources available in Global South universities, to fight back the damage from neoliberal globalism to emancipatory research and higher education. Looking forward, the authors seek to expand the innovative horizon of transformative research and education through dialogue with colleagues at ALARA (Action Learning, Action Research Association), SPARC (Swedish Participatory Action Research Community), SIRA (Swedish Interactive Research Association), 'Red Universidad y Compromiso Social' (Seville, Spain), the Global Tapestry of Alternatives (GTA) and other innovative academic spaces. This introductory chapter ends by highlighting some unique features in this book:

(1) A coupling of perennial insights from classical authors with contemporary debate and research.
(2) The experience of writing this book validates Mertens' assertion that 'transformative researchers have the potential to contribute to both personal and societal transformation'.
(3) It supports the view that universities are capable of producing and extending social knowledge useful for the common good.
(4) Last but not least, this book shows the workings of an alternative paradigm and praxis of research and higher education, grounded in experience, which is amply illustrated and empirically documented in the enclosed chapters.

Notes

1. Misuses of the social sciences for colonial and social control purposes are public knowledge today. One finds examples of this kind of research in the work of social scientists to deconstruct post-war welfare societies.
2. The Stockholm and Cambridge schools of political economy helped to design effective ways to manage the 1930 economic and financial crisis of the world system.

Chapter 1

Active Learning, Participatory Action-Research and Intercultural Dialogue in the 21st Century

Azril Bacal Roij

Abstract

My aims in this chapter are to discuss alternative ways of doing education and research, and thereby highlight key contributions from Paulo Freire, Orlando Fals-Borda and Dorothy Lee, to active learning, participatory action-research and intercultural dialogue. These scholars were heirs of the university reform movements of the twentieth century, and their vital legacy is alive as shown in this book. The enclosed ideas and illustrations of transformative research and education draw from my academic experience in various corners of the world and points in time.

Keywords: Active learning; intercultural dialogue; participatory action-research; Paulo Freire; Dorothy Lee; Orlando Fals-Borda

Prologue

The next paragraphs illustrate how personal biography intersects with our academic work, also disclosing why and how this chapter differs from the other chapters in this book. First conceived as a book containing three articles, it became a chapter in this anthology as suggested by our editor. This change of gears entailed the difficult task to collapse three articles into one coherent whole. In this regard, the contents of these articles roughly correspond to three main sections in the body of this chapter, namely active learning, intercultural dialogue and participatory action-research (PAR). While written in a narrative style that might recall 'free association', there is a unifying link weaving these sections together. The alluded link lies in Paulo Freire's critical pedagogical legacy, meant to transform society, culture, research and education. This is a timely homage, as the world celebrates this year Freire's 100th birthday anniversary, in a context of

Transformative Research and Higher Education, 11–44
Copyright © 2022 Azril Bacal Roij
Published under exclusive licence by Emerald Publishing Limited
doi:10.1108/978-1-80117-694-120221002

a deep Brazilian crisis. In addition to a catastrophic poor management of the COVID-19 pandemic that has killed over 500,000 Brazilians, Saldaña (2019, p. 1) tells us that/'Bolsonaro's education plan means to expunge Paulo Freire's influence from the school system'/. As earlier hinted, there is a personal dimension to this chapter. My friendship with Dorothy Lee (1986, 1987), Paulo Freire (1970, 1973, 1997, 2014), Orlando Fals-Borda (1987), and Ulf Himmelstrand (1982), the authors named in this work, lasted pretty much until they passed away. The *pedagogical eros* inherent in Freire's sense of *amorosidade* is a fertile soil for lasting personal relations in the world of learning. This learning context breeds relationships developed between teachers and students who over time turn into co-learners, co-researchers and friends. My life as a university teacher is also largely indebted to inspiration received from Peter Ulrich Ritter and Paul Kimmel, just to name a small sample from a large list of my extraordinary teachers, friends and distinguished students. In this light, I accepted a recent request to review *Atropellos, arreglos y regocijos*, a book written by Andrés Solari Vicente (2018), one of my former students who became a close friend. He is a Peruvian sociologist, economist, university professor, political analyst and talented writer. Solari analyzes in this book the structure and culture of violence in Peru and Mexico, adorned with a depth and richness of language, rarely found in academic texts.

Thanks to time opportunities provided by the COVID-19 pandemic, another former student popped in my screen. I asked him about his memories from the sociology course in question. He first recalled meeting in the botanic garden instead of caged in a classroom. When pushed for more substance, he recalled reading 'Todas las Sangres', a novel that conveys a vision of a pluri-national and multicultural Peru, by José María Arguedas (1964), one of the best Peruvian writers of all times. I used this novel to introduce Dorothy Lee's methodology of intercultural education to teach/learn values from Andean culture. What I learned with Dorothy Lee about remote cultures rendered fruition when teaching a course on ethnicity and culture, as a humanities endowed scholar at Otterbein College (USA) in 1995. Looking at transformative research, my early positivist and quantitative training in agricultural and social science research methodology changed in the 1970s. I adopted at that time a qualitative and PAR methodology influenced by C.W. Mills (1959), Paulo Freire and Fals-Borda better suited for an experiential study of the ethnic identity orientations of Mexican Americans (Bacal, 1994a). PAR methodology was also appropriate for studying the process of self-management, training and organizational development, with textile workers in Lima, Peru (Bacal, 1991b). During my academic working years in Mexico in the 1980s, I used a collaborative teaching/learning approach to teach a variety of subjects such as development theories, rural sociology, sociology, social psychology, clinical and industrial psychology, sociology of education and communication. PAR methodology was applied in the research project entitled 'prototype of integrated farms'. when working for the post-graduate college (COLPOS) in San Pedro Tlaltenango and Juárez Coronaco, two peasant communities in Puebla (Bacal, 1981–1985). During the 1990s, experiential PAR methodology was helpful in the study of assumed ethnic identity changes among

Latino elderly in Sweden (Bacal, 1996). I used this style of participatory and collaborative teaching/learning approach during the first decades of the new century in Spain, Peru, México and Sweden. Since 2017, I work as a guest lecturer at the graduate programme on PAR, jointly organized by the University of Mällardalen-Eskilstuna and the Swedish Association of Participatory Action-Research (SPARC). By supervising students' research projects in education, health, popular theatre, education and other study fields, my intellectual and practical horizon continue to expand.

My research in the past decades dwells with ethnicity, racism, citizenship, national identity and ethno-politics (Bacal, 1994a, 1997, 2021), lines of enquiry in the International Sociological Association linked to research committees 10 (Participation, Organizational Democracy and Self-Management), RC 05 (Nationalism, Racism, Ethnicity and Indigeneity) and RC 26 (Social Innovation, Intervention and Socio-Techniques). In the next paragraph, we address the question of how context helps us to explain the ways in which conventional research and education operate, as well as the conditions under which these can be de-constructed and transformed.

Context Matters

Anchored in the tradition of the sociology of knowledge, Bell (2018) reminds us that context matters in trying to explain sociocultural phenomena in the social sciences. This view suggests that particular conditions of place and time exert considerable influence on our earlier perceptions and primary definitions of reality, beliefs and the values and attitudes that precede and frame our behaviour in the realms of research and education. In other words, the interpretation of context varies according to our selective perception of natural and social reality, as well as on our relevant location, particular stage in history, individual needs, culture, social class, ideology, occupational status and particular interests. We find ourselves nowadays catapulted into a critical watershed in human history. As a platform to observe social reality, the *Anthropocene* era urges and enables us to both examine the causes and finding collective solutions to the world crisis. Evidence of this crisis (Beck, 2009) comes in the guise of increasing global inequalities, climate emergency, structural racism, police brutality, faulty public health services, environmental devastation, sixth extinction of species, forest fires, tens of millions of refugees brutally forced to flee from home and homelands, accounting for the worst humanitarian catastrophe of the century. The creation of the United Nations Organization for Education, Science and Culture (UNESCO) and adoption of the Universal Declaration of Human Rights in 1948 were corrective educational measures adopted by the international community to overcome the misery, devastation and prejudices leading to the madness of two world wars in the past century. These measures relied on science, education, reason, culture and the quest for peace, intended to reconstruct a world left in ashes by war and totalitarianism.

This also explains why active learning, intercultural dialogue and PAR are called for today in helping to shape the outcome of the ongoing cultural war. This war is currently being fought between the kind of reactionary tribalism denounced by Umberto Eco (2018) as *il fascismo eterno* and progressive forces struggling for democracy, justice and cultures of peace. One understands against this background, why and how different contexts variously frame, facilitate and/or block the educational game, as discussed by Mészáros (2004) in (Bacal, 2011, p. 69). Freire viewed the sociopolitical context of education of his time as being problematic, exploitative, oppressive, alienated and alienating, hence calling for sociocultural change. For Freire, the context was to be 'read' through critical lenses. This kind of reading would raise the awareness, understanding and empowerment of persons, otherwise conditioned and oppressed by their sociocultural circumstances. In this respect, Paulo Freire and Orlando Fals-Borda were active participants and intellectual heirs of the early university reform movements in Cuzco (Peru) and Córdoba (Argentina), while Dorothy Lee participated at a later stage in several teach-ins organized by the 1968 Free Speech movement in Berkeley, California, USA. Next follows a brief introduction about the context that framed the university reform movements in Latin America, the conditions of my encounter with Paulo Freire and the consequences of his pedagogical legacy for my own approach to transformative research and education, as transcribed in Gadotti (1996, pp. 232–233). The next section also describes the decisive impact that the 1910 Mexican Revolution had on the 1917 and 1918 student reform movements in Latin America.

The Mexican Revolution and the Student Reform Movements

One finds much information in the literature on the structural and cultural conditions prior and leading to the 1910 Mexican Revolution, the first social revolution of the twentieth century. The Catholic Church owned at that time 90% of the Mexican land. In this light, this revolution primarily was a 'Peasant Revolution'. The Mexican and Soviet Revolutions and World War I changed the world order inherited from the nineteenth century and provided the intellectual humus for creating an engaged university for the common good, as illustrated by Schugurensky (1983), in Bacal (2018b, p. 66):

> By securing cost-free and open access to the universities, the 1918 Reform constituted an unequivocal pledge for university democratization, both in quantitative and qualitative terms. In the five year period after the reform, enrollment grew by approximately 80% relative to the previous period. During the same period, graduation rates increased 244%...The success of the reform was not fortuitous. It was the result of a variety of social, political, and economic forces operating at the international, national, and institutional levels...At the international level, three major events – World War I, the Mexican Revolution, and the Soviet

Revolution – had important repercussions on the political and cultural attitudes of Argentine students. The war created disillusionment with Europe and shifted students' attention towards their own region...The Cordoba Reform had a tremendous impact in most Latin American universities, and would even inspire the leaders of the 1960s student movement in industrialized countries.

Elsewhere, I have summarized my views on the consequences of the Latin American history and crisis on the university reform movements, covering the period between the Mexican Revolution and World War II (Bacal, 1981, p. 26) as follows:

The progressive penetration of U.S. economic-political and military power in Latin America...continuing immigration from Europe, ...growing influx from the rural population into the cities, ...emergence of an upwardly mobile middle social strata, the organization of the first workers' groups and...demands for better working conditions...post-war deflationary crisis that exploded around the year 1930, the university reform movement, the emergence of populism, nationalism, and Latin American solidarity in the form of anti-Yankee imperialism.

As heirs of the Latin American Student Reform Movement, Freire's work was related to the Peasant Movement in Northeast Brazil, known as the *legas camponesas* (peasant leagues); while the pervasive violence in Colombia led Camilo Torres and Fals-Borda to organize the first faculty of sociology to study the structure and culture of violence in this country. Against the background of the university reform movement, I wrote my views on how to transform the Ibero-American University in the context of neoliberal globalization, from the vantage points of sustainable human development and a culture of peace (Bacal, 2000, pp. 161–218). Next follows a brief introduction to the historical background of the nationalist progressive reforms in Peru, appraised by Hobsbawm (1971) as a 'peculiar revolution', in Bacal (1998):

Perú was defined as underdeveloped, within the capitalist system. Within the former there existed semi-feudal or pre-capitalist features, mostly in the agrarian sector. Another distinguishing characteristic remains its cultural heterogeneity and associated features of ethnic oppression and discrimination...The degree of penetration of foreign capital significantly increased during the 1960s...Most of the economic power groups (landowners, exporters, bankers, industrialists, business, energy and communications) corresponded to foreign interests and...neo-colonial intermediaries...Together these groups controlled not only the means of production and political power, but also the means of communication.

Between 1969 and 1976, in this spirit of social transformation, teachers and students from the National Agricultural University La Molina (UNALM), supported the Agrarian Reform process. The latter included a national peasant radio programme created by the author, based on a participatory and dialogic media approach suggested by Freire himself (Bacal, 1988). This progressive reform process stopped in 1975 by a military conservative coup, which in the next decades led to a hurricane of violence, with an estimated 70,000 lost lives and missing people. The violence of this internal or civil war accounts for a vast migratory flow from the rural Andean population to Lima and other urban coastal and jungle areas. After the Fujimori regime (1990–2000) collapsed, the country returned to a liberal regime. The following regimes were unable and unwilling to solve the pervasive problems of poverty, huge socio-economic gap, criminal violence and human insecurity linked to the traffic of narcotics, as well as other forms of systemic corruption. Latin America has not managed yet to solve its structural problems of poverty, socio-economic and educational gap and unequal development up to present time. The context of active learning under conditions casted by the hegemonic globalization of neoliberal education is 'read' from a critical perspective on dialogue and hope, as follows.

Dialogue and Hope as Critical Perspectives

In addressing the need of value perspectives in rational science, Gunnar Myrdal (1973) wrote:

> Science can only be rational if you have explicit value premises. One needs value premises to ascertain facts. There are no answers except to questions. No questions except from viewpoints.

At a time when econometrics prevailed in the reified field of economics, the position held by Myrdal (1986) on the role of values in scientific enquiry went against the mainstream. Myrdal argued that the science of economy was not value-free, taking into account its frame of political economy. In a similar critical vein, Paulo Freire, Orlando Fals-Borda and Dorothy Lee revolted against the elitism and dominance of positivism in university research and education. 'Dialogue' and 'Utopia' in Freire's work reflected the influence of Martin Buber (1929, 1955). Both reflected, in turn, the influence of the critical theory of alienation by Marx (1961). Freire argued that there was no neutral pedagogics as such. For him, pedagogics was always political pedagogics, intended to 'domesticate' or liberate students. Dorothy Lee challenged the emphasis of 'scientific' anthropology at the expense of humanist anthropology, as later discussed. Looking at context from these perspectives, the reader finds that the present situation shares similar features with the societal conditions confronted by these authors. In other words, society continues to be problematic, exploitive, oppressive, alienated and alienating. These conditions demand a critical reading of society, oriented towards the transformation of society, culture, research and education. Freire's answer to this quest was to foster citizen education to help raise the awareness of the population. The process of conscientization was for Freire a precondition for people engaging in cultural action and social transformation. In this regard, the higher status and influence of teachers makes their role either emancipatory or demeaning. Active teaching and learning takes place within spatial–temporal boundaries, and is a socio-educational construct, in principle susceptible to be de-constructed and re-constructed. Some of the most important progressive changes of the educational systems resulted from the struggles of the historical socio-educational reform movements, aiming for knowledge democracy and social inclusion. From a dialectical perspective, in our status as teachers, researchers, educational decision-makers, planners and school administrators lies the potential to reproduce and/or change the educational system. We are not merely bystanders in the educational scene, but players with an upper hand in helping to re-shape educational rules, routines and outcomes. Active listening, dialogue and hope have an important role to play in this respect. Paraphrasing Marin (2010), is there a place for listening, dialogue and hope in this age of global distrust? While the COVID-19 pandemic clouds the horizon with anguish and uncertainties concerning the future of humankind, the need for hope, trust and dialogue is higher than ever before.

For Dorothy Lee, dialogue paves a way to break and overcome our ethno-centric biases by learning values from other cultures. Dialogue for Freire and Fals-Borda is a method to raise critical awareness, hope and empowerment of citizens, engaging them in social and institutional transformation. These authors approached their teaching and learning from a viewpoint of freedom and autonomy rooted 'in' community. Their view stands in contrast to hegemonic neoliberal views of freedom, mostly based on individualistic selfish motivation, competition and greed. These authors did not view research and education as separate ventures. Paulo Freire and Orlando Fals-Borda viewed research and education as two activities nourishing each other. They argued likewise for the need to bridge theory and praxis. The view on how research and education might help to transform institutional policies and practices was used in a recent inter-national research project on higher education in Latin America, in which I was involved (Bacal, in Velezmoro et al., 2013). In this context, I led two workshops on PAR applied to higher education for teachers and graduate students at the Graduate School of UNALM. After the completion of our research, our research team presented a report to the university authorities with recommendations, guidelines and targets for the adoption of policies and actions, to make improvements on the existing poor levels of social inclusion. This chapter freely draws from and elaborates the three alluded publications written by the author (Bacal, 2018a, 2018b, 2018c). It also conveys an attempt to bridge my reflections on theory, research methodology and social practice, as proposed by Himmel-strand (1982).

Before going further, it is pertinent to spell out what do I mean by 'trans-formative', a big task in itself. To make it simple, by transformation I mean to change the present state of affairs, from an emancipatory and consciousness-raising perspective, to overcome prevailing sociohistorical conditions of alienation and oppression. Freire (1976) conveyed his views on education and change, from a vantage point concerned with a just society and participatory democracy. This transformative perspective frames the next section on active learning as follows.

Active Learning as Transformative Education

Michael Price (2004) in Bacal (2018c, p. 342) tells us that 'active learning requires students to do meaningful learning activities'.

> Active learning has received considerable attention over the past several years...is generally defined as any instructional method that engages students in the learning process.

The literature tells us that active learning is an educational enterprise with a reputed label as a trademark. Looking at the sources of active learning, we acknowledge valuable contributions from philosophers, psychologists, pedagogues, researchers and practitioners, covering a vast range of disciplines and study fields. Authors like Freire, Vygotsky, Montessori, Freinet, Revans, Barnes, Glenda, Bandura, Prince, Brookfield, Weltman and Martyn were selected from a long list of scholars, who contributed to the development of active learning (Bacal, 2018a). Much of the accumulated and fruitful development in the field of active learning came however to a halt at the 1989 Fall of the Berlin Wall, thereby triggering the hegemony of the neoliberal world disorder. The term active learning is *quasi* tautological, since learning is a human activity *par excellence*. The following general lines on active teaching/learning borrow from Moacir Gadotti (2000), the general director of the Paulo Freire Institute in São Paulo. This seminal Brazilian pedagogue recalls the triad of actors envisioned by Rousseau in the educational game: (1) One-self ('I'), the active learner, (2) other (significant) persons in our lives, such as teachers and parents and (3) the term 'things' alluding to nature and human-made cultural artefacts in our particular habitat. The role of teachers and educational administrators as 'significant educational others' entails a dual potential to facilitate and/or block the innate curiosity and active exploratory learning process of our students. 'Things' acquire practical use and existential meaning and value through human interaction of students with significant others. The concept 'significant others' refers to meaningful persons and socialization agents that exert most influence our life story. The interpersonal process of transferring beliefs and information about the world and ourselves takes place through a filter comprised by particular set of values, language and the personal teaching style of 'significant teachers'. Dorothy Lee and Paulo Freire viewed education as a life-learning process of transformation. In this respect, several questions come to mind about, for example, how much are teachers willing to look at and to correct the consequences from policies and practices decided from above, by the educational decision-makers? Are the contemporary schools and institutions of education offering students a formative learning space that fosters their ability to think critically? Are educational authorities enabling students to partake in the educational decision-making process? Is it reasonable to expect that democratic values in education will help students to act as concerned citizens in society, culture and their local community? From this vantage point, I search for clues in the pedagogical legacy of these authors that might help us to understand and overcome the main causes and consequences of the world crisis.

The next paragraphs introduce selected theoretical inputs from Dorothy Lee and Paulo Freire, and illustrate their insights with examples of their use in the classroom, with vignettes drawn from my teaching experience on intercultural education and communication.

Education and Culture as Mind Battlefields

A starting point for introducing the notion of cultural war as 'the battle for the mind', is to look at culture, education and media and examine how these institutions help to shape the norms and values that frame our perceptions, beliefs and definition of reality. Cultural anthropology teaches us that we do not perceive the surrounding natural and symbolic environments in 'objective' or neutral ways. The norms, values and attitudes framing our ways to read and related to the context are acquired constructs, filtered, communicated and coloured through cultural lenses. When shared group definitions of situations turn into internalized norms, mores, values, myths, stereotypes and prejudices, these personal imprints condition and shape our personal and collective behaviour. The correspondence of individual values with societal norms explains why and how education and mass media constitute such a hotly contested locus today, between public and private agencies of social control, on the one hand, and social movements striving for freedom, justice, peace and democracy, on the other. It is my contention that active learning has suffered much in the past decades resulting from neoliberal educational 'reforms', like the increased commodification and privatization of all levels of education. This regressive shift points to the reliance on cost-benefit methods of evaluation, the rise of 'public management', treating education as if it were a commercial enterprise, focussed on market competition, technological development and instruction, at the expense of formative education. Castells (1998) tells us that in our times many of today's educational strategies respond to the demands made by emerging Information and communications technologies (ICT) networks in knowledge-based and complex societies. These pressures entail measures to enforce and standardize curricula and praxis of education impregnated by neoliberal directives. Under such conditions, the educational focus is restricted to the incorporation of technical innovations, participatory methods and fun games, hence neglecting education's formative mission. How valid is in this respect the view that new technical innovations are required to awaken students from their assumed slumber?

A perusal of the pertinent literature points to the fact that most schools and universities adhere to the avowed premises of active education. One also finds available as a reader a wide battery of methods and techniques in stock to support active learning in the industrialized world. In other words, the existing literature tells us that theory, research, methods and techniques of active learning are no scarce commodities. If all is seemingly under control, what is there to add to the debate about active learning? A preliminary answer to this question leads us to look at the neglect of formative values and citizen education associated with the humanistic and critical traditions in social sciences and education. These issues invite us to look, for example, at peace education. The reader finds information about my experience and reflections on peace education in Bacal (2002). Since the root causes of war and violence lie in the human mind, much hope and resources have been invested in advancing the socio-educational conditions for democracy, rule of law, justice, peace and development, especially after the second world war. It is evident to most readers that the educational system has failed in helping to solve the alluded problems, above, leading us into the crisis of the twenty-first century. As done in the past, the world resorts once again to education, science and culture, as the best human artefacts at hand to identify, mitigate and overcome the main problematic features of the world crisis. In this respect, to what extent are the mainstream educational theories, policies and social practices providing the corrective actions for solving pressing institutional problems of society and education? Available empirical evidence points to a set of negative consequences resulting from unequal globalization for education, research and social exclusion. I argue in this regard that we are witnessing today the failure of the contemporary public and private educational systems. I attribute a large part of this failure to the hegemony of the human capital doctrine of education, largely enforced by globalism. In my view, hope lies in an alternative educational project that endows students from all social backgrounds with equal access and tutorial support to quality and formative education as a universal human right. A classic sociological tenet on the consequences from self-fulfilled prophecies postulates that: 'What is defined as real has real consequences'. If we believe that students lack self-motivation to learn, our educational efforts will likely seek to motivate them via external methods and techniques.

If we consider, however, that students are born with innate curiosity to learn, efforts to improve on their learning might focus instead on their genuine interests and active attention. This alternative view leads into designing schools and universities that effectively support the creativity and development of their human potential. I look next at ways in which Dorothy Lee and Paulo Freire approached formative values in the active teaching/learning process.

Humanist Anthropology and Critical Pedagogics

What is the role of formative values in active learning? I examine in this regard selected views from Dorothy Lee on: (1) cultures that 'value the self', (2) community as identity anchor and (3) the formative values of freedom, autonomy and structure, in the active learning process. While Freire and Lee are both great educators of the twentieth century using dialogue in their praxis, they differed in their teaching style. Lee developed a method of slow reading of selected texts with biographical content, intended to expand our cultural–linguistic boundaries. Lee's psycholinguistic methodology in humanist anthropology helps to expand beyond our ethnocentric doors of perception, enabling us to 'discover' and learn values from 'remote cultures'. In contrast, Freire's aims with critical pedagogics are to raise the awareness of students making use of dialectics and dialogue via the pedagogy of the question. Dialectics is a method that enables students to reflect about their own thoughts and beliefs and to grasp the contradictions inherent in their culture, society and in themselves. Dialogue entails the act of attentively listening to each other. It fosters empathy by inviting students to 'wear the shoes of the other'. Dorothy Lee, who was able to bridge humanist anthropology and transformative education, was as a unique voice in the academic world. The next paragraphs drawn from Jeffrey Ehrenreich (1986, p. 176) give a flavour of Dorothy Lee's philosophical views on the role of culture and language in education.

> The original impetus to inquire into the philosophical dimension of culture came from my husband, Otis Lee (a philosopher), for whom all experience and behavior has its philosophical content, and all reality held value...My search into the cultural codification of experienced reality, and into the conceptual and value implications of language and other aspects of culture, came through an attempt to find answers for his disturbing questions...In recent years, I have been concerned with questions revolving around freedom, individual autonomy, responsibility, creativity, the self.

In respect to the question raised by Dorothy Lee,/'Are the contemporary institutions of higher education able and willing to respect and support student's autonomy?'/, her answer about the intimate link between culture and freedom *cum* autonomy in Ehrenreich (1986, pp. 76–180), in Bacal (2018c, p. 347), reads as follows:

> Through comparative analysis of numerous cultures both Western and primitive, Lee suggested that in order for the individual to achieve autonomy it was essential that the community truly values the self.

According to Dorothy Lee, different cultures vary in value orientation towards the 'self' and the freedom and autonomy of children. From a comparative perspective, certain cultures do value and support the self and the autonomy of students, while others are cultures 'against man'. Jules Henry (1963) wrote about cultures that place high value on obedience, discipline, social control, conformity, epitomized but not restricted to Nazi-like pedagogy. In contrast to liberal and neoliberal views on freedom based on individualism, Dorothy Lee and Paulo Freire regarded freedom in terms of the autonomy in persons who are socioculturally rooted in and supportive of community. In the learning space envisioned by Dorothy Lee, students are innately curious, actively engaged in exploring and learning about, thereby developing an intimate relation with their relevant universe. For Lee, students do not need external motivation nor rewards or punishment as advocated by educators with a behaviourist orientation. In this respect, she was critical of B.F. Skinner, her colleague at Harvard University, for his lack of respect towards his students, often mistreated as research pigeons. Skinner's views on social control were spelled out in his novel Walden II (1948), depicting a dystopian society build on behaviouristic scientism. Her misgivings concerning the assumption of student passivity extended into the proposed remedial measures. She questioned the assumed 'need' for external motivation and reinforcement, even if these corrective measures had good intentions, namely, to turn apathetic students into active learners. Instead, Lee looked at the interface between the student's inner motivation and their learning contexts. Her analysis leads us to examine the educational context, here regarded as a spatial–temporal *locus* mediated by the quality of the teacher-learner interpersonal relation.

Meaningful Learning as an Existential Challenge

When we met at our first lesson, Dorothy Lee invited us to close our eyes, imagine and decide whether we would stay in the room were the world suddenly to end. She thus confronted us with an existential choice: To stay in the classroom or to go elsewhere. In our days plagued by anomie, existential crisis, lack of meaning, hopelessness and political distrust, her provocative question has infused my work as educator with the quest for meaning. The teaching/learning context includes the world, the classroom and the educational *locus* referred by Dorothy Lee as 'relevant universe'. In other words, students travel their educational journey bounded by a symbolic environment, populated by a community of significant people, grounded in meaningful places and times. It follows from the previous train of thought that when the context for learning is irrelevant, the learning process suffers. The conventional claim made about student apathy was in her eyes a misguided diagnosis based on the faulty assumption of student innate passivism. Dorothy Lee was critical of conventional claims that students needed external motivation and viewed the grading system as an institutional sign of disrespect degrading the value of the student's personal integrity. Dorothy Lee regarded students as intrinsically self-motivated and self-driven by values and interests. Their apparent apathy or passivity of students was a result in her eyes from the lack of relevance and meaning in their educational environments and curricula. Paul Goodman (1960) captured this sense of educational banality when he wrote on growing up absurd in the USA as an alienated society. Similarly, Dorothy Lee regarded community as the basis for meaning, in a society plagued by meaninglessness, anomie, consumerism, narcissism and hopelessness. The lack of meaning in education was for Dorothy Lee a symptom of an existential crisis, indicated by the fast pace, massive consumerism and drug culture of our time. One cause of this existential crisis was in her eyes the demise of community in modern society. I find her views concerning the need to re-build community in modern society closely related to works by Martin Buber (1996) and epidemiologists Wilkinson and Pickett (2018). To end this line of thought, an alternative vision of institutions of higher education begins with learning communities able to acknowledge the self, freedom, autonomy, human potential, creativity and critical thinking of their students. Paulo Freire's significant contribution to transformative dialogue in the open *locus* of active teaching and learning follows next.

Monologue or Dialogue in Intercultural Communication and Education

I trace my personal encounter with the work of Paulo Freire, when teaching a master's course on agricultural extension at the UNALM in Peru.

Freire (2020) regarded extension as a kind of monologue and persuasive type of oppressive communication, in contrast to 'dialogical' communication. His views on dialogue were influenced by Socratic enquiry, as well as by the social and political writings of Buber (1955, 1996), who distinguished between two opposite ideal types of interpersonal interaction. Buber's modes of communication roughly correspond to Freire's two alternative educational paths: (1) 'I–It', alluding to structured situations when the teacher relates to students as an 'it', namely an object to be taught and moulded at will and (2) 'I–Thou', pointing to a kind of education based on interpersonal respect, mutual care and appreciation. This kind of teaching entails learning via dialogue, where the roles of teacher and students mesh, enabling them to learn from each other as co-learners. Considering the pertinence of dialogue in primary school and higher education, I contend that in learning settings that prize the 'I–It' mode of teaching active, learning suffers and, vice versa, when primacy is assigned to the 'I–Thou' mode of teaching, active learning flourishes. Freire argued that one is not able to know everything, and neither is the other. In this way, Freire regarded humility as the proper attitude required to facilitate dialogue and mutual learning in the active teaching/learning game. While Freire is widely acknowledged as an early pioneer of active learning, the formative tenets of education associated with his work are neglected due to the fast pace of life and work in the hegemonic neoliberal world. In this train of thought, how valid is the assumption that students are passive and thus in need of external motivation and reinforcement, a view widely spread in behaviourist educational quarters? Dorothy Lee presents us with a radically different viewpoint on active teaching and learning. This view invites us to look at the early curiosity and eagerness of young students to learn what genuinely interests them, a feature often neglected in the current management of the learning process. The previous reflections explain why education, media and culture together play such a critical role in deciding the outcome of the ongoing cultural warfare, in favour or against democracy. This chapter argues that freedom, self, autonomy, community and citizenship are formative values, calling for their incorporation at the centre of the curricula and praxis of active learning.

For Dorothy Lee, meaningful learning takes place in meaningful contexts, where students learn through life activities shared with a community of significant others, located in relevant universes and times. In contrast, if the learning context is irrelevant, it is equally irrelevant to the pupils. I owe to Dorothy Lee my coming to understand the nexus between freedom and culture, as well as why it is of the utmost importance to learn values from what she called 'remote cultures'. She was interested in the consequences for education from how different cultures value (or not) an autonomous self, in contrast to cultures that put a prize on discipline, homogeneity and social control. This line of enquiry leads us to examine the role of dialogue in active learning in intercultural situations framed by complexity and unequal societies. I explore in the following paragraphs the nexus between the pedagogical legacies of Paulo Freire and Dorothy Lee in the realm of intercultural dialogue and the practical and theoretical barriers confronted by immigrants and refugees, in an increasingly hostile Swedish society.

Paradigmatic Change: Intercultural Dialogue and Social Inclusion in Sweden

The context of this section looks at the world's migratory crisis, humanitarian refugee catastrophe and hostile environment to refugees in the twenty-first century, which further complicate the structural features of the Swedish Dilemma. This dilemma refers to the gap between the ideal values of immigration and policies based on equality, freedom of choice, solidarity and multiculturalism, on the one hand and the structural, cultural and institutional barriers, behind the increasingly restrictive and hostile migratory policies that block the attainment of these goals. A commonly accepted view in Swedish public opinion is that the past policies of multiculturalism and social integration have failed. A new insurgent theoretical trend has emerged in this respect in the Swedish academic arena, appealing to the social science community to replace multiculturalism and adopt instead the paradigm of intercultural dialogue, as an alternative model to guide immigration policies and praxis. In this respect, FID (2017, p. 2) in Bacal (2018c, p. 321) raised the following question:

> A key question is whether the conceptual shift from multiculturalism to intercultural dialogue will really lead or has already led to a corresponding shift in the political management of questions related to migration?

The above question and the related paradigmatic shift reflect an attempt to move beyond the prevailing theoretical and methodological horizon, hoping to effectively deal with the challenges, problems and new possibilities entailed by ethno-cultural diversity. As a theoretical development, cultural dialogue entails an intellectual effort to respond to the growing threats to social democracy from the rise of white nationalist populism in Sweden. In this respect, Abraham (2017, p. 1) recently wrote that the growing inequalities of globalization have become a source of collective resentment, which lies behind the backlash of xenophobia and national populism. Sweden is no exception to this global trend, with its own version of nativism emblematized by the far-right political parties Swedish Democrats and National Democrats. The influx of large numbers of immigrants and refugees expelled from their homes and home countries of origin, by violence, poverty, intolerance and oppression entails for Sweden as a host country, a complex set of benefits, problems and challenges. The enhanced human power and creativity that comes along with diversity are added benefits to society. Against this background, how do we account for the causes of international migration and the growth of a hostile environment of refugees in Sweden and Europe? Saskia Sassen (2014) provides us with a theory to explain this drama supported with empirical data and disclosing the consequences of the increasing inequality gap for the expulsion of refugees, in turn pointing to the worse humanitarian catastrophe of this century. One observes that, paradoxically, instead of effective and humane solutions to help overcome this human tragedy, we observe a chain reaction of increasing xenophobia, hate media, racism, national populism and neo-fascism. Similar developments correlate with growing inequality gap and a new wave of white national populism in Sweden. These problems are not that new. There was, for instance, an upsurge of national populism and racist violence in Sweden in the 1990s, denounced by Ålund and Schierup (1991) in the following terms: /'Sweden is moving closer to the exclusiveness, selectivity and increasing brutality of Fortress Europe'/. The authors of this line also quote Peter Nobel's condemnation of Swedish refugee policy at that time:

> (It) is stupid, inhumane and void of any solidarity. Moreover, quite personally, I am unwilling to live in a society, which is a glossy supermarket for some nationalities and a rigid police state for others.

Returning to the present time situation, inequality, social inclusion, social integration, ethnic discrimination and segregation, remain unsolved as structural social problems, which in turn correlate with the growth of far-right forces. These forces have acquired increasing power and influence at all levels of the Swedish political system. Several research centres and *ad-hoc* commissions appointed by the Swedish authorities are some of the institutional measures to help understand, mitigate, and correct these sociopolitical developments. These issues stand however beyond the issues of ethnic diversity and multiculturalism and currently pose a factual threat to Swedish Social Democracy.

Multiculturalism or Intercultural Dialogue?

The notion of multiculturalism was an attempt in the past century to assert the uniqueness of each culture, while avoiding the cultural flattening process in the ideology of the 'melting pot' of Americanization. The three key principles of Sweden's 1975 immigration policies were equality, freedom of choice and cooperation changed to multiculturalism in the 1980s. These changes were fashioned after the Canadian approach to manage immigration, sociocultural inclusion and integration. Rex (1986) raised a critical question in respect to multiculturalism:/

'How, then, is it possible to ensure both equality of opportunity and...toleration or encouragement of cultural differences?'/. Given his experience with Apartheid in South Africa, Rex (1986) was concerned about/'a fraudulent alternative which dissociates multi-culturalism from equality of opportunity and...opens the way for de-facto differential incorporation'/. We witness in this respect a paradigmatic shift from multiculturalism to intercultural dialogue in the academic scene. While the paradigm of multiculturalism continues to be used, for example, at the Multicultural Centre, in Botkyrka, Stockholm, the research council for intercultural dialogue (FID) has adopted the paradigm of 'intercultural dialogue'. FID researchers advocate the centrality of intercultural dialogue as a conceptual platform to facilitate the encounter between Europeans and non-Europeans in Sweden. The reader finds an example of PAR applied from the perspective of intercultural dialogue in a case study led by Pirjo Lahdenperä, seeking answers to the question of how to improve the conditions for the social integration of refugees in Sweden. Another recent example of PAR methodology applied to study similar problems of social integration of immigrants in the United Kingdom is found in the chapter in this book written by Umut Erel and her colleagues at the Open University.

It is worth taking note that researchers at FID are fully aware that intercultural dialogue still is an open question about making changes in the political decision-making process. As a line of enquiry, intercultural dialogue calls for a collective reflection on the quality of public services dealing with health, schools, housing, labour and issues of human rights, justice, democracy, equality, diversity, social sustainability and intersectionality. I argue in the end that solutions to current problems resulting from cultural diversity in a social context framed by structural class and ethnic inequality cannot be resolved only in the realms of theory and culture. In short, intercultural dialogue must go hand in hand with long-range policies and sustained actions to diminish the vast economic, cultural, educational and sociopolitical gap in Sweden and elsewhere. The next paragraphs present how Paulo Freire bridged the worlds of education and social transformation in terms of 'cultural action' meant to re-define the world and thus overcome the consequences of the 'banking' system of instructional education and the 'human capital approach to education'.

Cultural Action

Freire's 'banking' model of education challenged the hegemonic conditioning for passivity, conformity and obedience. Freire's *Pedagogy of the Oppressed* (1970) was his answer to Marx's question and theory of alienation (and its transcendence) in terms of critical education, consciousness-raising and transformative education. Freire's key contributions to intercultural dialogue was first developed in *Extension or Communication* (1973), where he thereby defined the following two types of communication: (1) 'Monological', namely, persuasive and oppressive communication, applied, for example, in the realms of agricultural extension, propaganda, political indoctrination, commercial publicity and 'domesticating' education for conformity and (2) 'dialogical' communication, envisioned as emancipatory, creative and transformative. Freire further develops Buber's influential work on the types of human interaction, where the 'I–It' mode alludes to a perception of the 'other' person as an 'it' a 'thing' that can be misused and manipulated, even for 'teaching' purposes. Buber contended that a new awareness and mutual possibility to learn emerges between participants in dialogue. In this sense, dialogue relates to the quest for justice and peace. When Freire received the UNESCO's Award as peace educator in 1974, he made clear that peace education for him entailed education and action for justice.

Freire coined the term 'cultural action' pointing to our potential to re-define reality, in order to change it, no longer conditioned and doomed to reproduce the culture of oppression; thereby combining intercultural dialogue with the quest for hope, democracy and equality. Moreover, Paulo Freire regarded educational theory and social praxis as the two faces of Janus, namely, as an effective way to engage people in cultural action in turn geared toward social transformation. Turning to the humanistic anthropological perspective on education, Dorothy Lee went much beyond 'cultural tolerance', demanding a mutual process of intercultural appreciation and co-learning. Dorothy Lee viewed intercultural dialogue as a way to raise awareness about our ethnocentrism and thus enabling us to break away from cultural conditioning and prejudicial misunderstanding of cultural otherness. This line of work recalls Freire's prescription to 'unlearn' our conditioned prejudices, as well as the voices from our 'internal enemy'. To overcome the rigidities of tribal ethnocentrism, Lee developed a sociocultural linguistic approach to intercultural education, which includes reading selected materials from what she called 'remote cultures'. This approach highlights how some cultures value and support an autonomous self, in contrast to cultures that value instead conformity, discipline, homogeneity and social control, like Nazi Germany. In the context of an unequal multicultural society, the Swedish Dilemma casts a shadow over a set of unsolved problems of social integration, social inclusion, that currently lack proper management in an increasingly diverse and complex society.

Sociopolitical Equality, Multiculturalism and Intercultural Dialogue

Whatever paradigm adopted on multiculturalism or intercultural dialogue, the 'Swedish Dilemma' of class, racial, ethnic and gender inequality persists as an unsolved structural problem of society and culture. It is not likely to change by virtue of a mere linguistic or conceptual shift. When asked for a solution to a similar dilemma, namely, *the American Dilemma*, Myrdal (quoted by Wallerstein, 1988) answered that power harnessed by those who have grievances enables the social conscience to become effective. Myrdal's assertion concerning the need by those with grievances to assemble power points to a way for engaged scholars to bridge the divide between universities and social movements; thereby coupling multiculturalism with socio-economic, cultural and political equality. Effective solutions to the existing problems of social inclusion and integration in unequal societies are not likely to result from limiting our horizon to the ideational realms of culture, linguistics and academic paradigm.

In this respect, Freire contributes to bridging: theory and praxis, cultural action and social change, transformative education and intercultural dialogue, in the frame of sociopolitical equality.

Transformative Intercultural Education

My teaching/learning work on intercultural education took place as earlier mentioned at different locations and points in time. The following vignette shows, for example, the syllabus designed to teach on ethnicity and culture at Otterbein College in 1995, which incorporated inputs from Dorothy Lee and Paulo Freire in Bacal (2018a, p. 353).

> This course is designed to provide a theoretical, methodological and an experiential approach to the study of culture, ethnicity and ethnic identity. The methodology of this course is built on participation and dialogue, combining individual, small-group projects and classroom levels of work and discussion...Daily personal reading and writing are combined with study-circles, which also function as support peer groups...The lecture format will be complemented with seminars and panel discussions....Films and field projects... enrich...collective learning experience...The kind and pace of individual reading in this course was to be extremely and consciously slow, providing enough time for the reader to walk, as a manner of speech, in the pages, to imagine oneself walking in the landscape, smelling the smells of nature, 'meeting' the places, 'listening' to and even 'relating' to the persons introduced by the authors in the books...meant to be slowly read...students were invited then to reflect and to write about their deep reactions and reflections, including gut feelings and/or intellectual ...analysis. These personal responses were later to be shared in the context of group dialogue in the classroom space...The discussion was enriched by the cultural diversity and perspectives of the students, mostly trained teachers from all corners of the world...In this way, the individual aha (!) sense of personal discovery is coupled with the analytical dimension via dialogue in an active learning space and process...The course assignments included tasks such as: a personal diary with comments about the student's reactions and reflections to their 'personal encounters', with the main characters and places 'met' in the pages of the books they read...These diary notes were discussed weekly on one-to-one basis with the teacher, in addition to group reports on the readings, and other activities related to the course.

This methodology to develop a sense of intercultural discovery and appreciation of cultural otherness was instrumental in the training courses for the Swedish International Development Agency (SIDA) in the 1990s, prior to their work abroad. This in a 1998 course on 'Learning from Remote Cultures', taught at the Department of Culture and Library Studies, Uppsala University. 'Juan the Chamula', a book written by Ricardo Pozas Arciniegas (1962) introduced Swedish students to the world of the Chamula Tzotzil Maya peoples. It enabled my students to grasp the conditions behind the 1994 Zapatista rebellion in Chiapas, Mexico. In another similar experience, a group of Mexican students met with Ricardo Pozas Arciniegas, my revered teacher at Universidad Autónoma de México (UNAM), who visited our classroom at 'Universidad de las Américas, Puebla' (UDLAP) in the 1980s. His visit to this private elite university provided an unusual learning opportunity to these privileged students, children of the elite in the Mexican racialized class society. The construction of this transformative educational approach took place during my early teaching years at UNALM, Lima, Peru. Students taking introductory and general sociology courses in the 1970s met weekly in small study groups and later conversed face-to-face with writer–anthropologist José María Argüedas, after reading and discussing 'Todas las Sangres' ('All Bloods'). The next section looks at transformative participatory action-research (TPAR).

Transformative Participatory Action-Research: A Latin American Perspective

This section presents selected inputs from Paulo Freire and Orlando Fals-Borda, shedding light on the promise of TPAR in the twenty-first century. Due to time limitations, this chapter focusses on the contributions of Paulo Freire. However, the reader finds a large number of bibliographical references to the seminal contributions made by Fals-Borda to TPAR in Bacal (2018b, pp. 68–69). These authors convey a sense of urgently needed hope, at a time of spreading political malaise, confusion, hopelessness, anomie and widespread distrust in authorities. Humanity confronts a severe world crisis caused by the coronavirus pandemic, the resulting economic and sociopolitical consequences and the lack of providence observed in the public and private health systems. Against this background, what might it be a good way to introduce the contributions of Paulo Freire to PAR? My choice is to present Latin America as the cultural and intellectual context that framed the lifework of these authors, as previously described in this chapter.

As a region, Latin America reflects a colonial heritage of enslavement, serfdom, exploitation and oppression, as well as by a legacy of contestation, emancipation, student reform movements, socialist reforms and liberation theology. To begin with, it is important to point out to the fact that these Latin American authors went beyond the usual separation between research and education. Paulo Freire and Orlando Fals-Borda treated research as an integral feature of education and learning and acknowledged the innate curiosity and exploratory activity of our animal species. These engaged scholars rejected the patterns of alienation and the elitist division of labour divorcing researchers from the persons researched. They regarded instead the two actors in the research process as co-researchers engaged in the shared exploration and transformation of their natural and social environment. In a similar way, they regarded teachers and students as co-learners, actively engaged in the process of teaching and learning from each other. The previous introduction to the Latin American context is meant to help the reader understand why Freire's and Fals-Borda's contributions markedly differ from traditions developed in other latitudes like the PAR approach built around Kurt Lewin. My perspective on TPAR in this chapter reflects my historical and theoretical anchor in Latin America, concerned with social constructivism and ethics. TPARin Latin America seeks to produce valid and reliable social knowledge to benefit the vast segments of the peoples commonly excluded from the benefits of the neoliberal project of globalization. In addition to the critical and constructivist perspectives in TPAR, it provides a central place to ethical concerns about whom is knowledge produced for, addressed in the next section. The chapter by Erik Lindhult in this book discussed the importance of ethics in terms of 'knowledge democracy'.

Socio-Constructivism and Ethical Concerns: Knowledge for Whom?

The methodological approach of PAR in this article adheres to the tradition of constructivism in the social sciences, and thus it is sharply opposed to essentialist claims on social reality. In the eyes of Thomas and Znaniecki (1918–1920) as quoted by Bacal (1994a), social reality is:

> The product of a continued interaction of individual consciousness and objective social reality...the human personality is both a continually producing factor and a continually produced result of social evolution, and this double relation expresses itself in every elementary social fact.

The value orientation in the methodological approach used by Freire and Fals-Borda to TPAR implied that the production of social knowledge should be relevant and useful in the struggle of the peasantry and other oppressed groups. TPAR methodology bridges social research techniques and social practice, geared in turn to raise the awareness of the situation of exploitation and oppression of oppressed people, thereby empowering them as agents of sociocultural transformation. Transformative research and education enable the oppressed to actively learn and participate, thus taking charge and transforming their social situation. This section also frames my work with PAR in the realm of self-management and organizational development with urban industrial textile workers in Lima.

Critical Theory: Freedom, Autonomy and Self-Determination

In their theorizing, Freire and Fals-Borda shared some influences from sources such as Socratic Dialogue, Marx's Theory of Alienation and Dialectics,

Phenomenology and Christian Theology of Liberation. These authors adopted critical social theory as best suited to interpret the reality and the needs of the peasantry and to support the global struggle against rural exploitation and oppression in the Third World. I found additional inspiration in the critical theory and method of socio-analysis, developed by C.W. Mills (1959) to examine how personal history intersects with the larger history. This method was developed to raise peoples' awareness about how deeply conditioned we are by global historical circumstances. This awareness would in turn empower us to recover our human potential and act as agents of historical change. Mills extended his views on how the past impinges on our inner psyche and also on how present history influences our psyche by intersecting public issues with private problems. These insights help in turn to develop our awareness and social action as informed citizens. In my elaboration of a paradigm of autonomy and self-determination in the social sciences and education, I also explored how our particular culture intersects with our individual personality to raise awareness and overcome its deep imprint on our cultural conditioning. This acquired understanding would empower and aware us to engage as citizens in 'cultural action', the term used by Freire alluding to our potential to re-define reality in order to change it, thereby pointing to the emancipatory potential of breaking away from our external conditioning and stop reproducing the culture of oppression inherited from the past. My attempt to summarize an epistemology of human freedom, autonomy and self-determination in Bacal (1994b, p. 1), reads as follows:

> As one moves away from biological and behavioristic accounts of human behavior, one also takes distance from causal explanations in psychology and other social sciences...The development of social-psychology as a separate and yet integrating discipline opened new theoretical and methodological possibilities...it paved the way to seriously entertain the human potential for personal autonomy and self-determination, within variable historical and socio-cultural conditions...The conceptual shift from organism to identity signals the road from psychology to social-psychology, from the causal paradigm to the alternative paradigm known as 'relative determinism', and from conditioning to the realms of freedom, empowerment, values, and social change.

From a value perspective on emancipatory research and education, Freire invites us to 'read' (interpret) the world context as being a problematic socio-cultural structure of exploitation and oppression, therefore in dire need of transformation.

Pragmatism or Transformation?

The conventional approach to social research based on philosophical positivism calls for 'value-neutrality' and 'objectivity'. Constructed in opposition to positivism, PAR explicitly points to value-tinged lenses held by researchers in the process of scientific inquiry. Awareness of the theoretical and methodological consequences from different regional ideological and cultural traditions, Lindhult distinguished between two kinds of PAR: (1) transformative and (2) pragmatic. Freire and Fals-Borda identified with the emancipatory features of critical PAR, nourished by a left-oriented Christian Liberation Theology. By contrast, in the Research and Development tradition, the pragmatic approach to PAR focus on such problem areas as efficiency, productivity, adaptive innovations and organizational development. Kurt Lewin emblematizes the Western tradition of PAR, influenced by the American philosophical school of pragmatism. He focussed on the post-war problems of enhancing job opportunities, the sources of prejudice, street gang socialization and training strategies of fostering democratic styles of leadership. The next section deals with how to bridge theory, methodology and social practice, from a transformative perspective on research and education for the common good.

Theory, Methodology and Social Practice

The following notes mirror views by Ulf Himmelstrand (1982) on PAR. He was a Swedish sociologist, actively engaged in the public debate, and a personal friend of Orlando Fals-Borda who regularly attended the international PAR congresses in Cartagena de las Indias, Colombia. Himmelstrand wrote about the key social issues of the Swedish agenda. As President of the International Sociological Association (1978–1982), he greatly contributed to internationalize sociology. Close to his heart and mind was to construct an organic bridge between theory, methodology and social practice. PAR has a close affinity with the realm of intercultural dialogue, given its participatory and dialogical nature. By linking theory, methodology and social practice, the 'researcher' and the 'researched' merge as co-theorizers, co-researchers and co-practitioners. For purposes of illustration on how this bridge works, theoretical views drawn from post-colonial authors provided guidelines to an empirical study of ethnic identity orientation among Mexican Americans via experiential methodology. Social practices to overcome the adverse psychological consequences of racism were inherent to this study. In the following paragraph, I examine the rationale for qualitative and experiential methodology.

Knowledge from What? Notes on Experiential Methodology

In correspondence with the previous reflections on PAR and experiential research, I endorse the following views on social science methodology by Blichfeldt (1987, p. 57):

> We need a social science where people matter, not as members of our sample, but as acting, reflecting and responsible. Where I inevitably as a researcher, am part of the process.

Can we envisage a social science where people matter? I proceed next to briefly introduce qualitative methodology, which in turn frames experiential research. The roots of qualitative research methods go back to Weber's *Verstehen* sociology and to Thomas and Znaniecki, among other. This perspective demands the immersion of the researcher in the everyday lives of the people and communities for a long time. My views on experiential research, drawn from John Heron, follow next drawn from Bacal (1994a):

> Heron...asked social researchers to reflect on their research practice and implicit orientations...he was particularly critical of those who advocate an absolute determination of human behavior... proposed...a view on relative determination...congenial with the emphasis on self-determination...in this particular study...The notion of relative determination recognizes the interaction between limiting socio-historical conditions and human freedom or self-determination...to assume that researchers are relatively free agents, while regarding research subjects as unfree or fully determined objects is plain elitism...the over-conditioned view of human beings is untenable, as evidenced by the researchers' own self-directed research activities...Summarizing, the notion of personal self-direction unfolding under conditions of relative determination provides a suggestive rationale for doing research in the social sciences...In the proposed approach, the researcher and the researched are regarded as co-participants in the research venture. Moreover, the enhancement of self-direction among...co-researchers is...an explicit research goal...in...the experiential orientation of this investigation...Social research can play a significant role in the process of developing a self-directive capacity among co-participants in research activities...Co-participants in this kind of social research get to review and reflect on their lives in a systematic manner, stimulating a process of individual/group learning and change...De Vos regards the experiential method as a novel approach to the study of ethnic groups...concerning the issue of self-directionality, Heron came to consider the experiential method 'as the central and crucial method for the systematic exploration of how human potential for self-direction can be actualized'.

Ethnic Identity Responses to Ethnic Discrimination: Learning from the Field

A real-life episode made me aware of what I later named 'ethnic hurt'. I was deeply struck when a Chicano classmate and neighbour broke down in deep grief and sobbing, because in his words and demeanour, he 'lacked Anglo features' (!). In other words, my friend felt painfully 'ugly' because he looked Mexican. This insight led me to reflect on social situations that are harmful to the self-regard of minority people. Previous research experience as a sociologist cum researcher in social psychiatry in Peru in the late 1960s had made me aware of the kind of mental problems resulting from the class structure of society. This episode led me to study ethnic identity research and to use a qualitative and PAR methodological orientation.

In the following years, this methodology was used in the study of organizational development and self-management of textile workers in Peru (Bacal, 1978/1991), to study peasant communities in a project of social rural development in Mexico (1981–1982) and to research identity changes among Latino elderly in Sweden (Bacal, 1996). The experiential PAR methods in these studies included: interactive group techniques, in-depth-interviews, natural and participant-observation, documentary research, content analysis, as well as more conventional data gathering methods. 'Self-selection', 'reputational' and 'theoretical' sampling procedures were of particular use in these studies. Special attention and listening to the 'definitions of the situations' by the participants is critical for this kind of co-research. The scope of experiential research within the larger horizon of PAR is open for imaginative and empirical exploration. It can contribute to bridging the realms of theory, methodology: new ways of gathering and sharing social knowledge with co-researchers and social practices. A note on social practice from the study of ethnic identity orientation follows next, alluding to concerted efforts to decolonize internalized ethnic oppression, as proposed by Rajne Kothari, in Wolf (1974):

> The worst result of the colonial experience was the destruction of self-regard and sense of dignity of those living under the conditions of ethnic domination... The restoration of this self-regard and dignity for minority group members has become a paramount task.

This study of ethnic identity responses of Mexican Americans used experiential methodology, a particular modality of PAR in social psychiatry. It examined the applicability of a social practice *cum* psychological counselling at the individual, dual and group levels of interaction, making use of the theory, methods and social practice of re-evaluation counselling. In this frame, co-counselling is a procedure designed to train lay peer counsellors to overcome psychological distress such as 'ethnic hurts', as described by Bacal (1994a, p. 72). These traumas that result from internalized racial and ethnic oppression are socially produced and unequally distributed and are thus susceptible of being mitigated or healed via, for instance, as it happened in this case study, at the Chicano counselling services at La Casa de la Raza, the Chicano Community Centre in Santa Barbara, California, USA. The re-evaluation of ethnic hurts often results in enhanced personal insight about one's own process of ethnic self-definition and self-esteem, which empowers people to take charge of their personal situation. From the perspective of community mental health, it entails the formation of ethnic self-help support groups fostering group solidarity and heightening awareness of the dynamics of oppression, internalized oppression and liberation in society. Participants take turns to speak about and openly express feelings associated with ethnic hurts, enabling them to learn about the scars left by Anglo ethnic discrimination on their psyche. These kinds of ethnic hurts underlie their experience of inadequacy and feelings of inability to cope with life tasks. How to summarize the main results of this particular case study of ethnic identity responses to ethnic discrimination of Mexican Americans? Let's assume that the methodological and social practice dimensions of this case study have been reasonably covered so far; let us next look at theoretical gains such as: (1) The confirmation that ethnic identity remains at the core of the self-image or identity of many people today. (2) The construction of an explanatory intersectional model in the social sciences seeking to explain four modal types of ethnic identity orientation among Mexican Americans, described below: (a) Ethnic Traditionalists or Loyalists, (b) Bi-Cultural, (c) Marginal and (d) Assimilated or Americanized. This model also explained the experience of Afro-Americans, concerning their process of ethnic identity orientation in an American-racialized society. (3) This study confirmed that changes in ethnic identity are associated with ethno-mobilization, as well as the reverse. Namely, a positive re-definition of ethnic identity among Mexican Americans after the Second World War led to affiliation in large numbers to the Chicano Movement in the 1970s, which shaped the cultural and political goals of these movements. One understands in this light the current saliency of ethnic identity and ethno-mobilization of Latinos in the USA, as they respond to hate media and the ethno-mobilization of white national populists who blindly support Trump's anti-Mexican politics. The current escalation of interethnic conflicts in the USA results in part from the stigmatization of Mexicans by Trump. A similar situation takes place in EU countries whose governments are poorly managing the problems resulting from the worst humanitarian crisis of the twenty-first century. Under current world conditions of racism, it is safe to expect the continuing saliency of racial and ethnic identity among ethnic minority group members, in turn bound to further lead to social polarization, ethno-mobilization, ethno-politics (Bacal, 2021) and a spiral of violence in our day and age.

Conclusions and Suggestions

Critical pedagogics helped me to differentiate knowledge from belief and prejudice, as well as to discern learning by fiat of dogma or revelation from learning by questioning. Dialogue entails an attitude of humility and self-examination in the ways found, for instance, in the lifework of Dag Hammarskjöld, whose attitude helped him to overcome personal prejudices and to reject dubious sources of hearsay, as narrated by Melber (2019). Such views on dialogue were useful in teaching Mexican teachers about peace education and cultures of peace, where hope in addition to dialogue help to correct the elitism, aloofness and cynicism, frequently observed among experts, technocrats, researchers and consultants. Devoid of hope, erudite scholars unwittingly reproduce the cycle of oppression in society. At the end of his prolific career, Freire realized the value of hope in the realms of education and politics. To illustrate the point just made about teaching peace education, I normally start my teaching with an exercise on what is 'new and good' in the lives of my students. This activity expands the emotional horizon and hope among students, which additionally provides a sense of empowerment. At times, one might start this exercise with an inspirational poem. Without personal coherence, hope and trust, the prospects for peace in a world plagued by societies and cultures of violence looks very deem. Research dealing with peace–conflict resolution, building peace, post-conflict and reconciliation are doomed to fail without peace education. When trying to make the point with my students concerning the quest for personal coherence and to explore the nexus between personal agency and general history, we read and analyzed 'the new page' written by Federico Mayor Zaragoza. One crucial lesson from this book is that if we want to write a new page on the culture of peace in world history, we need to write at the same time a new page of peace in our personal life history and praxis. Otherwise, the discourse on replacing the culture of violence with a culture of peace remains a platitude. The view of combining peace–conflict research with peace education was put to practice in a series of short-courses/workshops in Peru, next described. Against a background of about 200 recognized conflicts between communities, state and mining corporations, I led three short-courses/ workshops about conflict prevention and management, supported by the Institute of Peace and Conflict Research, Uppsala University and the UNALM in Peru, in the years 2013, 2015 and 2017.

These activities succeeded in recruiting mixed audiences that included representatives from different segments of society and *stakeholders*, including graduate students, university teachers, social movements, mining companies, practitioners and the Peruvian Ministry of Foreign Relations. They all benefitted from the rich insights drawn from peace–conflict research, small-group analysis of several case studies and peace education/cultures of peace.

Challenges and Possibilities of Active Learning

> The transformation education should assume today is to become a real social movement, not a political or economic one. In the past, there have been movements for the emancipation of working people and for that of women. Today we need a movement for the raising of the spiritual and intellectual values hidden in every human being.
>
> Maria Montessori (2016)

My suggestion to improve on active teaching/learning reflects an effort to re-enchant the classroom and bring back the joy of learning, as postulated by Paulo Freire. From another perspective, I question the imported notion of quality education as a trademark of the Bologna guidelines of higher education. The notion of quality education originated in the context of the industrial process of production and consumption, having in mind the final quality of merchandise. Are we able to conceive an institution of higher learning in which the different *tempos* of the students are taken into account and receive due support from teachers and school administrators? Is it possible to change the individualistic, competitive and commoditized higher education of our times? Taking into account the heavy demand of time, attention, effort and commitment, which are required by the 'I-Thou' approach to the teaching/learning process, one understands why it is rarely found in contemporary institutions of higher learning. This approach to active learning sounds unrealistic in our age of fast food, fast reading, one-week long courses, neglect of critical thinking and citizenship education, noticeable in contemporary institutions of higher education. In my attempt to shed light on the controversial meaning of quality education to Mexican doctoral teacher-students, I shown a video film interview with a student who had just graduated from high school in Finland, the country with the highest PISA scores. The interviewer asks, 'now that you graduated from school, which job interests you most?' His answer: 'I want to become the manager of Coca-Cola' (sic!). Is this a good example of what 'quality education' is about?

The term quality of education originated in the realm of the quality of products in the product market. In such a reduced scope of education, value is lost concerning the formative and ethical dimensions of active learning. If democracy worth its name is to have a sustainable future in the twenty-first century, formative values in the curriculum design and daily praxis of active learning should be acknowledged and incorporated by the key planners and players in all the educational spheres. This remark on the ethics of personal coherence in the realm of active learning in education confronts us with our stance as teachers and administrators in the educational game. These reflections led me to raise a few questions to conclude this section: are we able to reflect on our own ways to reproduce and to help to change the conventional ways to deal with the educational problems we seek to solve? What can we do in this respect? Paulo Freire and Dorothy Lee provide a communitarian sociocultural educational perspective that combines teaching/learning and research. Moreover, both Freire and Montessori regarded education as a social movement, to intervene in the socio-educational arena. Are we ready to engage in the task of transforming education in the institutions that pay our salary checks? This question is bound to cause cognitive dissonance, discomfort, and haunt us with an existential challenge: are we ready to take the leap of commitment and engage with our students as unique individual persons and co-learners in the educational game? The insights from Dorothy Lee, Paulo Freire, Orlando Fals-Borda and Maria Montessori, regarding education as a social movement, deserve their incorporation in the curricula, structure and praxis of academic and popular education. Christina Marouli addresses these issues with particular sensitivity in her chapter, based on her valuable experience with education on sustainability.

Paraphrasing UNESCO, the authors in this anthology contribute to a treasure of transformative educational experience in various corners of the world. How are active learning and intercultural dialogue pertinent to the Swedish educational and research situation? I contend in the frame of the Swedish debate on these issues, that an enlarged conceptual framework should couple intercultural dialogue with public policies promoting socio-economic, political and educational equality. This extended intellectual platform enables PAR to help solve practical problems like the integration and social inclusion of immigrant pupils in the school system.

These tasks have become more complicated in the past decades, due to Swedish nativism via political parties such as the so-called Sweden Democrats and National Democrats, previously known as National Socialists. In the next section, I summarize my views on TPAR.

The Promise of Transformative Participatory Action-Research

TPAR is a normative, meta-theoretical and meta-methodological approach to social research. It provides a conceptual framework to guide the process of investigation and sociocultural transformation. It additionally has the potential of helping to solve problems in the realms of education, development, health, climate change and democratization. The Latin American tradition of TPAR postulates an organic bridge between theory and praxis and a commitment to share social knowledge co-produced with fellow co-researchers to benefit the exploited and oppressed segments of the population. Different regional contexts account for the different theoretical approaches to PAR. The critical science approach prevails in Latin America, while in USA and Europe the pragmatic approach to problem-solving is prevalent. The view of self-direction under conditions of relative determination provides a suggestive theoretical platform for PAR in the human sciences. In this framework, both the researcher and the researched team up as co-researchers and co-learners in the research venture. The experiential method provides research with the means to explore ways to realize the human potential for autonomy and self-direction. In this regard, the development of self-direction among co-researchers is as an explicit objective of the research process. TPAR entails a promise to enhance active citizenship, and participatory democracy, through its learning dimension (critical thinking) by inviting the innate human potential of co-researchers and co-participants in the research process. It should be evident by now that the elitist assumption in conventional positivist research is untenable. Otherwise, we must be prepared to argue that the human population is divided in two segments regarding research conducted with 'human subjects', an elite of self-directed elite group of researchers endowed with freedom and a large segment of the world population devoid of that human attribute.

Words of Caution: The Two-Edged Sword of PAR and Social Knowledge

Experience casts a shadow on PAR here viewed as the two-edged sword of social knowledge. While I searched for answers to the questions raised in this article, concerning the potential use of social research and knowledge (for what, for whom?), I contend that social research might be irrelevant or used for both social control and emancipatory goals. Fals-Borda expressed his concern during the 50th Anniversary of the launching of PAR at the Dag Hammarskjöld Foundation in Uppsala. This concern points to the centrality of values, ethics, personal coherence and integrity in PAR, at a time when liberal and social democracies are being challenged, eroded and threatened by the rise of racism, tribalism and white nationalist populism. I end my reflections on TPAR contending that it is a legitimate scientific research methodology, capable of producing valid and reliable social knowledge for the common good and human emancipation. These final reflections have in mind the ongoing debate on the world likely to emerge in the post-COVID-19 viral era, pointing to the demand to build a bridge between the academic world and social movements, next discussed.

A Bridge between Academia and Social Movements

Along with tragic deaths and suffering, the COVID-19 pandemic has brought an unexpected occasion and time to observe and understand the root causes and unsustainable features of the old world disorder. This pandemic has unexpectedly brought the first possibility, after many decades of being shocked into passivity, to engage in active learning via a myriad of local, national, regional and global teach-ins, discussing how to go about building other possible worlds organized on the bases of justice and peace for the coming generations. We should plainly not return to the previous world's disorder. This is high time to apply international and intercultural dialogue to coordinate global efforts to overcome the damage caused by the COVID-19 and climate pandemics, as well as their underlying causes. In fact, we are witnessing a growing international demand for transformative research, education and social action. As an engaged scholar, I worry about the fate of liberal and social democracy and agree with Göran Greider (2017), *albeit* going beyond the Swedish political landscape:

> The only thing that means anything in the long view is working at the grassroots.

How is it possible to build bridges between academia and social movements? Gustavo Esteva (2014), a Mexican anthropologist, who is actively engaged in supporting the Zapatista project of resistance to the capitalist world system, has constructed new alternatives ways of production and consumption based on autonomy, cooperation and solidarity. In this respect, he created an alternative university model known as *Universidad de la Tierra* (Earth University) in Oaxaca, Mexico, published as a chapter in Manzano-Arredondo and Bacal (2014). This project is in turn part of the Global Tapestry of Alternatives Network (GTA) created in India. Another tentative answer to this question lies in the following argument by Vicente Manzano-Arredondo and Bacal (2014, p. 15):

> The university constitutes a privileged space to contribute in the creation of 'other possible worlds,' primarily intended to enhance

the so-called 'common good.' Rather, it can be found being immersed in processes which deny its mission, and to such a counter-productive degree, that it may be considered an 'Absurd University'...At the same time, a rainbow of overall social movements emerges, being much closer to the human longing for the 'common good', with a deep action experience...The confluence between 'university and social movements' might open a door to hope, as a powerful and mixed hybrid, decisively oriented towards 'Another Possible World.'

In this light, I wrote about the bridge suggested above between social movements, regarded as agencies of socio-educational intervention and transformative education (Bacal, in Macedo, 2011, pp. 65–84). To conclude, it is worthwhile to pay attention to the hope associated with the World Social Forum (Whitaker, 2005) and the awakening of a global awareness and social mobilization, in the shadow of the COVID-19 pandemic and the world climate emergency crisis. Time rarely available in the academic world has stimulated reflection, learning and debate on every conceivable issue between heaven and earth. These unusual times provide the unlikely opportunity to look at the structural causes and consequences from the pandemics, as well as opportunity to entertain the vision of other possible post-pandemic worlds. Thousands of cultural flowers are blooming in the guise of webinars, global teach-ins and Zoom discussions, such as the Tapestry of Global Alternatives (TGA), the World Social Forum 2021, social economy, human rights, Black Life Matters, Fridays for the Future, Popular Education, against apartheid and the annexation of Palestine by Israel, and the like.

The university is a contested battleground between producing useful knowledge for the common good, on one hand, and the neoliberal absurd university, on the other. The chapter by Vicente Manzano-Arrondo in this book unveils the workings of an absurd university in our time. The above examples about 'learning beyond the classroom' are reminiscent of the teach-ins of the university reform movements in the past, as well as of the utopian task to envision and construct other possible worlds, that in turn demand other ways to conceive research and education for the common good. The meeting of kindred souls taking place today in the forms of global teach-ins and webinars illustrates UNESCO's advocacy of education as a treasure and upholds the promise of active co-learning, co-research and intercultural dialogue. I hope that the readers of this chapter will realize why the perennial insights of Dorothy Lee, Paulo Freire and Orlando Fals-Borda, introduced in this work, defy the arrow of time.

References

Abraham, M. (2017). Presidential Message. International Sociological Association (ISA), *January Newsletter*.

Ålund, A., & Schierup, C.-U. (1991). Paradoxes of multiculturalism. In *Research in ethnic relations series*. Avebury: Academic Publishing Group.

Arguedas, J. M. (1964). *Todas las Sangres*. Buenos Aires: Editorial Losada.

Bacal, A. (1981). Capacitación de Educadores para Áreas Marginales: Desafíos en la Capacitación de Educadores en el Medio Rural, Unesco-OREALC, Santiago de Chile, Enero (1982). "Seminario-Taller Subregional sobre Innovaciones en la Formación y Perfeccionamiento de Educadores en el Marco de los Objetivos del Proyecto Principal de Educación en América Latina y el Caribe." Bogotá, Colombia, (3–10 Noviembre 1981).

Bacal, A. (1988). On people's media: The peasant radio-forum experience in Perú. In A paper presented at the XVIth Conference and General Assembly, on Mass Communications and Cultural Identity, International Association for Mass Communication Research, Barcelona, Cataluña, España, July 24–25.

Bacal, A. (1991a, February). Quality of working life & the level of economic and industrial democracy in Latin America. In A. Bacal (Guest Editor, Special Issue), *Economic and Industrial Democracy (EID). An International Journal, 12*(1). London: SAGE.

Bacal, A. (1991b). A participatory organizational & training strategy for the self-management sector: A case study of action-research in Perú. *EID, 12*(1), 119–135. London.

Bacal, A. (1994a, March). Types of ethnic identity responses to ethnic discrimination: An experiential approach to Mexican American identity, *KIM-Rapport* 18. Gothenburg: University of Gothenburg.

Bacal, A. (1994b). *From organism to identity: The road from psychology to social psychology (towards an epistemology of self-determination* (p. 1). Working Paper 94. Karlstad: University of Karlstad, Department of Social Sciences, Section of Communication.

Bacal, A. (1996). Permeando muitos projetos, Cap.5, parte II. In M. Gadotti (Ed.), *Paulo Freire: Uma Bibliografía, Cortes Editora* (pp. 232–234). São Paulo: UNESCO, Instituto Paulo Freire (IPF).

Bacal, A. (1997). Citizenship and national identity in Latin America: The persisting saliency of race, nation, class and ethnicity. In T. K. Oomen (Ed.), *Citizenship and national identity: Between colonialism and globalism* (pp. 281–312). New Delhi: SAGE.

Bacal, A. (1998). Reflections on cultural diversity and institutional human development, in red. Karin Apelgren och Ann Blückert, Universitetet som kulturell mötesplats: Verkligheten – utmaning – möjlighet!, Uppsala universitet. Rapportserie från Enheten för utveckling och utvärdering. *Rapport nr, 15,* 51–64.

Bacal, A. (2000). La Universidad Iberoamericana en el context de la globalización. In *Ongreso Internacional sobre la Universidad Iberoamericana. Actas II.* Valencia, CA: OEI. Colección Extrem América.

Bacal, A. (2002). Culturas de Paz y Desarrollo Humano Sustentable en América Latina: Educación para la Paz. In M. Salinas & U. Oswald (Eds.), *Culturas de Paz: Seguridad y Democracia en América Latina* (pp. 431–469). Cuernavaca, Morelos, and México: CRIM/UNAM, El Colegio de Tlaxcala, CLAIP y Fundación Heinrich Böll.

Bacal, A. (2011). Movimientos Sociales y Educación Transformadora (edición aumentada y corregida), en Porque uma educação outra é possível: Contributos para uma praxis transformadora, *Colecção querer saber 4,* Eunice Macedo (coord). Porto: Instituto Paulo Freire de Portugal, Centro de Recursos Paulo Freire FPCEUP.

Bacal, A. (2018a, November 23). The contributions of Paulo Freire to intercultural dialogue. In R. Nejadmehr (Ed.), *Anthology on "Interkulturell dialog"*. Gothenburg: FID.

Bacal, A. (2018b, October 5). The promise and challenges of transformative participatory action-research in the 21st century (the legacy of Paulo Freire and Orlando Fals-Borda). In A. Bilfeldt & J. Andersen (reds.), *Den ufaerdige fremtid – Aktionforskningens potentialer og udfordninger*. Aalborg: Aalborg Universitets förlag.

Bacal, A. (2018c). The legacy of Dorothy Lee and Paulo Freire to active learning in higher education. In A. Misseyanni, M. Lytras, P. Papadopoulou, & C. Marouli (Eds.), *Active learning strategies in higher education: Teaching for leadership, innovation and creativity*. Bingley: Emerald Publishing.

Bacal, A. (2021). *Ethno-politics*. Uppsala: Uppsala University.

Beck, U. (2009). *The world at risk*. Cambridge: Polity Press.

Bell, M. (2018). *City of the good: Nature, religion and the ancient search for what is right*. Princeton, NJ: Princeton University Press.

Blichfeldt, J. F. (1987). A case of action research. In S. Selander (Ed.), *Perspectives on action research* (p. 57). Stockholm: Institute of Education, Department of Educational Research, Reports on Education and Psychology.

Buber, M. (1929/1996). *Paths in Utopia*. Syracuse, NY: Syracuse University Press.

Buber, M. (1955). *Between man and man*. Boston, MA: Beacon Press.

Castells, M. (1998). *The rise of network society*. Oxford: Blackwell.

Eco, U. (2018). Contra el fascismo. In E. Lozano (tr.), *Il fascismo eterno*. New York, NY: Penguin Random House.

Ehrenreich, J. (1986). Prologue: Valuing Dorothy Lee. In D. Lee (Ed.), *Valuing the self: What we can learn from other cultures* (p.vi). Prospects Heights, IL: Waveland Press, Inc.

Esteva, G. (2014). *La libertad de aprender*. In V. Manzano-Arrondo & A. Bacal (co-editores), *Revista Interuniversitaria de Formación del Profesorado* (RUFOP), Madrid, Diciembre 14.

Fals-Borda, O. (1987, December). The application of participatory action-research in Latin America. *International Sociology*, 2(4), 329–347.

Forskningsrådet för interkulturell dialog (FID). (2017). Call for abstracts.

Freire, P. (1970). *Pedagogy of the oppressed*. New York, NY: The Seabury Press.

Freire, P. (1973). *Extensión o Comunicación: La Concientización en el Medio Rural*. México, MX: Ed. Siglo XXI y Tierra Nueva.

Freire, P. (1976). *Educación y cambio*. Buenos Aires: Debates del Tercer Milenio. Galerna – Búsqueda del Ayllu.

Freire, P. (1997). *Pedagogia da Autonomia*. São Paulo: Editora Paz e Terra.

Freire, P. (2014). *Pedagogy of hope: Reliving pedagogy of the oppressed*. London: Bloomsbury Publishing PLC.

Gadotti, M. (1996). *Paulo Freire: Uma Biobibliografia*. São Paulo: Cortez e IFFP. Brasilia: UNESCO.

Gadotti, M. (2000). *Pedagogia da terra: Ecopedagogia e Educacao Sustentável*. CLACSO.

Goodman, P. (1960). *Growing Up absurd: Problems of youth in organized society*. New York, NY: A Vintage Books.

Greider, G. (2017). Politikerveckorna gör mera skada än nytta. In *Metro*. Duellen, NJ: Behovs politikerrveckorna? 22 juni.

Henry, J. (1963). *Culture against man*. New York, NY: Vintage Books. A Division of Random House.

Himmelstrand, U. (1982). Innovative processes in social change: Theory, method, and social practice. In T. Bottomore, S. Nowak, & M. Sokolowska (Eds.), *Sociology: The state of the art. ISA* (pp. 37–66). London and Beverly Hills, CA: Sage Publications Ltd.

Hobsbawm, E. J. (1971). Perú: The peculiar "revolution". *The New York Review of Books*, December 16.

Kothari, R. (1974). Education for autonomy and diversity. In C. Wulf (Ed.), *The handbook on peace education*. Oslo and Frankfurt/Main: International Peace Research Association (IPRA).

Lee, D. (1986). *Valuing the self*. Epilogue by Jeffrey Ehrenreich. Prospect Heights, IL: Waveland Press, Inc.

Lee, D. (1987). *Freedom and culture*. Prologue by Jeffrey Ehrenreich. Prospect Heights, IL: Waveland Press, Inc.

Macedo, E. (2011). Movimientos Sociales y Educación Transformadora (edición aumentada y corregida), en Porque uma educação outra é possível: Contributos para uma praxis transformadora, *Colecção querer saber 4*, Eunice Macedo (coord), Instituto Paulo Freire de Portugal, Centro de Recursos Paulo Freire FPCEUP, Porto, Portugal.

Manzano-Arredondo, V. & Bacal, A. (2014). Co-autors & Co-editors (2014/2015), "La Universidad y movimientos sociales: la universidad absurda y la esperanza de las praxis universidad-calle" (Introducción) en La Universidad y movimientos sociales en 2014, Vicente Manzano arredondo y azril Bacal Roij (co-editores). *Revista Interuniversitaria de Formación del Profesorado (RUFOP)*, Madrid, Diciembre 14.

Marin, L. (2010). *Can we save true dialogue in an age of mistrust?* Uppsala: Dag Hammarskjöld Foundation. *Critical Currents*, no. 8 (January).

Marx, K. (1961). *Economic and philosophic manuscripts of 1844*. Moscow: Foreign Languages Publishing House.

Melber, H. (2019). Dag Hammarskjöld on dialogue. *Development Dialogue*, 64 (pp. 19–25). Uppsala: Dag Hammarsjköld Foundation.

Mészáros, I. (2004). Education beyond capital. III foro mundial de Educación. Porto Alegre, RGS, Brasil, in Bacal (2011, op.cit, p. 69).

Mills, C. W. (1959). *Sociological imagination*. New York, NY: Oxford University Press.

Montessori, M. (2016, November 9). Montessori quotes. Retrieved from www.montessorieducation.com

Myrdal, G. (1973, November 2). At a lecture at Campbell Hall. University of California at Santa Barbara.

Myrdal, G. (1986). *Against the stream: Critical essays in economics*. London: Macmillan.

Pozas Arciniegas, R. (1962). *Juan the Chamula; an ethnological re-creation of the life of a Mexican Indian*. Berkeley, CA: University of California Press.

Prince, M. (2004). Does active learning work? A review of the research. *Journal of Engineering Education*, 93(3), 223–231.

Rex, J. (1986). *Race and ethnicity*. Milton Keynes: Open University Press.

Saldaña, P. (2019, January 7). Bolsonaro's education plan means to expurge Paulo Freire's influence from the school system. *Folha de São Paulo*.

Sassen, S. (2014). *Expulsions: Brutality and complexity in the global economy*. Cambridge, MA and London: The Belknap Press of Harvard University Press.

Schugurensky, D. (1983). Selected moments of the 20th century. A work in progress. In *Department of adult education, community development and counselling psychology. The Ontario Institute for studies in education*. Toronto, ON: University of Toronto.

Skinner, B. F. (1948). *Walden two*. Indianapolis, IN: Hackett Publishing Company, Inc.

Solari, A. (2018). *Atropellos, arreglos y regocijos*. Lima.

Thomas, W. I., & Znaniecki, F. (1918–1920). *The polish peasant in Europe and America. Monograph of an immigrant group (5 Vols.)*. New York, NY: Dove.

Velezmoro, C., Julio Chavez, A., Mandujano, Bacal, A., Rodrich, H., & Chacón, H. (2013). Politicas de Equidad y Cohesion Social para la UNALM (2011–2013), ALFA/Riaipe-3, UNALM.

Wallerstein, I. (1988, November 10). The Myrdal legacy: Racism and underdevelopment as dilemmas. Lecture at the University of Stockholm. Faculty of Social Sciences.

Whitaker, C. (2005, March). The world social forum: What is it really about? *The OECD Observer, 248*, 26.

Wilkinson, R., & Pickett, K. (2018). *The inner level: How more equal societies reduce stress, restore sanity and improve everyone's well-being*. London: Penguin.

Chapter 2

Critical Pedagogy for Environmental and Social Change: What Helps? What Obstructs? Theory and Practice in Dialogue

Christina Marouli

Abstract

Contemporary societies face serious environmental and social challenges that require decisive action. In the 1970s, Environmental Education (EE) was conceived as an important method for raising awareness and bringing about the needed changes in social practices that can lead to environmental protection and more recently sustainable development (transforming EE to Education for Sustainability (EfS)). Since then, many EE/EfS programmes have been implemented and some change has been observed despite the persisting problems. EE/EfS – especially when aiming to change behaviours – has been akin to critical pedagogy which aims to prepare independent and critical thinkers and empowered citizens that can effectively address social problems. What pedagogical approaches and educational methods are more effective in bringing about changes in attitudes and social practices? What instructional design and practices facilitate this transformation? What are the challenges? These are questions that have troubled environmental educators and are worth reflecting on in the present context of knowledge societies and Higher Education that is significantly impacted by a neoliberal ideology.

This chapter aims to contribute to the ongoing discussions around these questions, via a dialogue between theory and practice. A discussion of critical theory and pedagogy and of EE/EfS is counterposed with theoretical reflections and insights from the author's more than three decades of teaching experience (primarily in Greece). A discussion of the instructor's key pedagogical influences and the evolution of her (my) instructional practices follows, with the aim to identify instructional practices that have a transformative potential, within the context of the challenges and the facilitating parameters of contemporary societies and educational contexts. The instructor's self-reflections and students' qualitative comments are used in a

Transformative Research and Higher Education, 45–72
Copyright © 2022 Christina Marouli
Published under exclusive licence by Emerald Publishing Limited
doi:10.1108/978-1-80117-694-120221003

variety of research methods: a self-study research approach drawing on the author's self-reflections as instructor and an analysis of students' qualitative comments in course evaluations and other informal evaluative situations.

Keywords: Environmental education; education for sustainability; instructional design; social change; pedagogical practices with transformative potential; challenges; critical theory

Introduction

Education has been repeatedly identified as a major mean for social reproduction as well as social change. Contemporary societies face serious environmental and social challenges, as evidenced by the economic crisis in the Western world and the 'natural catastrophes' (like floods, wildfires, intense hurricanes) that we have been recently experiencing. This reality points to the need for changes in our cultural values, the organization of our societies, the premises of our economies and our relationship with the environment. Thus, education today is called to realize its transformative potential for the sake of humanity as a whole and nature.

In the 1970s, Environmental Education (EE) – later transformed to Education for Sustainability (EfS) – was proposed as a tool to stimulate the needed changes in the relation of human societies with the environment. Given the 50-year long history of EE/EfS and the continuing and ever more intense environmental problems, one can argue that the good intentions of EE/EfS efforts are not sufficient to lead to critical self-reflection, let alone altered attitudes, behaviours and social practices. Still, EE and EfS experiences, along with theories like critical pedagogy, have provided important insights regarding effective transformative educational experiences as well as the challenges and limitations such efforts face.

What helps EE/EfS achieve its transformative goal – to entice learning, interest and action for the environment and sustainable societies? What pedagogical approaches and educational contexts are more effective in bringing about changes in attitudes and social practices? What instructional design and practices facilitate this transformation in contemporary societies? These are the questions this chapter aims to tackle.

Methodological Approach

I believe that theories can provide important guiding principles for thought and action, but actual practice provides fresh insights highlighting strengths and potential weaknesses of theories as well as the significance of everyday experiences and tacit knowledge. For this reason, I will choose to investigate the aforementioned questions via a dialogue between critical pedagogical theory, theory of EE/EFS and the educational praxis, building on my personal experiences as educator (for 30 years now, mostly in Higher Education, but with experience in earlier ages as well and in non-formal education in the context of Non-Governmental Organizations).

Due to my educational background, I will discuss both environmental and social education as I do believe that they should be very much interrelated. Starting from a discussion of literature relating to critical pedagogy and EE/EfS, I will extract insights for transformative instructional (and course) design and contexts. I will subsequently discuss the design of select courses and my (the instructor's) goals. Then, I will analyze students' comments regarding their learning experience including the instructional practices and the instructor, with the intention of gaining a deeper understanding of the impacts of the instructional design. Student comments are compiled from the official course evaluations (an online questionnaire with mostly close-ended questions and two to three open-ended ones), qualitative in-class evaluations (written – with open-ended questions only regarding what they liked and what could be enhanced in the course, the instructional activities, the instructor, the readings) or oral feedback that was spontaneously provided to the instructor at unexpected times.

Theoretical Insights from Critical Pedagogy and Education for the Environment

Learning implies change, although this could range from adjustment/shifting of one's own thinking to change in behaviours and social practices. According to traditional pedagogical theories, education transmits (past) knowledge, changing individuals for social reproduction – 'formation from without' according to Dewey (1938). Progressive pedagogical theories focus on transformative educational practices and creation of new knowledge, leading the way to personal and social change.

Critical Pedagogy

Critical pedagogy emphasizes social change. According to Freinet, a French pedagogue, 'education was a way, if not *the* way, to change humanity' (Legrand, 1993, p. 9). Gramsci has argued that culture in all its forms – including education and beyond high and low culture – is not merely a superstructure, an expression of the material basis of society but also a significant force constructing reality (Mayo, 2014). Critical theorists like Gramsci (1971) and Freire (1970) have argued for the political nature of education; education is not apolitical or neutral. Hegemony, according to Gramsci, is a social condition in which a certain social group exercises influence but also wins consent. In order for that to happen, hegemony in its manifestations also educates people in order for consent and influence to be possible. At the same time, Gramsci advocates that critical pedagogy can lead to change in hegemonic practices. Freire (2000) reinforces this view and identifies cultural work inside the educational institutions as well as in other social loci as important for social transformation, referring to 'cultural action for freedom'.

Freire (2000) advocates the pedagogy of praxis, viewing the educational practice as a continuous dialectic between reflection and action connecting theorizing with common sensibility for critical consciousness. The learning process should start from learners' experiences and common sense, and with further knowledge, skills and critical reflection transform these to a new body of knowledge that can empower them to act on their lives and societies. The instructor should validate learners' prior experiences and create a learning process that builds on and transcends them. According to Freire, the 'pedagogy of praxis' aims for a transformative understanding of reality towards liberation and a free society. Ira Shor (1987) poignantly argues that education should stimulate learners to experience the ordinary in an extraordinary way; to problematize the socially taken-for-granted. Berry (1998) says, 'In fact, in postmodernism, challenge and chaos are the agencies out of which knowledge is created' (p. 54). This insight provides a handle for the translation of critical pedagogical theory into critical pedagogical practice as well as a guide for the actual design of the educational praxis.

> Students use this chaos to create knowledge.... In order to do so, changes are required that dismantle and reposition the multiple dimensions of educational sites. Teachers, materials, structures, content, logic, methodologies, educational discourse, mainstreaming, administration, policies, classroom management and planning are only a few of the sites that would be accused of hegemonic practices that function to block students' creation of knowledge.
>
> (Berry, 1998, p. 55)

Acting and changing social reality require the use of diverse bodies of knowledge and skills. Gramsci opposes the division and different valuation of high and low culture. Giroux (2011) proposes interdisciplinary approaches. Freire's and other critical pedagogues' approaches highlight the significance of learners' prior experiences and knowledge. Barnes as quoted in Goodson (1998) states: 'In so far as we use knowledge for our own purposes... we begin to incorporate it into our view of the world, and to use parts of it to cope with the exigencies of living. Once the knowledge becomes incorporated into our view of the world on which our actions are based, I would say it has become "action knowledge"' (p. 38). Feminist theorists have also highlighted the different ways people (women and men) know, as well as the fact that some of these ways are considered valid while others – the ones connected with marginalized groups – are either undervalued or ignored (Belenky, Clinchy, Goldberger, & Tarule, 1986; Berry, 1998). In a learning context, the instructors should validate these ways of knowing for action knowledge to be possible.

Contemporary educational settings generally target learners' thinking process, at best leading to critical thinking and questioning. However, as Freinet indicated, wonderment is the point of departure for knowledge – otherwise a lesson is a bore; then comes the need to share this feeling with others and simultaneously search for explanations (Legrand, 1993). An uninterested mind is not available for new knowledge and surely, it is no fertile ground for the creation of knowledge.

Furthermore, contemporary educational settings disembody knowledge, requiring students to stay immobile for the duration of a lesson. Critical pedagogues call for the involvement of the whole learner – mind, emotion and body – (e.g. Clandfield & Sivell, 1990) as a way not only to critical thinking (knowledge as an entry point) but also to critical consciousness and critical action; different levels of criticality as Habermas has aptly indicated.

But an important component of an empowering pedagogical praxis that can lead to social change is hope. This is a prerequisite for action (Freire, 1998; Giroux, 2001; Marcuse, 1966; Van Heertum, 2006). Bloch (1986) argues that we should move away from a condemnation of present societies toward an alternative vision that can inspire people. In this effort, the instructors have a significant role to play. Van Heertum (2006) writes:

> Critical teachers and researchers must also embody the change they are advocating, showing students an alternative through their actions together with their words. This requires more than critique, activism and alluding to the great refusal; it also must include a positive dream that can inspire others to follow, embracing their creativity and beliefs.
>
> (p. 49)

Freire also underlines the significance of the educators as intellectuals. They are needed to help learners develop a critical consciousness and organize the pedagogical praxis for social transformation. Freinet states that teachers should create question-provoking environments. Ada (2007) highlights the significance of caring and loving environments. She advocates that these are the environments where learning can take place; and learning environments are created by educators. Giroux (2011) furthered Freire's view of 'organic intellectuals' by proposing the term 'public intellectuals', those who work for social change by targeting a larger audience, with the aim of mobilizing them to socially transformative action.

Environmental Education – Education for Sustainability

Foley, Morris, Gounari, and Agostinone-Wilson (2015) state 'Critical pedagogy's project [is] rooted in critique, challenge, hope, transformation and construction' (p. 131). EE, from its conception, is akin to this project, but more practical. EE has been conceived as critical education that aims to bring about change in behaviours and social practices that relate to the environment (United Nations, 1975, 1977). It started as outdoors education, bringing learners in contact with nature, just as Freinet advocated (Legrand, 1993). Thus, experiential learning (Dewey, 1938) is at the heart of EE. It has aimed to raise people's awareness about environmental issues and to develop their knowledge about nature and the way it works. Its ultimate goal has been to contribute to contemporary societies' concern with finding solutions to environmental problems and fostering a harmonious relation of human societies with nature. After some years of experience, EE was reconceived as Education for Sustainability or Education for

Sustainable Development (EfS) as it became clear that environmental issues alone could not be effectively addressed. An integrative approach, combining social, economic and ecological knowledge, was proposed (UNESCO, 2005; UNESCO, 2016), requiring integrative and widely interdisciplinary (or better yet trans-disciplinary) approaches to sufficiently address the complexity of the environment–society–economy nexus.

EE has proposed a useful categorization of pedagogical efforts: education *on, in* or *for* the environment. Education on the environment focusses on knowledge acquisition and awareness-raising; education in the environment brings learners into contact with the natural and human-made environment and aims to emotive learning; while education for the environment aims at behavioural and social change for a better and healthier environment.

The main pedagogical methods used include projects (often in the form of group work), emphasizing learning as a process; problem-solving, with an emphasis on real – usually local – problems; and pedagogical games, creating fun and enjoyable learning environments, that stimulate learners' ability to critically understand diverse viewpoints. The EE pedagogical methods not only aim to engage learners in the creation of knowledge but also to involve them in actual environmental problem-solving and ultimately to stimulate their interest in environmental action. In this effort, the boundaries between the classroom and educational institution on the one hand and the local community and nature on the other dissolve, with the learning praxis occurring in multiple loci, sometimes within the context of a collaborative effort between students, instructors and community members – i.e. action research.[1] EfS has emphasized integrative learning, drawing from diverse disciplines and bodies of knowledge. Efforts to resolve environmental problems require good understanding of social and ecological systems – systemic thinking, which is based on but is not the same as integrative thinking.

Some contemporary thinkers have criticized EfS for overemphasizing inte-grative approaches, ignoring issues of power and inequalities and sinking into a transmissive form of pedagogy. They argue that EE, with its evolution to EfS, has lost its transformative and empowering edge (Jickling & Wals, 2008; Kopnina, 2014). Jickling and Wals (2008) proposed an interesting heuristic highlighting the significance of two independent dimensions – first from the individual to the collective level and second critical and creative learning (critical thinking) to participation in society (action) – both of which should be considered in the design of EE/EfS initiatives. This framework is in line with the Habermasian distinction between critical thought, critical consciousness and critical action, as they relate with three fundamental dimensions: knowledge, self and community/world (Blackmore, 2001). Marouli (2016) and Marouli, Misseyanni, Papadopoulou, and Lytras (2018) enhanced this heuristic and proposed that learning is a process, with increasing depth of enquiry and action, from critical learners, to empowered learners (both of these at the level of knowledge and individual personal change), to engaged citizens and then empowered ones (both at the collective level, moving from theory to action for the common good). Critical and empowering education and EE/EfS should consciously reflect on each of them and create educational contexts, instructional and assessment methods, tools and institutional settings that best support them. As a guide, Marouli and Duroy (2019) suggest five dimensions (see Fig. 2.1) instructors should consciously reflect on while designing classes and along which, they should aim at the more transformative end of the continuum in each one of them.

In summary, critical pedagogical theory perceives education as a way of bringing about social change and promoting the common good; thus, it goes hand-in-hand with critical social theories. EE/EfS is akin to this perspective of education. At a more practical level, critical pedagogy views education as learning based on action often around real-life issues. Thus, it advocates a pedagogy of praxis, aiming to a transformative understanding of reality, and provides useful insights in regard to what contributes to such a pedagogy. Wonderment and challenging the taken-for-granted reality constitute important starting points. The integration of a variety of bodies of knowledge is fundamental in the query process, while starting from learners' prior experiences (knowledge) validates their reality and provides a secure ground for the cultivation of new knowledge and understandings of reality. The active involvement of the whole learner – mind, emotions and body – in interactive learning contexts is fundamental for an empowering pedagogy that can lead to action and more so social action. EE/EfS talks about education *on, in* and *for* the environment. This holistic involvement supports the connection between theoretical knowledge and real-life action. Dissolving boundaries between classroom and community and between disciplines, as well as addressing power issues in society and in the classroom, are useful approaches. The instructor plays a crucial role in the empowerment of the learners, as s/he orchestrates the educational setting (including instructional design, learning context, pedagogical methods and tools, and assessments)

	Transmissive learning → Transformative learning			
Goal / Dimension	Critical learners	Empowered learners	Critical citizens	Empowered citizens
Instructor role	Expert	Mentor	Mentor - collaborator	Facilitator
Instructional design	Authoritative classroom	Interactive classroom	Democratic classroom	Democratic & social learning spaces
Pedagogical methods	Interactive discussions	Interactive learning in context / problem solving	Sociological imagination / systemic learning	Social learning in service / real problem solving
Assessments	Measuring output	Measuring outcome	Documenting / Measuring learning process	Supporting learning process
Context – Higher Education institutions	Disciplinary expertise	Interdisciplinary approaches	Socially responsible institutions / sustainable universities	Partners with society for the common good

Fig. 2.1.   Framework for Transformative Learning in Contemporary Societies. *Source:* Marouli and Duroy (2019)

rendering it caring, democratic and collaborative, or mechanistic, hierarchical and individualistic; s/he cultivates (or not) social responsibility and hope with his/her example and words; and s/he mobilizes (or not) to action.

In the following sections, I will discuss some of my experiences as a critical educator, aiming to counterpose practical experience with the theory and extract lessons regarding critical (EE/EfS) education and its transformative potential in contemporary societies, focussing on its form and content (class environment, instructional and assessment methods).

Insights from the Pedagogical Experience

Course Design: My (the Instructor's) Intentions and Viewpoints

I will discuss four Higher Education courses that I have taught several times, allowing for a longitudinal reflection: an introductory Environmental Studies (Contemporary Environmental Issues) course, a Research Methods course (Integrated Methods for Environmental Studies); a course on Environmental Justice; and one on Sustainable Cities. I designed the last two courses myself; the Research Methods course was co-designed, while the Introductory Environmental Studies (Intro ES) was not designed by me. I selected these courses as I consider them representative of the different modes of teaching indicated in the heuristic of Marouli et al. (2018) as Table 2.1 below indicates.

Introductory Environmental Studies/Science Course

The Introductory Environmental Studies (ES) course (from now on: *Intro ES*) is an overview course aiming at acquainting students of different fields – except Environmental Studies – with scientific knowledge relevant to contemporary environmental issues and natural laws underlying ecosystems. It also aims at raising awareness about the responsibility of humans for these problems and about sustainable solutions, hoping to change environmental attitudes. This is a multi-section course, taught by different professors, with two in-class exams common for all sections.

In this context, the instructor is an expert in the field sharing knowledge on the subject. Lessons involve interactive presentations, involving PowerPoints and discussions and one or two field visits to the nearby forest for an in-nature experience. I usually start with questions regarding their prior knowledge and experiences regarding the subject. When I started teaching the course, I offered students the possibility of investigating a specific environmental issue (with sources I provided) which they then presented to the class. This was a voluntary activity. In later iterations, I decided to change the instructional approach and vary it in different sections in order to investigate the impact of different peda-gogical methods on students' learning. I introduced more experiential collective activities (e.g. a collective waste measurement at the recycling points of the campus, documenting the actual situation, reflecting on it and discussing proper ways of recycling) and/or flipping the classroom instruction (e.g. the class was

Table 2.1. Basic Information about the Courses and Their Design.

	ES4017	ES4229	ES4343	ES1005
Educational institution	Higher Education – College	Higher Education – College	Higher Education – College	Higher Education – College
Level	6 (senior)	6 (senior)	6 (senior)	4 (introduction)
Times taught	7 (taught once a year)	2 (once per year)	8 (taught once a year)	9 (per semester; usually 2 sections)
Number of students	Average 7 (between 4 and 11)	Average 9 (between 5 and 12)	Average 5 (between 2 and 9)	Average 21 (between 20 and 24)
Goal	Empowered learners; critical consciousness – in future: policy makers with power awareness; social change	Critical knowledge and consciousness about cities; contribute to better cities; social change	Critical knowledge about scientific methods; critical scientists capable of using scientific methods fit for purpose and aware of hidden biases	Knowledge, awareness-raising; critical learners; preparing future citizens sensitive to environmental issues and more ready to change and contribute to change
Goal – type of learners/ citizens	Critical and empowered learners; critical citizens	Empowered learners; critical and engaged citizens; empowered citizens	Critical and empowered learners; critical scientists and citizens	Critical learners – critical citizens (if possible)
Class environment relations	Teacher co-ordinator; students take	Teacher co-ordinator; much group work; connection with	Teacher as mentor and facilitator of interactive discussions; sessions	Teacher at the centre – lecturer and discussion facilitator

Table 2.1. (*Continued*)

	ES4017	ES4229	ES4343	ES1005
	responsibility for some classes	community (community problem-solving)	discussing their capstone proposals (connecting theory with their practice) – exchanges; sometimes small group discussions	
Pedagogical methods	Group discussions without PowerPoint presentations; students leading some class meetings; field experiential visits; recently: collaboration with course in the USA	Group projects; on problems of community interest (service-learning); individual investigation; interactive lectures (only 1/2); student presentations	Interactive discussions; PowerPoint presentations used; occasional group discussions in class; practical (design, apply, analyze a questionnaire related to an issue of interest on campus); guided capstone proposal preparation	Interactive lectures; field activities; occasional small groups for engagement; recently: plant experiment (for emotion and bodily involvement). Started with voluntary projects (research); then: some exercises (like waste measurement) for experiential learning; now: plant experiment (as example of science and contact with nature)
Assessment method	Take home exam; paper/ project	Take home exam; group project with an individual investigation of a sustainable city	Take home exam; report on practical exercise; capstone proposal	2 in-class exams

divided into groups, and each took responsibility of presenting different parts of the chapter on water resources). In more recent iterations, I have introduced many more small group discussions on different topics brought up in class.

In this class, students are predisposed to passively receive knowledge from the expert instructor. With the aforementioned instructional approaches, I aim at going beyond the expert role and at creating an interactive classroom with opportunities for critical thinking, peer and experiential learning, with the ultimate goal being active and critical learners.

Environmental Studies Research Methods Course

The ES Research methods course (from now on: *Methods*) is a core and higher level course of the Environmental Studies programme and aims to impart a large body of methodological knowledge to the ES students, with a critical perspective. I have participated in its design, and I have taught it since its inception (eight times).

This annual course has changed form over these eight years. In the first five iterations, it was one course, including both natural science and social science methods, as well as methodological discussions, while instruction was based on interactive discussions and one of the main products of the course was a capstone proposal. It was co-taught with other ES faculty, with myself as the main instructor and each one of the other colleagues presenting a natural science method depending on their expertize. As this course was too heavy, it was divided into two separate courses, the first one focussing on natural science methods and the second one on social science methodological approaches. After its division into two courses, I teach the second course which focusses on methodology and social science methods and leads to students' capstone proposals.

Students were assessed via an in-class exam and their capstone proposal in the first five iterations; while in the last three iterations, assessment in the second course of the series comprises a take-home exam, a practical exercise (usually designing and administering a survey) and the capstone proposal. The take-home exam questions have turned the individual assessment exercise into a learning experience, where students are encouraged to discuss the questions (peer-learning) but answers should be written and submitted individually. Instructional methods have also evolved from mainly interactive discussions in the class and some laboratory demonstrations, to more experiential learning involving field measurements and laboratory analysis for the natural science component (first course of the series), and practice assignments on surveys and questionnaires, a mock-up exercise on interviewing and group activities in the social science component (second course).

In the class, I act as a mentor, and students learn with each other in an interactive context, with some practical components, i.e. practising surveys and interviews and group activities where students help each other understand and reflect on the material. This instructional approach and assessment method allows the involvement of the whole learner – mind, emotion and body – too. Although this course's main aim is inevitably methodological knowledge, its connection with the capstone proposal provides a practical component to the course – a real application – making all the theoretical knowledge about research methods relevant and directly useful to the students.

Environmental Justice Course

The Environmental Justice course (an annual course that I have offered seven times) aims to sensitize the ES students (a science degree) to the political dimensions of environmental issues. I act as a facilitator asking many 'how', 'why' and 'who' questions, while different theories of explaining environmentally unjust situations and their implications are discussed with the aim of facilitating critical and systemic thinking.

This course has a very different classroom environment: the instructor facilitates discussions without PowerPoints, while students organize and lead selected class meetings. I designed this course as a 'seminar' where students should have done the readings before the class meetings, while in class discussions based on the readings and students' reflections on them, as well as debates take place. Thus, knowledge is co-created by students and instructor together, in a class which rather resembles a think-tank. After two or three iterations of the course, I added an initial internet-based exercise (search for audiovisual materials related to environmental justice as students understand it) with the aim of mobilizing emotion and self-reflection, as well as role-playing activities to stimulate students' capacity to critically understand and empathize with other viewpoints and experiences. I also organize walks to the local community so that students experience the city reality in a new/extraordinary way (with an environmental justice perspective), the relevance of students' experiences and prior knowledge is revealed and emotive learning is triggered.

In the first iterations of the course, students were assessed via a research paper and an in-class exam. After the first five years, I replaced the in-class exam with a take-home exam, again in order to render the exam one more step of the learning process and less of an assessment tool.

This instructional and assessment design provides an example of a learning process that is organized to cultivate critical engagement in the commons (of education in this case), in line with the logic that we teach by our example more than with our words.

Sustainable Cities Course

The Sustainable Cities course could have been taught as a higher-level knowledge-centred course. However, I have chosen to emphasize knowledge creation (rather than critical knowledge acquisition) via a rather interactive classroom, with firstly interactive presentations and discussions based on a set of readings students are expected to have done before class and secondly considerable group work time in class. Group projects relating to real issues of neighbouring local communities (action research) constitute a central axis of this course. Oftentimes, the topics are decided after consultation with local authorities and the findings of the projects are shared with them. In the context of their group work, students are often expected to find literature, collect information from city inhabitants, interview municipal authorities, etc.

From the beginning, the assessment strategy of this course included a take-home exam and a group project. In the second iteration, I added an individual exercise where students had to collect information about and critically present a sustainable or smart city and its actions. This has provided a wealth of cases demonstrating the concept of sustainable cities and allowed students to critically assess its reality. This has also provided an opportunity for students to collaborate with and help a primary school in Athens that also worked on the ideal city. Finally, students of this course have participated in real competitions for urban issues (e.g. Climathon in Athens – for problem-solving; or a contest for a new city vision). Connection with community issues shows the relevance of the learning process, provides opportunities for real problem-solving (a more empowering experience) and constructive involvement in the community, nurturing skills as well as hope for social change.

Students' Perspectives

Students' qualitative comments provide some interesting insights regarding the impact of the pedagogical methods. They are also valuable inputs for instructors' reflection on the course design in comparison to their intentions. Below, students' qualitative comments from course evaluations (organized by the College itself) and informal evaluations in class or other informal comments are discussed per course. They are also presented in a tabular format, along with the important dimensions that critical pedagogy and EE/EfS, have identified: pedagogy of action (action–reflection; experiential learning–action research), extraordinarily experiencing the ordinary, knowledge boundary crossings, power in theory and practice (class environment, assessment), systemic thinking, mind–emotion–body involvement, hope and imagination. Students' critical comments or concerns are also presented in the discussion below. Then, an overall comparison of students' evaluations in the four courses is attempted.

Introductory Environmental Studies/Science Course

The quantitative course evaluations show that students are generally satisfied with the course, and the level of satisfaction has increased after the introduction of more experiential activities. In the first year and before the introduction of more experiential collective activities and small group discussions, students appreciated the interactive character of the class and the encouragement they received for participation. A student indicated that lots of in-class interaction enabled them to think. Students' critical comments usually asked for more practical activities, e.g. field trips, while some asked for less material. A couple mentioned as a complaint that disrespectful students obstructed their learning process, again revealing the significance of interaction in the learning process. More recently, students' comments showed appreciation of the active learning approaches and referred to increased critical thinking, increased awareness of environmental issues and concern for the environment, as well as efforts to adopt more environmentally friendly behaviours as a consequence of the course.

> I loved the experiential component and how the professor encouraged students to participate. She would ask us to present course material and would challenge us instead of letting us be passive learners.
>
> (2018)

> The teaching method enabled me to think critically and be more conscious/aware of the world we live in.

> I really liked that the instructor ... always went beyond the ordinary exam materials encouraging everyone to think and act in a more critical, free (in terms of thinking) manner.

> The course increased my sensitivity towards environmental issues and I have started taking small steps in integrating the course's learning outcomes to real life.

Generally, students appreciate and ask for more videos, and more so field visits and outdoor experiential activities (like the waste measurement), pointing to the significance of contact with nature (as Freinet advocates) and the involvement of the entire person (mind–emotion–body) in the learning process. It appears that the adopted instructional approach mobilized interest and made the class enjoyable and inspiring, at least for some.

> Everything was very interesting in this course – I really enjoyed the lectures!!! (2019)

> This course inspired me a lot!!!

Another interesting point that arose from students' comments was the significance of my emotional involvement with the issues. It appears that the instructor's deep and obvious interest and involvement with the topic positively influences the students' stance towards their learning. Some commented:

> She [the instructor] was really passionate about it. She made me concern a little more about the environment.

> The passion the instructor had for the subject made the class easy to engage in.

The most usual suggested amendment related with less material (one specifically indicated less exam material), and although this can be construed as a complaint from indifferent or 'lazy' students, it may also be a message regarding overview courses that seek to cover huge amounts of material for maximum 'knowledge acquisition'. Other comments reflected the desire for more field trips and contact with nature, more videos, more practical/experiential activities, more questionnaires before and after instruction on a topic.

Environmental Studies Research Methods Course

Generally, students expressed a high level of satisfaction with this course. Students have indicated that the interactive/dialogic learning approach was useful for their learning in all the formats of this course. In the first iteration when no PowerPoints were used, a student stated:

The fact that no PowerPoints were used was very appealing in my opinion; sole teacher to student interaction was very effective and made the course very interesting!

Furthermore, students have appreciated the collaborative teaching approach when it was used. They liked the interdisciplinary character of collaborative teaching.

The fact that we got to be taught by all the instructors we ever had throughout all our science-oriented courses was very interesting.

After the division of the course into two, regarding the second course of the research methods series, students indicated that they liked the interactive learning and the cooperation and discussions amongst students and with the instructor, as well as the practical exercises (for instance, mock interviews or the proper referencing exercise). Furthermore, they stated that take-home exams facilitated learning.

> [I liked] the fact that there is no final exam and instead we have to do take-home exams that help us learn the material much better.

In this course too (Methods II), a student commented positively on the 'instructor's enthusiasm', highlighting the impact of the instructor's emotional involvement with the subject on the students.

The only real concern for this course was the amount of material to be studied and of the work needed. However, students also appreciated the value of this knowledge and significance of this course for their degree and further environmental career.

Environmental Justice Course

Students of the Environmental justice course unequivocally positively evaluated the dialogic and debate-like character of the class meetings and highlighted its contribution to the development of critical thinking, while they noted as a positive characteristic of the course the question-provoking environment created by the instructor.

> Interaction helped significantly.

The materials were covered through discussions, which helped in critical thinking, and had an effective learning outcome.

... [The] professor challenged us to take our learning to the next level.

Several students also appreciated the opportunity to facilitate a class meeting and noted the significance of students' taking a leadership role in the class and responsibility for their learning.

It allowed for students to take a leadership role that helped us all learn and become comfortable with the material.

It was important for us as students to carry responsibility for the classroom environment. Ideally that makes the classroom space better, as we are prepared and already knowledgeable as we enter the classroom space, and the class discussions are a place to further knowledge.

Others stated that the experiential components (e.g. field trips – walks in Athens and the local community or participation in Climathon) were very interesting and conducive to deeper understanding of the concepts and theories discussed. They also appreciated the challenge to relate and apply their knowledge to real-life situations.

She [the professor] challenged us to think outside the box and to apply what we are learning to problems and injustices that are occurring in the world around us. The field trip was great and was really important for applying our knowledge. I am better all around for taking this course.

Two were the main concerns of the students: the amount of assessments (which was reduced in later iterations) and students' 'lack of total accountability' – i.e. some students not doing readings ahead of time – undermining the in-class creative interaction. The concern for others' lack of accountability underlines how learning occurs in interaction; it is not an individual, isolated process, unaffected by other class participants. Collaboration and responsibility for the class community is significant for learning. Furthermore, I have noted that students are sometimes uneasy with the organization of the learning environment of this class at first, primarily in relation to how they will be assessed; this leads to an initial anxiety about the dynamic nature of the classroom, which is overcome after the first assessment.

During informal (uninvited) exchanges after the completion of the course, several students have indicated that the course influenced them deeply. One ES graduate indicated that the Environmental Justice course influenced him to select the topic of his postgraduate studies. Another ES student shared with me that during a pleasure trip he undertook after the class, he noticed that he had developed a new way of experiencing the world as a consequence of this course, noting things that he did not pay attention to before. These are real indications of personal transformation.

Sustainable Cities Course

Students consistently noted as very positive aspects of the course are its highly interactive character, with group projects, facilitating peer-to-peer interaction, as well as engagement of the students with the instructor, and its positive atmosphere. In the first iteration of the course, some students expressed a discomfort with the group work or the take-home exam (others liked them) due to their prior educational experiences; however, students generally characterized the class as fun, interactive and practical. Some characteristic quotes say:

> The instructor used unconventional methods of teaching, creating an extremely friendly and warm environment.

> Class never boring.

> The city was our lab.

In the more recent iteration, students also appreciated the individual exercise to investigate a sustainable or smart city and its different dimensions and share this with the class. A student noted that it was helpful that this started early in the project as it provided a context for deeper understanding of the later discussed theoretical aspects of sustainable cities. Deeper understanding was also facilitated by the voluntary extra activities (e.g. participation in a competition for the future city vision) the class participated in.

> The assignments, the additional topics taken voluntarily by the class and encouraged by the instructor heavily facilitated deep diving in the concept and learning.

Group projects that relate with actual concerns of the local community facilitated practical knowledge and called for creative problem-solving with obvious relevance to real life. The significance of the instructor's contribution in supporting creative problem-solving (imagination) and positive thinking were noted by the students.

> I liked how you encouraged us to think creatively and find solutions.

> Your positive energy and encouragement allow me to think deeper and attempt complex assignments, issues and tasks.

As students indicated, the course impact on them included critical thinking, presentation skills, 'desire to improve quality of life and to live sustainably', as well as being 'glad that I could offer to the class'.

Students' comments reveal that this class touched considerably on their emotions (e.g. 'Loved the class! Beautiful atmosphere!', fun, 'class never boring'), while it appears to have cultivated a sense of community (e.g. 'glad that I could offer to the class'). It is also noteworthy that the three of the five students of the second iteration – a class that participated voluntarily in several community activities (e.g. Climathon, competition for the future city vision, collaboration with/contribution to a primary school working on the ideal city) – actively expressed their desire to respond to the Athens Municipality's invitation for collaboration beyond the class with the aim to make the city more sustainable, a practical evidence of their desire to improve the urban quality of life (transformative impact of the course).

Students' concerns referring to the first iteration of the course pointed to the need for a clearer organization and for reassurance when unconventional forms of assessment are provided. In the second iteration, scheduling and stress were the concerns expressed.

This course demonstrates how group work and interaction among all participants can enhance learning and cultivate emotive learning too. Community projects are challenging enough to stimulate new knowledge as well as to reveal the valuable connection between education and community work. This course seems to have motivated students to wish to work for change in cities and individual life and to have cultivated their connection with the class and general community (e.g. happy that they contributed to the class). However, inflexible scheduling of classes causes stress and circumscribes possibilities for knowledge creation via collaboration, usually a time-demanding process.

Some General Observations

A comparison of the four courses reveals that the most transformative courses are on the one hand, those that are fun and intriguing and depend on collaborative problem-solving of real community/local problems, and on the other, those in which students have responsibility for their learning in the context of a collaborative process (see Table 2.2 for the average scores from all iterations of a course at relevant questions of the course evaluation). Such learning contexts often facilitate the involvement of the whole learner – mind, emotion and all senses (body). The least satisfying ones are those that aim to an overview of a knowledge domain, removed from students' interests and dependent on a teacher expert. In this latter context, creating interactive educational contexts with experiential learning activities and emotive learning is fundamental. However, experiential and emotive learning activities that are isolated instances in a generally mainstream educational context are not as effective as experiential learning processes (lasting throughout the course).

Table 2.2. Average Scores to Selected Questions from the Official Student Course Evaluations.

	Environmental Justice	Sustainable Cities	Methods Course	Methods Course II (Only)	ES Introductory Course
Number of iterations/classes	7	2	8	Last three of 8	9
Question					
Q10/Q4 – course encouraged critical thinking	4.70	5.00	4.45	4.89	4.02
Q16/Q1 – class interaction facilitates learning	4.76	4.67	4.72	4.72	4.14
Q24/Q16 – instructor's teaching methods helped me acquire knowledge on the subject	4.66	4.50	4.53	4.67	4.14
Q27/Q19 – instructor motivated me to seek knowledge on my own	4.75	4.84	4.47	4.56	4.07

Note: With perfect score being 5.

Revisiting Critical Pedagogy and Environmental Education – Education for Sustainability in Contemporary Societies

The social context in which education is enacted has changed. '[I]n the context of the shift from an industrial to a knowledge economy with globalization and the emergence of the new information and communication technologies' (Blackmore, 2001, p. 353), the role of education has changed too. Knowledge is a main currency in the job market and a valuable 'commodity' produced primarily in higher education institutions. Innovation, based primarily on science and new technologies, is a main goal of contemporary 'advanced' societies and is considered the main vehicle for solutions to social and environmental problems. The prevalent neoliberal ethic, which values only what is sold and purchased in the market, contributes to this overemphasis on knowledge, science and technology. Thus, knowledge that is fundamental for living or social cohesion (i.e. useful knowledge), if it is not marketable, is undervalued and less desirable. In this context, knowledge is fragmented into often very narrow slices of expertize that can be acquired and then sold as a skill in the job market. Instrumental logic most often guides young people's selection of their studies. Education is now sought for self-development and for better career opportunities; certified knowledge is the goal, rather than knowledge as a social good. This was also revealed by a couple of student comments to the Introductory ES course ('I was surprised that I would be satisfied with this course as it was a general [education] course for me'; '[I wanted the instructor] to explain things better for good grades'). Education has become an individualistic affair. Performativity – 'be efficient or die' (Blackmore, 2001, p. 362) – has become a main goal of education, especially Higher Education. Finally, with the expansion of mass media and information and communication technologies into practically every aspect of life, contemporary societies are societies of spectacle (Debord, 1994) – we are used to watching but not acting.

How should the critical educational praxis be designed in this context? What is the key or keys in instructional design and educational contexts that can mobilize learners and facilitate the transformation towards sustainable and caring societies today? What are the challenges in this process? Based on the educational experiences shared above, systemic thinking, posing questions that seek critical reflection, creating extraordinary learning experiences, involvement of the whole person and the role of the instructor are important.

Given the present fragmentation of knowledge and with globalization affecting practically all aspects of life, from the economy to the news, to cultural norms, to health and education, acquiring an understanding of the workings of the system and its underlying power relations is a challenge. *Systemic thinking and analytical capacity* constitute an urgent need for the transition towards sustainable and caring societies but also for the effective resolution of contemporary problems. EfS has pointed to the need for integrative and interdisciplinary approaches. However, a systemic analytical capacity goes beyond integrative thinking to reveal the connection between personal and political (Mills, 1959), power dynamics and the mechanisms that maintain present social practices and may obstruct needed social change. Educational environments should problematize the taken-for-granted reality, 'extraordinarily experiencing the ordinary'. Authentic questioning (Berry, 1998) that deconstructs existing pre-packaged knowledge, thus leaving space for creation and reconstruction of knowledge, is a useful tool. Such questioning reveals the framing process, who is the author, how s/he has constructed the topic, what claims s/he makes and how these relate with his/her social positionality, etc., putting students in a position of power.

But just theorizing is not enough. Transformative educational contexts should also demonstrate *alternative power relations in the classroom*. This is verified by the Environmental Justice course, which focusses on political analysis of environmental issues – with many who, why and how questions – and is organized as a think-tank where the instructors and students co-create knowledge and cultivate critical consciousness. This course has attracted several student comments – well after the end of the course – about its transformative impact on them, including their choice of postgraduate studies, and their worldview. However, as students are not used to this pedagogical approach, they should be 'educated' into it via consistent and steadfast implementation throughout the semester, along with caring support towards them. Furthermore, instructors generally have been educated (via example too) in the traditional, planned and controlled approaches that see the instructor as the expert and planner and the learners as willing receptors that do not upset the instructional plan. The democratic classroom approach makes the learning process rather unpredictable and maybe unsettling for the instructor too.

Learning occurs in *interaction*. According to one student of the Methods course, a direct face-to-face interactive learning setting is more interesting than the mediated one (e.g. via PowerPoint presentations). But beyond interaction, fostering a *sense of community* facilitates learning. Ada (2007) notes that 'we learn better in an interactive, supportive and non-competitive environment. As we live in a competitive society, it takes intention and effort to establish a co-creative atmosphere'. However, with the prevailing individualistic ethic in contemporary education and societies, creating spaces for the development of a learning community (e.g. group activities) can be a transformative experience. Such learning spaces challenge learners to think for the group and reveal their inalienable connection with each other, thus cultivating a sense of collective responsibility. Collaborative teaching (see the Methods course) can also provide a good example.

Critical pedagogues also advocate that education should be a 'pedagogy of action', a dialectic process of *action and reflection*. This *dialectic process* seems even more important and challenging in contemporary societies that educate spectators, too accustomed to virtual reality, and where fragmentation and the fast pace of life are not conducive to long processes. In courses that have time for reflection built in them – like Sustainable Cities and Environmental Justice – students seem to report 'deeper knowledge'. Experiential activities were also adopted in other courses too (like the Introductory ES or the Methods course), but in a more 'instantaneous' way. A project approach with some significant duration (learning as process) is needed to allow for cycles of preparation, action, reflection and follow up. This appears to be significant for the consolidation of learning and the possibility for action. When reflection and action are coupled in a spiral learning methodology (Papadopoulou, Lytras, & Marouli, 2016), as in the case of Sustainable Cities, students reported that they could 'think deeper and attempt complex assignments, issues and tasks' as well as think more creatively. Furthermore, in this class, all students voluntarily participated in diverse community activities, offering their services and learning at the same time, while several of them tangibly expressed their desire to work for better quality of life in the city.

According to the Habermasian model, three aspects need to be stimulated in the educational praxis: knowledge, self (including emotion and reflection) and a community-orientation (Blackmore, 2001). This distinction gives a very significant handle for action in contemporary knowledge societies which emphasize thinking and pacify action, while they focus on the individual without a sense of and responsibility for the community. *Bridging academia with the local community* in a way where thinking and action are closely intertwined is a transformative experience. Freinet advocated that learning should start from observations of the natural and human environment – going out of the classroom (Nowak-Fabrukowski, 1992). 'The study of the environment is once more the point of departure. But for Freinet observation is not an end in itself: the need to understand and the need to act are paramount' (Legrand, 1963, p. 6). However, this attempt requires that the instructor undertakes considerable and intricate organization and coordination activities. Furthermore, institutional constraints make this effort challenging – not impossible – as issues of scheduling, safety, etc. arise. Good planning and cultivating collective responsibility help.

Some critical pedagogues (e.g. Marcuse, Freinet) and EE/EfS call for the involvement not only of the mind but also of *emotion and body* in learning. Present educational practices fragment the learner and require a passive body without emotions and an active mind. But emotion triggers the desire for knowledge. It is no surprise that students frequently state that they like and ask for more audio–visual learning material or experiential learning (e.g. videos or field trips). However, emotive learning by itself can be disempowering (Firth, 2016). Feeling but not knowing how to constructively act on your feelings can be a numbing, if not socially destructive, experience. Marcuse (1966) argues that all senses should be involved in the learning process and the exploration of the world. Freinet's argument that all education should start with contact with nature is extremely relevant today. Experiential activities that involve the whole person – mobilizing the now immobile body of the learner – have the highest trans-formative impact on learners in contemporary societies that breed sedentary people, sedentary learners, passive spectators of (often virtual) reality. I believe that this is one reason that the Sustainable Cities course has the highest impact on students' real desire to act and contribute to solutions to real urban issues (or even better for a 'better urban quality of life', as they put it).

Empowering education, however, should be well-grounded on *hope and imagination* as several critical pedagogues have indicated. Without hope, only inaction is possible. Recently, in the Introductory ES class I am presently teaching, I showed a video on climate change and then asked the students about their thoughts; they remained silent staring at me. After a few seconds of silence, I asked what they felt; they immediately responded 'hopeless', 'powerless', 'should we have children?'. The video was effective in mobilizing feelings and the desire to know what they could do, but alone it was disempowering, leading to passivity. In this context, I decided to involve students in an online exchange regarding their vision of the world, what can be done and good examples of environmental ini-tiatives as a follow-up activity. The instructor and the learning activities should cultivate hope and provide space for learners to imagine the 'good' world of the future – a dream that can inspire. This is probably one of the most important parameters that critical education/critical EE/EfS should take into consideration in contemporary societies, where there is too much information about all the problems of the world, little information about alternatives, and even less hope, a very disempowering mix.

The *instructor's role* in this process is pivotal. Students learn from their teachers' example what is mainstream, acceptable – boring – practice, but also what is possible/imaginable. As demonstrated by aforementioned students' comments (e.g. 'Your positive energy and encouragement allow me to think deeper and attempt complex assignments, issues and tasks'; 'She [the instructor] was really passionate about it. She made me concern a little more about the environment'), the instructor's passion can mobilize students' interest in the topic and lead to deeper learning as well as to action for social change. But this should be accompanied by encouragement and a caring learning context, as this constitutes a fertile ground for critical and empowered learning. This is in agreement with Ada's (2007) observations:

> ... we learn better in an environment that offers love and respect, and allows us to experience and honor the truth of our thoughts, emotions and feelings.

> ... we learn better in an environment that allows us to learn at our own pace and in our own way, that honors what we care about, and that builds on what we have already learned from our life experience.

Critical pedagogues (Marcuse, 1966) indicate that the instructor–intellectual should embody the change they advocate. In my view, collaborative teaching or supportive collaborations among colleagues can buttress instructors when they lose sight of hope. At a more systemic level, teachers' education is an important entry point for the desired social change.

However, as Legrand (1993) suggests, 'The application of these [critical pedagogy] methods obviously requires radical changes in the institutional environment, beginning with the *physical surroundings* [sic]'. Present institutional constraints include the organization of time, assessment requirements, boundaries between educational institution and local community, rigid organization of space in the classroom, organizational obstacles for co-teaching, etc. When institutional changes do not happen, the instructor can use them as opportunities for critical reflection and can provide windows of hope. Furthermore, despite the institutional constraints experienced in all educational settings including education of future teachers, the observation that educators influence emotive learning is hopeful because present critical educators were once learners themselves in traditional educational settings, where just one or two instructors and/or experiences made the difference for them. Some teachers leave an indelible mark in students' minds and souls, and it is always because of their extraordinary and inspiring instructional practice. These instructors are the ones that open a window to the possible utopia that speaks to learners' hearts and mobilizes action for a 'better world'.

Concluding Thoughts

Critical pedagogy and critical EE/EfS have significant insights to offer contemporary societies and the needed transition towards sustainable and caring societies. But which are the crucial elements of an enlightening and empowering educational praxis in contemporary societies? Plato's cave allegory is still relevant today and instructive, as it provides a view of contemporary societies, the type of education that is needed and the challenges.

Plato envisages the society as a cave with only one entrance allowing light to come in. In the cave, people are bound with their backs against a wall since their childhood, unable to move and always facing only shadows. 'To them, ... the truth would be literally nothing but the shadows of the images' (translation from ellopos.net/elpenor/greek-texts/ancient-greece/plato-paideia-cave.asp). Only when someone is released from his/her chains, can s/he turn and see the light entering from the entrance.

At such state, if an instructor freed someone and told him/her that what s/he previously saw was an illusion and the instructor then leads him/her to the entrance to see the light, s/he will first resist and then it will take him/her a few minutes before the eyes get accustomed to the light. People's eyes, accustomed to shadows, ache when they first face the light. After seeing the sun, the person will reason about it and its relation to life, and s/he will be happy about this change in him/herself.

If s/he returned to talk with the other prisoners, 'Men would say of him that up he went and down he came without his eyes; and that it was better not even to think of ascending; and if any one tried to loose another and lead him up to the light, let them only catch the offender, and they would put him to death'. In this world of knowledge, Plato states that 'the idea of good appears last of all, and is seen only with an effort'.

This allegory refers to 'the ascent of the soul into the intellectual world' and underlines the crucial elements of a transformative and empowering educational praxis:

- First, you need to free the body, make it supple and involve it in the educational praxis. Movement, dance, contact with nature facilitate learning. This also implies that breaching and reconceiving spatial boundaries between the individual, the classroom/educational institution and the local community or nature are prerequisites for a liberating educational experience.
- Intrigue, curiosity and imagination are fundamental for the step outside the dark cave. Education should aim to arouse these emotions. In this process, a caring, supporting and hopeful environment is fundamental with the instructor having a pivotal role in this process.
- Learning is a long process, with painful moments of transition from darkness to light and vice versa. Thus, educational contexts should treat knowledge as a process (not an instance) of enlightenment, involving projects (learning objects with duration), having a more flexible organization of time and a more democratic organization with students having initiative and responsibility for the learning process.[2] Changes in the institutional setting are also required.

• Given the pains of moving between the generally accepted views (Plato's darkness) on the one hand and knowledge and the good (Plato's light) on the other, building a community is a necessary context for learning as well as a source for support. It is particularly useful at the uncomfortable moments of enquiry and certainly in the process of enticing others – still in the cave – towards enlightenment and leaving the cave setting (i.e. social action).

> But then, if I am right, certain professors of education must be wrong when they say that they can put a knowledge into the soul which was not there before, like sight into blind eyes. They undoubtedly say this, he replied. Whereas, our argument shows that the power and capacity of learning exists in the soul already; and that just as the eye was unable to turn from darkness to light without the whole body, so too the instrument of knowledge can only by the movement of the whole soul be turned from the world of becoming into that of being, and learn by degrees to endure the sight of being, and of the brightest and best of being, or in other words, of the good.
>
> (Plato, 518c & d)

Notes

1. For more information on Environmental Education and Education for Sustainability, as well as more recent developments, please refer to Flogaiti (1998), Georgopoulos and Tsaliki (1993), Goncalves (2012), Kalaitzidis and Ouzounis (2000), Tilbury (2004), and Bowers (2002) (Eco-justice pedagogy) and Marouli (2002) (Multicultural Environmental Education).
2. For a discussion of learning objects, indicatively see Wiley (2002) and Papadopoulou, Marouli, Misseyanni, and Apostolaki (2018).

References

Ada, A. F. (2007). A lifetime of learning to teach. *Journal of Latinos and Education*, *6*(2), 103–118.

Belenky, M. F., Clinchy, B. M., Goldberger, N. R., & Tarule, J. M. (1986). *Women's ways of knowing*. New York, NY: Basic Books.

Berry, K. S. (1998). Nurturing the imagination of resistance: Young adults as creators of knowledge. In J. L. Kincheloe & S. R. Steinberg (Eds.), *Unauthorized methods: Strategies for critical teaching*. New York, NY: Routledge.

Blackmore, J. (2001). Universities in crisis? Knowledge economies, emancipatory pedagogies, and the critical intellectual. *Educational Theory*, *51*(3), 353–370. doi: 10.1111/j.1741-5446.2001.00353.x

Bloch, E. (1986). *The principles of hope*. Cambridge, MA: MIT Press.

Bowers, C. A. (2002). Toward an eco-justice pedagogy. *Environmental Education Research, 8*, 21–34.

Clandfield, D., & Sivell, J. (1990). *Cooperative learning & social change: Selected writings of Celestin Freinet.* Montreal, QC: Our Schools/Our Selves Educational Foundation.

Debord, G. (1994). *The society of the spectacle.* New York, NY: Zone Books.

Dewey, J. (1938). *Experience and education.* New York, NY: Touchstone.

Firth, R. (2016). Somatic pedagogies: Critiquing and resisting the affective discourse of the neoliberal state from an embodied anarchist perspective. *Ephemera: Theory and Politics in Organization, 16*(4), 121–142.

Flogaiti, E. (1998). *Environmental education.* Athens: Ellinika Grammata. (in Greek).

Foley, J. A., Morris, D., Gounari, P., & Agostinone-Wilson, F. (2015, December). Critical education, critical pedagogies, marxist education in the United States. *Journal for Critical Education Policy Studies, 13*(3), 110–144.

Freire, P. (1970). *Pedagogy of the oppressed.* New York, NY: Continuum.

Freire, P. (1998). *Pedagogy of freedom.* Lanham, MY: Rowman & LittleField.

Freire, P. (2000). *Cultural action for freedom* (Revised edition). Cambridge, MA: Harvard Educational Review.

Georgopoulos, A., & Tsaliki, E. (1993). *Environmental education: Principles—Philosophy, methodology, games and exercises.* Athens: Gutenberg. (in Greek).

Giroux, H. (2001). *Public spaces, private lives: Beyond the culture of cynicism.* New York, NY: Rowman and Littlefield Publishers, Inc.

Giroux, H. A. (2011). *On critical pedagogy.* New York, NY and London: Continuum and Bloomsbury.

Goncalves, F. (2012). *Contributions to the UN decade of education for sustainable development.* Frankfurt am Main: Peter Lang AG. Retrieved from http://web.a.ebscohost.com. acg.idm.oclc.org/ehost/ebookviewer/ebook/bmxlYmtfXzQ4ODAwOV9fQU41? sid=51f8c226-1e86-4cd4-a3b8-a861526442e@sessionmgr4003&vid=6&format=EB &rid=2

Goodson, I. F. (1998). Towards an alternative pedagogy. In J. L. Kincheloe & S. R. Steinberg (Eds.), *Unauthorized methods: Strategies for critical teaching.* New York, NY: Routledge.

Gramsci, A. (1971). *Selections from the prison notebooks* (Q. Hoare & G. N. Smith, Eds.). New York, NY: International Publishers.

Jickling, B., & Wals, A. E. J. (2008). Globalization and environmental education: Looking beyond sustainable development. *Journal of Curriculum Studies, 40*(1), 1–21.

Kalaitzidis, D., & Ouzounis, K. (2000). *Environmental education: Theory and practice.* Xanthi: Spanidi Publications. (in Greek).

Kopnina, H. (2014). Revisiting education for sustainable development (ESD): Examining anthropocentric bias through the transition of environmental education to ESD. *Sustainable Development, 22*, 73–83.

Legrand, L. (1993). Celestin Freinet (1986–1966). *Prospects: The Quarterly Review of Comparative Education, UNESCO, XXIII*(1/2), 403–418.

Marcuse, H. (1966). *Eros & civilization: A philosophical inquiry into freud.* Boston, MA: Beacon Press.

Marouli, C. (2002). Multicultural environmental education: Theory and practice. *Canadian Journal of Environmental Education, 7*, 26–42.

Marouli, C. (2016). Moving towards a circular economy: The need to educate. Why and how? In 4th International Conference on Sustainable Solid Waste Management, Limassol, Cyprus, 23–25 June 2016. (e-proceedings).

Marouli, C., & Duroy, Q. (2019). Reflections on the transformative power of environmental education in contemporary societies: Experience from two college courses in Greece and the USA. *Sustainability, 11*(22), 6465. doi:10.3390/su11226465. Special Issue: Education for Pro-Environmental Behaviors.

Marouli, C., Misseyanni, A., Papadopoulou, P., & Lytras, M. D. (2018). A new vision for higher education: Lessons from education for the environment and sustainability. In A. Misseyanni, M. D. Lytras, P. Papadopoulou, & C. Marouli (Eds.), *Active learning strategies in higher education* (pp. 361–387). Bingley: Emerald Publishing.

Mayo, P. (2014). Antonio Gramsci's impact on critical pedagogy. *Critical Sociology*, 1–16.

Mills, C. W. (1959). *The sociological imagination*. New York, NY: Oxford University Press.

Nowak-Fabrykowski, K. (1992). Freinet's concept of teachers and theory of teaching. *McGill Journal of Education, 27*(1), 61–68.

Papadopoulou, P., Lytras, M., & Marouli, C. (2016). Capstone projects in STEM education: Novel teaching approaches, mentoring and knowledge management for empowering students. In EDULEARN16 Proceedings, pp. 5675_5685. doi:10.21125/edulearn.2016.2358

Papadopoulou, P., Marouli, C., Misseyanni, A., Apostolaki, S. (2018). Improving learning environments through use of "smart" learning objects in STEM courses. In Proceedings of the 10th International Conference on Education and New Learning Technologies, Palma, Spain. 2–4 July 2018 (pp. 385–395).

Plato. (n.d). Politeia (514a–518d). (B. Jowett, Trans.). E-book by www.elpenor.org. Retrieved from https://www.ellopos.net/elpenor/greek-texts/ancient-greece/plato-paideia-cave.asp

Shor, I. (1987). *Critical teaching and everyday life*. Chicago, IL and London: University of Chicago Press.

Tilbury, D. (2004). Environmental education for sustainability: A force for change in higher education. In P. B. Corcoran & A. E. J. Wals (Eds.), *Higher education and the challenge of sustainability* (pp. 97–112). Dordrecht: Kluwer.

UNESCO. (2005). United Nations decade of education for sustainable development 2005–2014. Retrieved from http://unesdoc.unesco.org/images/0013/001399/139937e.pdf

UNESCO. (2016). *Education for people and the planet: Creating sustainable futures for all*. Paris: UNESCO Publishing. Retrieved from https://unesdoc.unesco.org/ark:/48223/pf0000245752

United Nations. (1975). The Belgrade Charter. Retrieved from http://www.gdrc.org/uem/ee/belgrade.html

United Nations. (1977). Tbilisi declaration. Retrieved from http://www.gdrc.org/uem/ee/tbilisi.html

Van Heertum, R. (2006). Marcuse, Bloch and Freire: Reinvigorating a pedagogy of hope. *Policy Futures in Education*, 4(1), 45–50.

Wiley, D. A. (2002). Connecting learning objects to instructional design theory: A definition, a metaphor, and a taxonomy. In D. A. Wiley (Ed.), *The instructional use of learning objects*. Bloomington, IN: Agency for Instructional Technology & Association for Educational Communication and Technology. Retrieved from http://reusability.org/read/chapters/wiley.doc

Chapter 3

Action Research in Planning Education – Lessons from Roskilde University[1]

Martin Severin Frandsen and John Andersen

Abstract

Roskilde University was established in Denmark in 1972 as a critical reform university based on the principles of participant directed problem-oriented project learning (PPL). In 2009, the university launched a new master programme in Urban Planning (Planning Studies). This chapter presents experiences from student projects working with action research in facilitating citizen-driven urban development. Firstly, we outline the key theoretical foundations of the Planning Studies programme: planning as social learning, empowerment and social mobilization. Secondly, we describe the principles of the Roskilde University pedagogical model (PPL) rooted in the tradition of experiential and critical pedagogy of Oskar Negt, John Dewey, Paulo Freire and others. Thirdly, we present two cases of problem-oriented projects working with action research in bottom-up urban planning and sustainable transition in Copenhagen. The first case concerns the involvement of local residents in the redesign of a public square through a series of aesthetic experiments. The second case concerns an experiment with alternative transport solutions and sustainable street transition through reduction of private car use and the creation of new public spaces on former parking lots. The article concludes that action research in problem-oriented project work is promising way of involving students in community empowerment processes. Doing action research strengthens the students understanding of 'the logic of practice' and their ability to master practical and ethical judgements in complex real-world empowerment and learning processes. This both prepares them for professional practice and provides them with an embodied and pragmatically empowered understanding of how transformations towards a more sustainable and just society can be brought about.

Transformative Research and Higher Education, 73–91
Copyright © 2022 Martin Severin Frandsen and John Andersen
Published under exclusive licence by Emerald Publishing Limited
doi:10.1108/978-1-80117-694-120221004

Keywords: Participatory planning; action research; transformative education; problem-oriented project learning (PPL); social learning; empowerment

Introduction

In 2009, Roskilde University (RUC) launched a new programme in urban planning (Plan, By and Process/Planning Studies). The purpose of the new programme was to educate planners that could supplement the traditional planning professions of the architect and engineer and on a theoretically informed basis would be able to design and facilitate interdisciplinary and participatory planning processes. From the start, action research was a core part of the curriculum and was taught in both courses and tried out in problem-oriented project work, the key element in the so-called 'Roskilde University model' of problem-oriented participant-directed project learning (PPL) (Andersen & Heilesen, 2015).

Whereas there is growing body of research literature on action research in higher education, there seems to be almost no studies that directly link action research to the principles of problem-based or problem-oriented learning (Gibbs et al., 2017; Laudonia, Mamlok-Naaman, Abels, & Eilks, 2018; Thorsen & Børsen, 2018). In this article, we will by way of two case studies of action research in problem-oriented project work explore the following research questions: What is the 'added value' of doing action research in problem-based learning and problem-oriented project work? And how do we ensure that value is created for all participants in ''student-directed' action research?

The criteria for the choice of cases followed Flyvbjergs strategies for information-oriented selection (Flyvbjerg, 2006, pp. 229–233). We chose two atypical cases (extreme/deviant cases in Flyvbjergs terminology). The first case was an unusually successful case that was chosen to obtain knowledge on the potentially 'added value' of working with action research in problem-oriented project work and the conditions for successful collaborations between students and external partners. The second case was a more complex and problematic case that we chose to reveal some of the potential tension points and challenges in student-led action research and to discuss strategies to cope with these. The qualitative data for the case studies we collected from field notes from supervision meetings (five to six meetings with the students per project), communications and feedback from external stakeholders and the final project reports (Dahlerup, 2018; Nielsen, Ullerup, & Fløyel, 2016; Schock, Rudolph, Skogbjerg, Lium, & Voss, 2017).[2]

The first part of the article outlines the key theoretical foundation of the Planning Studies (PS) programme: planning as social learning and social mobilization (empowerment). We highlight the affinities between participatory planning and action research and outline a model of prototypical phases in community-based action research. Secondly, we describe the Roskilde University pedagogical model of problem-oriented project learning (PPL). In the third section, we describe how we have worked with action research on Planning Studies in the framework of PPL, exemplified by the two cases of project work. Finally, we reflect on the potentials and challenges of working with action research in problem-oriented project work and draw conclusions in relation to the two research questions.

Participatory Planning Traditions

The civil rights movement in the United States in the 1960s and the upcoming urban movements and revolts fundamentally challenged the legitimacy of mainstream planning based solely on technical expert knowledge. Inspired by massive community mobilizations (Jacobs, 1961), critical planners challenged the idea of planning as a value-free activity purely based on 'objective' scientific and technical knowledge. The theory and practice of advocacy and participatory planning was born. Drawing on a tradition and 'canon' of progressive community activism that can be traced back to the progressive era and pragmatists like Jane Addams and John Dewey (Fisher, DeFilippis, & Shragge, 2012), advocacy planning (Davidoff, 1965) wanted to put poor people's needs first, facilitate community empowerment and challenge the power of economic, bureaucratic and political elites at all levels. The participatory and social justice-oriented planning tradition (Marcuse, 2011) has, with varying degrees of success, struggled to create a form of planning that emphasized social justice, local needs and the empowerment of citizens.

Planning theorist John Friedman speaks of two participatory planning traditions, *social learning* and *social mobilization* (Friedmann, 1987). In brief, *social learning* is a typically bottom-up orientated form of planning where planners, community workers, citizens and other stakeholders collaborate in common problem-solving and mutual learning processes (Frandsen, 2018). Through these learning processes, the capacity for collective problem-solving is strengthened while the involved actors learn about themselves and their community and society. *Social mobilization* is a form of planning based on people's empowerment in social movements with a transformative potential to create more socially just development paths in society (Andersen, 2007). In both (much overlapping) traditions the understanding of learning is similar to Paulo Freires 'Pedagogy of the Oppressed' (Freire, 1972), where learning is seen as a process of overcoming disempowerment and alienation and of developing critical consciousness through transformative action for social justice.

Participatory Planning and Action Research

The kind of knowledge production that is characteristic of the critical planning traditions is closely related to the participatory knowledge creation that characterizes the action research tradition. Action research facilitates collective action and change while at the same time producing new knowledge. Action researchers see themselves as co-producers of knowledge together with social actors struggling for social justice and people's empowerment: they share a commitment to democratic change (Brydon-Miller & Aragón, 2018).

Social learning-orientated planning has traits in common with Pragmatic Action Research, where the aim is to support social enquiry and problem-solving (Frandsen, 2016; Greenwood & Levin, 2007), and it also bears resemblance to the Critical Utopian Action Research tradition (CUAR) that has a strong focus on the creation of 'free spaces' and social experiments (Egmose, 2015; Gunnarsson,

Hansen, Nielsen, & Sriskandarajah, 2016). Planning as social mobilization has strong ties to both the North American (Brydon-Miller, 1997) and the Latin American Participatory Action Research (PAR) traditions (Bacal, 2018; Fals Borda, 2001; Freire, 1972).

In the following, we shall briefly outline a simple heuristic and prototypical model for phases in participatory and community-based action research, drawing upon the sources and action research approaches mentioned above (see Fig. 3.1). In other words, we draw upon several traditions and concepts of action research – action research as empowerment facilitation (Andersen, 2007), action research as experimental and social learning (Frandsen, 2018), action research as social innovation (Moulaert, MacCallum, Mehmood, & Hamdouch, 2013) and the work of Brydon-Miller and Aragón (2018) on the multiple roles of action researchers – from participatory enquiry to advocacy vis-à-vis authorities, trust building, etc.

The starting point is social tensions, everyday troubles and social injustices where some kind of collective action is needed to break away from, to find solutions to or to better cope with the situation. The first phase in the action research process is to make contact and engage in dialogue with the relevant

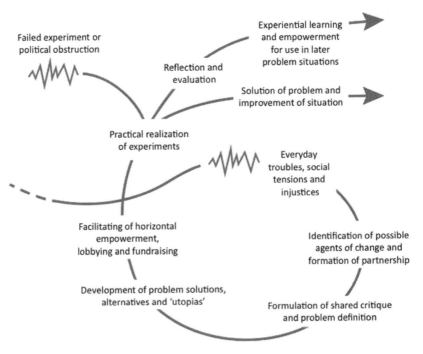

Fig. 3.1.   Prototypical Phases in Community-Based Action Research.
Adapted from Frandsen (2016).

actors and citizens affected by the situation in order to identify possible partners in an action research collaboration based on a joint understanding of the problem(s) that can guide further enquiry.

If this phase works out successfully, the next phase can be a deeper participatory enquiry of the problem and its context, where the creation of contextualized knowledge is linked directly to trust building, awareness-raising and development of mutual commitment (horizontal empowerment) in relation to citizens and local stakeholders. Based on this deeper and contextualized understanding, the next step is to jointly create suggestions for collective action and problem solutions with a broader group of citizens and stakeholders. In the following phase, an action committee or coalition (partnership) of actors either with their own resources and/or with support from private foundations or public funds can engage in an experimental test of the problem solution. If the problem solution requires changes at the political level, e.g. changes in legal regulations, public funding, etc., the knowledge and arguments for the problem solution can be advocated in the public and political sphere (vertical empowerment). If the problem solution improves the situation the initial everyday troubles and social conflicts will be reduced.

The final step can be to 'upscale' the knowledge, ideas, practical capacity-building, narratives, etc. to other communities, organizations and to higher levels: regional, national and transnational levels. If experimentation fails due to opposition or obstruction from political or private actors (e.g. investors and property owners), this knowledge about structural obstacles for progressive change can be shared to the wider public to stimulate deliberation about transformative empowerment and changing opportunity structures promoting more social justice in society.

In other words, if action research fails in the first round, it does not mean that it is useless. Both less successful experiments and experiments blocked by political and economic elites can be useful for reflection, narratives and deliberation in similar problem contexts. In other words, the learning process in action research consists of both successes and failures (Greenwood & Levin, 2007, pp. 109–113).

As stated before: the above is a prototypical model for transformative education and research (see introduction chapter to this book). As the experienced American (North and South) action researchers Brydon-Miller and Aragón argue, the conditions for action research are extremely dependent on the political, institutional and sociocultural context, which shapes the way in which the various stages of the action research process can be played out in practice.

> In some cases, the community may be well-established, and [...] the process can be focused on bringing the researcher into an existing set of relationships. In other cases, [...] more time must be spent in [...] building relationships within the community [...] Some communities are extremely hierarchical requiring the researcher to negotiate and sometimes challenge systems of power [...] while in other cases the lack of any hierarchy at all or any authority makes it difficult to establish communication and

to assign responsibility for carrying out tasks. And finally, in some cases communities may be so divided that nothing can be accomplished until lines of communication and basic trust have been established.

(Brydon-Miller & Aragón, 2018, pp. 35–36)

In many cases, there will be iteration where the same phases (e.g. problem identification or (re)design of solution strategies) are reworked and repeated again.[3]

Problem-Oriented Project Learning

The pedagogical model at RUC is based on problem-oriented participant directed project learning (PPL) (Andersen & Heilesen, 2015; Olesen & Jensen, 1999; RUC, 2017) and can be seen as an advanced model of transformative education. In practice, this means that 50 percent of the students' work is dedicated to project work while the remaining 50 percent consist of courses in different forms, ranging from traditional lectures to experimental workshops. The PPL model in its original form in the 1970s was in many ways in line with the critical pedagogical ideas of Freire: education as facilitation of a 'critical consciousness' working with 'real' problems and challenges in society. PPL was also influenced by the radical student movement emerging in the late 1960s and the idea that higher education should promote 'dual qualification':

> Firstly, it should provide suitable academic and professional qualifications for today's society, including those of an innovative and creative nature. Secondly, higher education should help students to develop critical judgement, enhance their societal involvement, and increase social equality and justice.
> (Andersen & Kjeldsen, 2015a, p. 5)

Although the interpretation of the PPL model has evolved over time due to changing circumstances and the influence of new pedagogical ideas, most of principles of the original model still exist. The key principles as they are interpreted today are as follows:

(1) *Project work.* Project work entails extended work on a well-defined problem and area of study within a given time frame of typically 4 months. At RUC, project work is organized in groups of two or more students. The students control the process under supervision and seek out and evaluate which theories and methods to use by themselves. Project work is based on the model of scientific investigation and enquiry. Students do projects that are similar to the ways in which researchers conduct research projects (Andersen & Heilesen, 2015, p. xi; RUC, 2017).

(2) *Problem-orientation.* Project work is problem-oriented. The point of departure for choosing and determining a problem is what Andersen and Kjeldsen term 'the trinity of personal, study-related and societal relevance' (Andersen & Kjeldsen, 2015b, pp. 24–25). The criterion of personal relevance ensures motivation and engagement, the criterion of study-related relevance ensures that the studies correspond to the curricular requirements, and the criterion of social relevance ensures that the studies are oriented towards existing and real-world social problems. Problem-orientation will thus often be driven by cooperation with stakeholders in society outside the university (RUC, 2017).

(3) *Interdisciplinarity.* Problem-orientation is linked to interdisciplinarity. It is the problem of a project rather than a traditional discipline that determines the choice of theories and methods. The interdisciplinary dynamics arise through analysis of complex problems that require solutions across subjects and research approaches (Andersen & Heilesen, 2015, p. xi; RUC, 2017).

(4) *Participant control.* Participant-directed learning is manifested in the students' choice of problems and in their own control of the project work under guidance from a supervisor. The terms participant control and participant-directed learning are preferred to the term student-directed learning firstly because project work is supervised by a teacher, and secondly, because projects have to conform to the curricular framework (Andersen & Heilesen, 2015, p. xii; RUC, 2017). To this, we would add that in cases where there is cooperation with stakeholders outside the university, like in action research processes, these collaborators act as a third kind of participant. Finally, with regard to courses, the learning process is more structured according to the subject and is largely determined by the lecturers (RUC, 2017).

(5) *Exemplarity.* Exemplarity means that an example or case is studied in such a way that it develops the students' insights into and overview of the investigative practices, methods and theories of the academic fields in question (RUC, 2017). Exemplarity can also mean that the content of project work should be related to and seen as exemplary of broader social and public issues – much similar to C. Wrights Mills notion of the 'sociological imagination' linking everyday 'troubles' and societal 'issues' (Mills, 1959) – and that the examples the students choose can be related to their own experience and as well as to the social conditions that influence their experiences (Andersen & Kjeldsen, 2015b, pp. 25–27).

(6) *Group work.* Project work is conducted in groups, and group work is also used in courses or workshops ranging from, for example, reading groups to smaller group exercises and 'mini-projects'. The main arguments for group work are that it promotes individual and collective cognitive processes and development, that it can illustrate a problem more comprehensively and more in-depth than the individual student can achieve alone and that the academic discussions within the group establishes a mutual learning process (RUC, 2017).

It is evident that the PPL model shares basic pedagogical principles with the variety of approaches that constitute Problem Based Learning (PBL) (Savin-Baden & Major, 2004). One of characteristics of PPL is that the emphasis on the students' participation in the formulation of problems is particularly strong (Andersen & Kjeldsen, 2015a, p. 14). This key element can be traced back to the early formulation of PPL in the writings of Knud Illeris. According to Illeris, a problem is a problem in the psychological sense only if it is formulated and chosen by the person who has to work with it:

> If the solution, or at least the elucidation of the problem, does not appear as a personal challenge, the conditions for accommodative learning are not present and thus neither the conditions for the development of creativity and flexibility (...) Accommodative learning is a demanding process that requires commitment. You accommodate only in situations that are relevant to yourself and what you are doing.
>
> (Illeris in Andersen & Kjeldsen, 2015a, pp. 7–8)

Students, however, have to argue for the relevance of the problem they choose to work with according to the trinity of personal, study-related and societal relevance as described above. At the same time, students in many cases start out from project ideas or suggestions proposed by supervisors or external stake-holders. In these cases, '... it is crucial that the proposals from the supervisor [or external stakeholder] are very brief so that the students can personalize the idea and make their own investigations and reflections in order to formulate a genuine problem for the project' (Blomhøj, Enevoldsen, Haldrup, & Nielsen, 2015, p. 99).

Action Research in Planning Studies

The relatively extensive time frame of project work at RUC of typically 4 months, together with the principles of problem-orientation and participant control, provides a distinct opportunity structure for doing action research with stake-holders outside the university, which to some extent makes it possible to escape from some of the institutional challenges for action research in contemporary universities (Thorsen & Børsen, 2018, p. 192) and from what Greenwood terms 'academic Taylorism' (Greenwood, 2012, p. 119).

In the Planning Studies programme, we have taught action research in courses and promoted action research in project work by facilitating 'matchmaking' with external partners through meetings at the start of each semester where stake-holders – ranging from NGO's, community activists, social housing associations to municipal planning departments – present ideas for possible cooperation.

Action Research in Courses

Teaching students action research within the framework of courses can be seen as a preparation for working more independently with action research in project work. The PS courses introduce the historical roots and principles of action research, present concrete cases of action research in cities and communities conducted with various stakeholders, i.e. community development projects, local councils, activist groups and 'ordinary citizens', and provide a framework for the students to try out action research in 'mini-projects'.

In PS, we have experimented with different activities that are often located in urban or rural neighbourhoods outside university walls. It is one thing to lecture on the epistemology and methodology of action research – it is another thing to develop the multiple 'hands-on' skills required to practice action research (Brydon-Miller & Aragón, 2018). This requires experiential learning processes with 'live cases'. It is our (and the students) clear judgement that placing courses *on location* makes a big difference (Rask & Andersen, 2016). It gives a completely different feeling to be in the thick of things, and it creates the possibility to organize city walks, mapping exercises, informal interviews on the streets and for relationship-building and dialogues with local stakeholders and citizens.

The aim of the courses are to show, *in germ form*, how action research can contribute to empowerment and learning among citizens and produce input and proposals for planning that is based on local needs. Through 'mini-projects', students are trained to analyze development plans for the neighbourhood, to design and use different methods for citizen involvement and community mapping, to conduct interviews with local stakeholders and to develop and sometimes realize small-scale initiatives and plans of their own. All of it to identify local needs and facilitate a shared problem definition among local citizens and stakeholders, to formulate proposals and visions for local planning and to develop the capacity to realize these.

Action Research in Problem-Orientated Project Work – Potentials and Challenges

To a large extent, problem-orientated project work provides an ideal framework for working with action research within planning education. The starting point for project work is typically concrete and practical public planning issues and, in comparison with the courses, the time frame is longer, with projects running for 4–5 months from the project's inception to its conclusion.

Working with action research in project work is, however, still somewhat of a balancing act. Even though the time frame is relatively long compared to the time allowed for in courses, it is still a short time frame in comparison with the time frame that characterizes a 'real' action research project, where the researcher often engages in longer running collaborations that sometimes go on for several years. There is therefore a risk that the collaboration becomes a frustrating experience for both students and external stakeholders, entailing what Thorsen and Børsen term a 'breach of expectation' (Thorsen & Børsen, 2018, p. 185) because the hopes for realizing an action or experiment that is valuable for both the students and the external stakeholder are not met.

Case 1: Aesthetic Experiments

In the following, we will outline an example of successful action research collaboration between a group of students from PS and an external partner in the form of a so-called 'area renewal project', *Områdefornyelsen Indre Nørrebro*, in the inner-city neighbourhood of Nørrebro in Copenhagen. 'Area renewal' is a 5-year integrated urban renewal programme targeted at disadvantaged neighbourhoods and housing areas. The integrated area renewal project was launched in 2014 in the inner part of Nørrebro, which underwent a prior urban renewal effort in the 1980s where many buildings, including tenements, were torn down. The renewal project in the 1980s was met with strong protests from local residents and sometimes led to violent conflict. Many of the new urban spaces that were created have subsequently shown not to be accommodating spaces for the social life of the neighbourhood. To make up for the errors of the past, the current area renewal project aims at involving local citizens in the redesign and improvement of a number of the central squares and spaces in the neighbourhood.

Experiences from earlier recent area renewal projects had shown that collaboration with student groups could sometimes be time-demanding, and the investment from the planners in the urban renewal project did not always yield a return in the form of valuable knowledge once the student groups had completed their project. Sometimes, students forgot to report their findings in an accessible way to the external partners once they had finished their exams and had moved on to the next project. In other cases, the students were seen as having a poor understanding of 'the logic of practice' in a real-world context, and their analysis, evaluations and judgements seemed to rest on very idealistic assumptions about planning with little value as practical guidance.

To make better use of the work of the students, the new area renewal project developed a practice of involving student groups in experimental test phases in the redesign of the local squares and urban spaces. The students, through experiments with smaller workshops, design prototypes and events, could map out and explore the potentials for future development before the area renewal project itself began the more permanent redesign and renewal process. Seen from the PS' and the students' perspective, the advantages of this type of partnership was that the area renewal project – in exchange for the practical experimentations of the students – made a lot of resources available in the form of local knowledge and gate keepers that helped to make action research possible within the time allowed for to do project work.

After themselves making contact with and consulting the area renewal project, a group of students doing their master's thesis chose to work with the renewal of a small local square named after the local and still existing social settlement 'Askovgården'. The theoretical and methodological starting point was a combination of diversity planning (Sandercock, 2004) and arts-based action research (Brydon-Miller, Antal, Friedman, & Wicks, 2011). From this starting point, the students drew the hypothesis that artistic and aesthetic methods held particular potentials to engage a diverse group of residents because aesthetic impressions and experiences speak to both emotions and to the imagination and communicate in a direct way to the everyday life of citizens (Nielsen et al., 2016, p. 9ff).

To test this hypothesis, the group designed a series of four aesthetic experiments with new forms, colours and materials and sought to engage local residents and organizations in all phases of the process. The whole process ran for two and a half months and was divided into three different phases: a prelude, realization of four aesthetic experiments and an evaluation (Fig. 3.2).

Although several obstacles were encountered on the way, the experiences from the experiments to a large extent confirmed the students' guiding hypothesis. Already the first aesthetic experiment showed that it did not take much more than a couple of people and a pile of coloured tape to engage a diverse group of citizens and change their image of what is possible in a given place. The activities that took place while the experiments unfolded drew people's attention and a broad group of people involved themselves out of curiosity and joy. The aesthetic experiments created a space where a diverse group of citizens could express

Fig. 3.2.   Impressions Form the Four Aesthetic Experiments.
Clockwise from left to corner: Children creating flags in the experiment Sky Space, street patterns made from coloured tape form the experiment Layouts, flags from the experiment Sky Space, decorated wire from the experiment Spaces in The Space and light installation from the experiment Lighting. (Photos: A. K. Nielsen, S. B. Ullerup, & S. Fløyel).

themselves physically and practically and not only through words. They created an 'aesthetic free space' on the square, where citizens on their own terms could get involved and develop and try out alternatives. The process became the focal point of 'a learning process at both an individual, social and cultural level, whereby participants [could] gain new perspectives on themselves, each other and the ordinary everyday life at Askovgårdens Plads' (Nielsen et al., 2016, p. 78).

Case 2: Sustainable Street Transition – From Parking Lots to Community Space

The second case of action research in problem-oriented project work concerns an experiment with sustainable transition in the local street Badensgade in the neighbourhood of Amagerbro also in central Copenhagen. In contrast to the publicly led urban renewal project on Nørrebro, the initiative on Amagerbro was civil society-based, and the project was more loosely tied to the municipal planning authorities.

The goal of the project was firstly to explore how the amount of privately owned cars in the inner city could be reduced and how the space now reserved for parking could be used for social and community activities. Secondly, the goal was to investigate how local residents themselves could lead a sustainable transition and transform and manage urban spaces. To achieve these goals, the experiment involved two logically linked sub-projects: The first sub-project aimed at reducing the local dependency on private cars through locally based initiatives like carpooling, introduction of a local bicycle library, arrangement of delivery services with local shops, free advice on sustainable transport solutions, etc. The idea behind the second sub-project was to involve the local residents in the design and co-creation of temporary and mobile urban furniture for community activities to explore the possibilities for future use of the space potentially freed from car parking.

Two aspects of the experiment on Amagerbro made it more complex and potentially conflictual than the renewal project on Nørrebro. The resident-led approach and the loose ties to the municipality made the collaboration with the planning authorities more difficult, and it meant that the experiment ran into more obstructions. At the same time, the potential removal of local parking spaces – creating less favourable conditions for private car ownership – was a potential subject of controversy internally among the residents. These difficulties also complicated the situation for the student project groups doing action research in partnership with the local stakeholders.

The project was initiated by the homeowner association in Badensgade together with architect and urbanist Henrik Valeur, who had a long record with participatory planning locally and internationally (Valeur, 2014). Valeur had been looking for a neighbourhood in Copenhagen that was willing to take part in experiments, where the aim was to reduce car use dependency and to redesign public places. The connection to Badensgade was made with the help of the local centre for environment (Miljøpunkt Amager) and the local district council

(Amager Øst lokaludvalg). The project was presented to the residents on a general assembly in the homeowners' association in May 2017, where Valeur received support to carry on with the project (Schock et al., 2017, p. 15). Following the meeting, Valeur and the board were successful in obtaining initial funds from the municipality for a pilot study to develop the project and later from the Danish Arts Foundation for the actual realization of parts of the experiment.

As part of the pilot study, alongside with developing the project brief, organizing a workshop for the residents, etc., Valeur contacted Roskilde University and PS with the aim of establishing partnerships with student project groups that could support the development and practical realization of the experiment. The experiment was presented for the students as part of the start of term activities, and in the following year, first a project group on master's level, and later a thesis student, collaborated with the project (Dahlerup, 2018; Schock et al., 2017).

The contribution of the first project group was tied to the pilot study and the development of a knowledge base for the experiment. The focus of the project was to investigate the mobility habits of the local residents and to enquire into their views and perspectives on the development of alternative transport solutions and transformation of the street. The group conducted 68 short interviews with residents followed by a focus group with six residents (Schock et al., 2017, pp. 26–38).

Whereas in the previously described case on Nørrebro there had been little contact and communication between the university supervisor and the external stakeholder and partner, the collaboration with the first project group showed that the more complex and potentially controversial project on Amager demanded a closer collaboration and alignment between the student group, the supervisor and the external action research partner to make sure the student project would contribute positively to the experiment. As mentioned, the potential removal of parking spaces was a 'touchy' subject among the local residents that had to be dealt with delicately. This meant that the aim and purpose of the experiment had to be communicated carefully to the local residents to prevent misunderstandings that could potentially create local opposition. The actions and interventions of the student group thus to a larger extent needed to be co-designed in collaboration between the students, the supervisor and the external partner.

A further complication for the action research partnership occurred when the Badensgade project reached the planned phase of realization in the spring of 2018. As mentioned, the idea behind the second sub-project was to design temporary and mobile urban furniture in the space potentially freed from car parking – in other words, this meant occupying parking space on the road surface (Fig. 3.3).

The 320-meter long street of Badensgade has a legal status of 'private community road', which means that the homeowners' association holds a certain authority over the street. However, they must comply with requirements for technically sound facilities, and they must ensure that the road is in good and proper condition and that private dispositions do not violate public planning and safety measures (Schock et al., 2017, p. 12). Although the temporary occupation of parking spaces was approved by the general assembly in the homeowners' association, the approval from the municipal planning authorities proved to be a much more complex and complicated affair due to the technical and safety issues

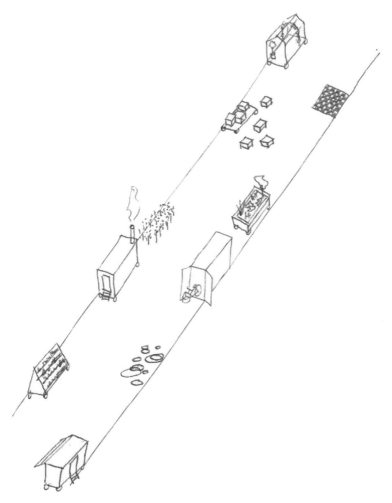

Fig. 3.3.   Sketch of Planned Furniture and Installations. (Sketch: Henrik Valeur).

involved in using the spaces on the actual road – and not just the pavement. As a consequence, the experiment had to be postponed for an indefinite period, and most of the experiments planned for the summer of 2018 had to be cancelled. This situation also caused complications for the master's thesis student who was collaborating with the project at the planned stage of realization. Whereas the initial idea behind the action research collaboration was that the student should contribute to the practical experimentations, the thesis project had to be re-orientated to focus more on uncovering the obstacles and difficulties for citizen-led bottom-up planning initiatives (Dahlerup, 2018).

Although most of the activities planned for the summer of 2018 had to be postponed, one activity was realized in the form of a prototype of the intended temporary and mobile urban furniture for community activities – without the official permission of the authorities (Fig. 3.4).

Concluding Reflections

In conclusion, we will propose some answers to the two research questions on the basis of the case studies. Firstly, we asked: 'How we can ensure that value is created for all participants in "student-directed" action research and project work?' The case studies indicate that collaborations work out best when local stakeholders and gatekeepers have clearly defined needs and a commitment to collective action, while at the same time being open for meeting the students' personal and academic motivations. Collaboration with students in experimental test phases or pilot projects seems to be a promising way of involving students in processes of planning and sustainable urban transition. Seen from the perspective of the external stakeholders, the students can contribute with valuable insights in the exploration of the potentials of places and the possible futures of communities, and they can also assist in providing a knowledge base for planned experiments and planning initiatives. In exchange, the students, from their perspective, are offered proposals for projects of societal relevance that they can choose from and personalize, and they are also given access to local knowledge

Fig. 3.4.   Co-creation of Street Furniture. (Photo: Henrik Valeur).

and gatekeepers that can help to make smaller action research projects possible within the time frame of project work.

In some cases, like the project on aesthetic experiments in Inner Nørrebro, the students can make contact with and create partnerships with external stakeholders with little facilitation from the university. In other and more complex cases where the potential for conflict is greater, like the case in Badensgade on Amager, alignment of interests, approaches and methods between students, supervisors and external stakeholders need to be facilitated more in depth, as tensions between students and external stakeholders can occur in the process.

In most cases there are also tensions between the requirements of the action research work and the annual cycle and timetable of academia. Our conclusion here is in line with Pain, Finn, Bouveng, and Ngobe (2013), who state that coping with these 'productive tensions' is a condition for following an action research orientation. Successful collaborations thus depend on close and flexible supervision of the students in order to make sure that the cooperation with the external partners can work and that the students can meet the requirements and time schedules given by the study programme.

Secondly, we asked: 'What is the "added value" of doing action research in problem-based learning and problem-oriented project work?' Our overall assessment from the case studies is that action research based on project work in local neighbourhoods is a powerful tool for 'double qualification' and education of engaged participatory planners. The huge potential with regard to learning outcomes is that students can complement academic skills with skills to engage and navigate in complex non-university contexts with different (and in some cases) potentially conflicting stakeholders. Students can develop a better understanding of 'the logic of practice' and acquire the ability to master practical and ethical judgements in complex 'real life' empowerment and learning processes. In relation to the goal of double qualification, this both prepares them for professional practice and provides them with an 'embodied' and pragmatically empowered critical understanding of how transformations towards a more sustainable and just society can be brought about.

Notes

1. Original publication details: Frandsen, M. S., & Andersen, J. (2019). Action Research in Planning Education – Experiences from Problem-Oriented Project Work at Roskilde University. *Journal of Problem Based Learning in Higher Education,* 7(1), 51–69. Reprinted in this volume with minor revisions.

2. Thanks to architect Henrik Valeur for sharing knowledge and illustrations, associate professor Simon Warren from the PPL Research and Development Unit at RUC for useful comments, and not least all the students who did the project work upon which the two case studies are based.

3. The model was developed for the purpose of this article and was thus not drawn on by the students in the two case studies.

References

Andersen, J. (2007). Empowermentperspektivet i planlægning. In E. Jensen, K. A. Nielsen, J. Andersen, & O. E. Hansen (Eds.), *Planlægning i teori og praksis* (pp. 46–63). Frederiksberg: Roskilde Universitetsforlag.

Andersen, A. S., & Heilesen, S. B. (Eds.). (2015). *The Roskilde model: Problem-oriented learning and project work*. Cham: Springer.

Andersen, A. S., & Kjeldsen, T. H. (2015a). Theoretical foundations of PPL at Roskilde University. In A. S. Andersen & S. B. Heilesen (Eds.), *The Roskilde model: Problem-oriented learning and project work* (pp. 3–16). Cham: Springer.

Andersen, A. S., & Kjeldsen, T. H. (2015b). A critical review of the key concepts in PPL. In A. S. Andersen & S. B. Heilesen (Eds.), *The Roskilde model: Problem-oriented learning and project work* (pp. 17–36). Cham: Springer.

Bacal, A. (2018). The promise and challenges of transformative participatory action research in the 21st century–the legacy of Paolo Freire and Orlando Fals-Borda. In A. Bilfeldt, M. S. Jørgensen, J. Andersen, & K. A. Perry (Eds.), *Den ufærdige fremtid* (pp. 48–68). Aalborg: Aalborg Universitetsforlag. (Serie om lærings-, forandrings- og organisationsudviklingsprocesser, nr. 9).

Blomhøj, M., Enevoldsen, T., Haldrup, M., & Nielsen, N. M. (2015). The bachelor programmes and the Roskilde model. In A. S. Andersen & S. B. Heilesen (Eds.), *The Roskilde model: Problem-oriented learning and project work* (pp. 79–106). Cham: Springer.

Brydon-Miller, M. (1997). Participatory action research: Psychology and social change. *Journal of Social Issues, 53*(4), 657–666.

Brydon-Miller, M., Antal, A. B., Friedman, V., & Wicks, P. G. (2011). The changing landscape of arts and action research. *Action Research, 9*(1), 3–11.

Brydon-Miller, M., & Aragón, A. O. (2018). The 500 hats of the action researcher. In A. Bilfeldt, M. S. Jørgensen, J. Andersen, & K. A. Perry (Eds.), *Den ufærdige fremtid* (pp. 19–47). Aalborg: Aalborg Universitetsforlag. (Serie om lærings-, forandrings- og organisationsudviklingsprocesser, nr. 9).

Dahlerup, C. (2018). *Konstruerede situationer og sociale byrum – en undersøgelse af Situationistisk Internationales unitære urbanisme og planlægningsprocessen fra bilgade til levende byrum i Badensgade. Specialeafhandling.* Roskilde: Roskilde Universitet.

Davidoff, P. (1965). Advocacy and pluralism in planning. *Journal of the American Institute of Planners, 31*(4), 331–338.

Egmose, J. (2015). *Action research for sustainability. Social imagination between citizens and scientists.* Farnham: Ashgate.

Fals Borda, O. (2001). Participatory (action) research in social theory: Origins and challenges. In P. Reason & H. Bradbury (Eds.), *Handbook of action research: Participative inquiry and practice* (pp. 27–37). London: Sage Publications.

Fisher, R., DeFilippis, J., & Shragge, E. (2012). History matters: Canons, anti-canons and critical lessons from the past. In J. DeFilippis & S. Saegert (Eds.), *The community development reader* (2nd ed., pp. 191–200). New York, NY: Routledge.

Flyvbjerg, B. (2006). Five misunderstandings about case-study research. *Qualitative Inquiry, 12*(2), 219–245.

Frandsen, M. S. (2016). Pragmatisk aktionsforskning – arven fra Hull House-settlementet. In A. Bilfeldt, I. Jensen, & J. Andersen (Eds.), *Social eksklusion, læring og forandring* (pp. 59–80). Aalborg: Aalborg Universitetsforlag. (Serie om lærings-, forandrings- og organisationsudviklingsprocesser; Nr. 7).

Frandsen, M. S. (2018). Sociale læreprocesser – John Deweys pragmatisme som udgangspunkt for aktionsforskning. In A. Bilfeldt, M. S. Jørgensen, J. Andersen, & K. A. Perry (Eds.), *Den ufærdige fremtid* (pp. 69–99). Aalborg: Aalborg Universitetsforlag. (Serie om lærings-, forandrings- og organisationsudviklingsprocesser).

Freire, P. (1972). *Pedagogy of the oppressed.* London: Sheed and Ward Ltd.

Friedmann, J. (1987). *Planning in the public domain: From knowledge to action.* Princeton, NJ: Princeton University Press.

Gibbs, P., Cartney, P., Wilkinson, K., Parkinson, J., Cunningham, S., James-Reynolds, C., … Pitt, A. (2017). Literature review on the use of action research in higher education. *Educational Action Research, 25*(1), 3–22.

Greenwood, D. J. (2012). Doing and learning action research in the neo-liberal world of contemporary higher education. *Action Research, 10*(2), 115–132.

Greenwood, D. J., & Levin, M. (2007). *Introduction to action research.* Thousand Oaks, CA: Sage Publications.

Gunnarsson, E., Hansen, H. P., Nielsen, B. S., & Sriskandarajah, N. (Eds.). (2016). *Action research for democracy: New ideas and perspectives from Scandinavia.* London: Routledge.

Jacobs, J. (1961). *The death and life of great American cities.* London: Jonathan Cape.

Laudonia, I., Mamlok-Naaman, R., Abels, S., & Eilks, I. (2018). Action research in science education–an analytical review of the literature. *Educational Action Research, 26*(3), 480–495.

Marcuse, P. (2011). The three historic currents of city planning. In G. Bridge & S. Watson (Eds.), *The New Blackwell companion to the city* (pp. 643–655). Oxford: Blackwell Publishing Ltd.

Mills, C. W. (1959). *The sociological imagination.* Oxford: Oxford University Press.

Moulaert, F., MacCallum, D., Mehmood, A., & Hamdouch, A. (Eds.). (2013). *The international handbook on social innovation: Collective action, social learning and transdisciplinary research.* Cheltenham: Edward Elgar Publishing.

Nielsen, A. K., Ullerup, S. B., & Fløyel, S. (2016). *Sanselige eksperimenter – udvikling og afprøvning af et metodisk værktøj, der skal fremme borgerinvolvering i en byfornyelsesproces. Specialeafhandling.* Roskilde: Roskilde Universitet.

Olesen, H. S., & Jensen, J. H. (Eds.). (1999). *Project studies: A late modern university reform.* Roskilde: Roskilde Universitetsforlag.

Pain, R., Finn, M., Bouveng, R., & Ngobe, G. (2013). Productive tensions–engaging geography students in participatory action research with communities. *Journal of Geography in Higher Education, 37*(1), 28–43.

Rask, L., & Andersen, J. (2016). *Dimittendundersøgelse 2016: En undersøgelse af undervisningsmetoder og kvalifikationer blandt dimittender fra Plan, by & Procesuddannelsen på Roskilde Universitet.* MOSPUS Research Paper Series No. 3. Roskilde: Roskilde Universitet.

Roskilde University (RUC). (2017). *Pedagogical profile at Roskilde University. Framework document for RUC's quality policy.* Roskilde: Roskilde University.

Sandercock, L. (2004). Towards a planning imagination for the 21st century. *Journal of the American Planning Association, 70*(2), 133–141.

Savin-Baden, M., & Major, C. H. (2004). *Foundations of problem-based learning.* Maidenhead: Open University Press.

Schock, S., Rudolph, M., Skogbjerg, J., Lium, A., & Voss, S. T. (2017). *Badensgades proces mod en grøn omstilling – et kvalitativt aktionsforskningsstudie om et stedsspecifik og samskabende planlægningstiltage for grøn mobilitetsomstilling. Projektrapport.* Roskilde: Roskilde Universitet.

Thorsen, N., & Børsen, T. (2018). Aktionsforskning på kandidatuddannelsen i Tekno-Antroplogi. In A. Bilfeldt, M. S. Jørgensen, J. Andersen, & K. A. Perry (Eds.), *Den ufærdige fremtid* (pp. 179–205). Aalborg: Aalborg Universitetsforlag. (Serie om lærings-, forandrings- og organisationsudviklingsprocesser, nr. 9).

Valeur, H. (2014). *India: The urban transition–a case study of development urbanism.* Copenhagen: B – Architectural Publisher.

Chapter 4

PAR: Resistance to Racist Migration Policies in the UK

Umut Erel, Erene Kaptani, Maggie O'Neill and Tracey Reynolds

Abstract

In this chapter we share research findings from our collaborative research project 'PASAR: Participatory Arts and Social Action in Research' (http://fass.open.ac.uk/research/projects/pasar), which combines participatory action research methods of participatory theatre and walking methods in order to understand the way in which racialized migrant women challenge their exclusion and subjugation in the context of the UK. The situation of migrant families in the UK is currently characterized by the 'hostile environment' policies. This policy 'is a sprawling web of immigration controls embedded in the heart of our public services and communities. The Government requires employers, landlords, private sector workers, NHS staff and other public servants to check a person's immigration status before they can offer them a job, housing, healthcare or other support' (Liberty, 2018, p. 5). The currently hegemonic political discourse, views migrants as outsiders to the nation and challenges their right to access welfare. Migrant families are cast as outsiders to citizenship, challenging the social and cultural cohesion of the nation. Indeed, UK immigration policies render it difficult for migrant families to secure their social and economic reproduction. Against this backdrop, the research explores how racialized migrant families develop their subjugated knowledges to claim belonging and participate in the society they live in. In this chapter, we share the key methodological findings, challenges and benefits of working with a PAR approach for co-producing transformatory knowledge with migrant families and advocacy organizations.

In line with the aims of this book, we reflect on the transformatory potential of research and knowledge for the common good through 'alternative collaborative system of co-researchers and co-learners engaged in dialogue with civil society and social movements' (Bacal, Introduction p. 1, see also Andersen and Frandsen, this volume).

Transformative Research and Higher Education, 93–105

Copyright © 2022 Umut Erel, Erene Kaptani, Maggie O'Neill and Tracey Reynolds

Published under exclusive licence by Emerald Publishing Limited

doi:10.1108/978-1-80117-694-120221005

Keywords: Participatory artsbased research; participatory action research; families; migration; racism; resistance

Introduction

This chapter introduces a participatory arts-based research project with migrant families, reflecting on how the elements of the project contribute to a wider political project of resisting racism in the contemporary UK. The chapter argues that by working together with migrant mothers and young girls, as well as organisations that focus on the rights of migrant and Black and Minority Ethnic people, research can co-produce knowledge that challenges racist and sexist subjugation of migrant girls and mothers. This project has the potential to not only generate new knowledge and insights, but it also illustrates that participatory arts-based research can be considered a challenge racist representations and generate consciousness of the injustice of contemporary UK policy of enacting a hostile climate towards migrants.

There is currently increased interest in creative and participatory approaches to research. This is in part due to the decolonial challenge to extractive and procedural research practices, which treat research participants' knowledge as 'raw material' for academics to 'interpret' and add value (Tilley, 2017). While such decolonial critiques have been formulated with a view to challenging the ways in which indigenous communities have been targeted by the intertwining of colonial and research projects (Smith, 2013), they also more broadly challenge the ways in which academic knowledge production is tied up with colonial conceptions and interests (e.g. Bhambra, 2014; Mignolo, 2012). Another reason for the increasing interest in creative and participatory research approaches comes as a result of the recognition of the sensual and affective aspects of knowledge (Ahmed, 2013). Furthermore, there is a need to explore how social research methods can address embodied knowledge (Kaptani & Yuval-Davis, 2008; Vacchelli, 2018). As creative methods are particularly apt at 'resisting binary or categorical thinking' (Kara, 2015, p. 14), these methods are also helpful for questioning and challenging the strict delineation of categories of 'researchers' and 'research participants' and the categorization of 'migrants' versus 'citizens,' a key concern of our research project (Jeffery, Palladino, Rotter, & Woolley, 2019).

We begin the chapter by describing the Participatory Arts and Social Action Research project on which we draw. Then we briefly present the arts-based methods of participatory theatre and walking used in this project to show how they can contribute to resisting racism.

The Participatory Arts and Social Action Research Project

This chapter draws on the Participatory Arts and Social Action Research project (PASAR http://fass.open.ac.uk/research/projects/pasar), which aimed to gain a better understanding of how participatory action research approaches engage marginalised groups in research as co-producers of knowledge.

Funded by the National Centre for Research Methods/Economic and Social Research Council, PASAR combined walking methods and participatory theatre to create a space for exploring, sharing and documenting processes of belonging and place-making that are crucial to understanding and enacting citizenship. Participatory Action Research, based on the principles of inclusion, valuing all voices and action-oriented interventions (O'Neill, Erel, Kaptani, & Reynolds, 2019; O'Neill & Webster, 2005). Our research is inspired by critical, collaborative approaches, including community based participatory research approaches which seek to benefit the communities they are working with through generating theories, knowledge and action collaboratively. The research itself is seen as a process of learning together (Minkler, 2005), instead of viewing academic researchers as generating theories and knowledge while collaborators and partners are simply providing data. It is located within a transformative, rather than pragmatic, ethos of Participatory Action Research, which is allied with movements for social justice, following the approaches of Freire and Fals-Borda (Bacal, 2018, p. 52). As Bacal points out in the introduction to this volume (p. 3), the project aimed to produce and share useful knowledge with vulnerable communities as co-researchers and co-learners.

The project created a model for bringing together practitioners and marginalized groups to engage with each other through creative and innovative methods for researching migrant families' citizenship, specifically, arts based participatory methods of walking stories and theatre. The project developed methods and methodological knowledge of participatory theatre and walking methods. To do this, we included three strands in the project. Firstly, we employed participatory methods with migrant parents' and young people, exploring issues of intergenerational communication (strand 1). Secondly, we employed participatory methods with families affected by the No Recourse to Public Funds Policy (NRPF) to facilitate conversation of participants with policy-practice (strand 2). The final strand (strand 3), building upon this, developed training tools for social science research (cf. O'Neill, Erel, Kaptani, & Reynolds, 2018).[1]

For reasons of space, this chapter focuses on strand 2, where we explored how theatre and walking methods can be used to research a particular policy issue and engage with policy makers and the people affected by the policy through these creative methods. We invited migrant mothers who are affected by the No Recourse to Public Funds (NRPF) policy to explore and reflect on their experiences through theatre and walking methods. Later in the process we organized a workshop in collaboration with Runnymede Trust that brought policy makers and practitioners into dialogue with the research team and mothers with no recourse to public funds. Here the participants presented their experiences, views and reflections through a short theatre performance piece, which allowed them a degree of control over how they presented their experiences. This facilitated a more equal level of discussions with attendees, who were practitioners, such as workers in local authorities and third sector organizations and policy makers, such as a member of the House of Lords. This short performance served to highlight the detrimental effects of the policy, and to enable participants to share their personal experiences in a way that enabled dialogue with practitioners and policy makers on a more equal footing (for more detail on methods see below).

The participatory theatre aspects of the project were led by Erene Kaptani, the research fellow and experienced theatre practitioner and drama therapist, who also trained team members in the early stages of the project. The idea of collaboration was very much at the heart of this project and we discussed our approach, limitations, challenges, opportunities and pitfalls with our partner organizations who also critically engaged with the design and process of the project. We worked closely with Counterpoints Arts an arts organization promoting work by migrant artists and about migration (see: https://counterpointsarts.org.uk). Film maker Marcia Chandra also accompanied the project throughout its different phases. We also worked closely with Renaisi, a family support organization (see: https://renaisi.com) and Praxis (see: https://www.praxis.org.uk), a migrant support and advocacy organization, who were both crucial in recruiting participants and, providing advice to participants where needed.

Finally, we collaborated with Runnymede Trust, a race equality policy organization, in particular on our policy workshop involving shared dialogue with practitioners and policy makers about the project (see below for more detail) and a briefing paper (Reynolds, Erel, & Kaptani, 2018) for social researchers (for more detail on collaborations see O'Neill et al., 2018). All of the resources produced during these collaborations, formed part of the project Toolkit (O'Neill et al., 2018). We will now discuss in more detail the context in which the project took place, that is how racialized migrant families in the UK are positioned and represented.

Migrant Families Resisting Racism

In our research we explored the experiences of migrant women as mothers and young girls from migrant families in London, from 2016 to 2018. The participants in the larger project came from a range of ethnic backgrounds and had a range of migration experiences (for more detail see Kaptani, Erel, O'Neill, & Reynolds, 2021; O'Neill et al., 2019). We sought in particular to understand how intersections of gender, age, racialization, mothering, and migration status shape migrants' experiences. Racialized migrant women are often not recognized as legitimately participating and socially, politically and culturally shaping the societies in which they live. Their belonging to the nation of residence is seen as tenuous, and their social positioning is that of racialized, gendered Others who are often relegated to a precarious status, engaging in poorly paid and unskilled employment (Erel, 2016). Often seen as cultural outsiders to the nation, black and racialized migrant women are positioned as a potential threat to the social and cultural cohesion of the nation (Lentin, 2003; Tyler, 2010). They are suspected of transmitting the 'wrong' cultural and linguistic resources to their children, with migrant mothers often blamed for a supposed lack of 'integration' of their children (Reynolds et al., 2018) or even their political radicalization (Ryan & Vacchelli, 2013; *The Times*, 18 January 2016).

While the cultural practices and resources of racialized and migrant communities are often marginalized and excluded from public representation (Reynolds & Zontini, 2014), when racialized migrant mothers, as part of their 'kin-work,' transmit such cultural resources to their children, this does not only serve to connect them with kin and family members, it is also an aspect of equipping them with the cultural identities to resist everyday racism (Reynolds, 2003; Reynolds, Erel, Kaptani, & O'Neill, 2017; Reynolds et al., 2018). This 'culture work,' essential for resisting and challenging racism, is an important part of racialized migrant women's mothering work (Collins, 2009; Reynolds, 2005).

When, despite racist and exclusionary immigration regimes, migrant families live, work, and engage in community building, they claim the right to participate, reside and belong. By claiming such a right to belong and participate for themselves and their children, migrant families bring into being new understandings of who can and who cannot be part of their locality, city and nation. Furthermore, by bringing up a multi-ethnic new generation of citizens, migrant families change our understanding of who can legitimately form the social and cultural community on which the polity is based. With this participatory arts based research project, we set out to learn more about how migrant families practice, imagine, reflect on and theorize their participation and belonging.

Participatory Theatre and Walking Methods

In this section we describe the research design and methods, in particular highlighting how participatory arts and action research methods can challenge existing knowledge on migrant families by foregrounding participants' own knowledges, which often in challenge official discourses on migrant families as problematic and potentially threatening social and cultural cohesion. By articulating their experiences in their own terms, positing which issues they would like to focus on in the theatre scenes and walks, participants shaped not only the research, but also began to share their experiences with each other, reflecting on their social positioning collectively and developing collective 'subjugated knowledges' (Foucault, 1980).

For reasons of space, here we focus on one strand of the larger project where we worked with a group of 20 mothers affected by the No Recourse to Public Funds Policy. Our partner organization, Praxis, a migrant rights advice and advocacy organization helped us recruit participants (https://www.praxis.org.uk). We also explored how the idea of 'legislative theatre' (Boal, 1998) could be used to allow those affected by the policy to voice their experiences and views of the policy to practitioners and policy makers. Boal developed the practice of legislative theatre during a period when he served as a councillor in Rio de Janeiro, he used participatory theatre to find out which issues mattered to poor and marginalized residents and how the law making process could address these issues in their interests. In our own project, of course, as researchers we have much more limited access to the legislative process. In addition, the project took place during a period when migrants' rights were under increasing attack from a government that introduced a range of policies that made access to housing, education, health care and other services more difficult for migrants, reinforcing a politics of bordering between those deemed to be 'migrants' and those deemed to be citizens with a broader range of social rights (Yuval-Davis, Wemyss, & Cassidy, 2019). That is why our work with legislative theatre focused on firstly making visible the effects of a policy on those it targets, and secondly involving the people affected by the policy into dialogue with practitioners and policy makers on the detrimental effects of that policy. This was important as the people affected by this policy have been marginalized and excluded from policy debates. For that purpose, we brought two social workers into the workshop space for three sessions, allowing participants to share their experiences, critiques and frustrations with them and reflect together on how this policy pushed families into poverty and destitution. This was important as social workers constitute the front-line staff whom families with No Recourse to Public Funds encounter when applying for support. The role of the social workers is to assess whether families are eligible to receive support and to refer them for housing and other support. While the law is clear in stating that families with children should receive support from their local authority, many professionals, including social workers try to deter families who have no recourse to public funds. This means that many families, despite being legally entitled to some minimal support because they have children, in practice take a long time to argue for this support (Flynn, Erel, O'Neill, & Reynolds, 2018, NELMA). We then produced a short play which was shown at the policy workshop to practitioners and policy makers (including social work professionals, migrant and family support organizations, race equality and children's rights organizations) and at the Houses of Parliament (facilitated by MP Kate Green, then the Chair of the All Party Parliamentary Group on migration).

The research workshops were based on a combination of participatory theatre (principally forum theatre) and walking methods (Erel, Reynolds, & Kaptani, 2017, 2018; Kaptani & Yuval-Davis, 2008; O'Neill & Roberts, 2019; Reynolds et al., 2018).

Our use of participatory theatre draws on Augusto Boal's body of work on Theatre of the Oppressed (2000). Forum Theatre is one key tool of the Theatre of the Oppressed, where participants are invited to show a particular situation of oppression or a dilemma they have experienced themselves. Once they have shown this dilemma, other participants are invited to step onto the stage, replace the protagonist, and change the course of action. This can be thought of as a 'rehearsal' for social change outside of the theatre stage (Boal, 2000; Ganguly & Jana, 2010). Theatre of the Oppressed transforms the role of audiences, they are not any more seen as passive spectators, but instead invited to take centre stage. Boal (2000, p. 98) broke down the boundaries between actors and spectators, audience and the 'sacred space of the stage' to allow participants to become 'spect-actors'. This form of theatre developed as part of wider social movements and campaigns, for example, for literacy and land reform in South America. Training participants in basic theatre skills through a series of games and exercises allows them to create theatre scenes as an arena to rehearse challenging inequalities of power. Participants' interventions were about trying out different solutions and experiencing the steps necessary for social change. While interventions may not be successful in achieving the spect-actors' aims fully, they can nonetheless lead to a changed situation (cf. Erel et al., 2017).

With regards to walking methods, walking as a methodology helps us to understand peoples 'routes and mobilities' and that 'social relations are not enacted in situ but paced out along the ground' (Ingold & Vergunst, 2008). As Clark and Emmel (2010) describe, walking interviews can be useful to understand how interviewees 'create, maintain and dissemble their networks, neighbourhoods, and communities.' Drawing on O'Neill (2017, p. 74) we see walking as an arts based, *ethno-mimetic* method that forms part of a biographical research approach that enables 'a deeply engaged relational way of attuning to the life of another that evokes knowing and understanding' for when 'walking with another we can engage in an embodied and corporeal way and attune to the narratives and lived experiences of research participants'. Taking a walk with someone can open a space for dialogue and communication in reciprocal ways because the 'physical embodied process of walking, remembering, sensing – attuning – is constitutive and the relational shared process opens up a discursive space that can also be a reflective space' (O'Neill, 2014, p. 76).

These participatory arts-based methods, forum theatre and walking methods, are not only helpful in understanding the everyday lives of participants, they are also generative, so that knowledge is not simply retrieved, but constructed in collaboration between arts practitioners, researchers and participants; it is 'collaboratively made' not found (Jeffery et al., 2019; O'Neill, 2008; O'Neill et al., 2019). Arts based approaches reflect 'the multidimensional, complex, dynamic, inter-subjective and contextual nature of human experience' (Jeffery et al., 2019, p. 7; cf. Kaptani & Yuval-Davis, 2008), and as such are particularly useful in challenging stereotypical racist representations of migrants.

Participatory theatre and walking in combination as a research method can be mobilized to reflect on shared experiences, building community and belonging. They can also lead to the articulation of collective subjugated knowledges to challenge racist representations of migrant families. Furthermore, as we will show in the following section, research using such methods within a socially transformative framework can become a way of constituting migrant families as rights claiming subjects.

Migrant Families with No Recourse to Public Funds Enacting Citizenship

The project explored how we can use participatory arts-based methods to enable a group of racialized migrant mothers to engage in dialogue with practitioners and policy makers about a policy which deeply affects their everyday lives. The No Recourse to Public Funding (NRPF) policy means that migrants subject to immigration control are not allowed to access many benefits, tax credits or housing assistance. While this policy has been effective for decades, since the introduction of hostile environment policies in 2012, it has been widened to cover all migrants deemed 'subject to immigration control'. It now applies to a wider range of different statuses, such as those on spousal or student visas, migrants with leave granted under family or private life rules, and dependents of a person with settled status, as well as those without legal residence status (http://www.nrpfnetwork.org.uk/information/Pages/who-has-NRPF.aspx). This policy is based on a racist system of immigration controls, defining migrants as outsiders who should not be entitled to social rights and has the effect of pushing racialized migrant families into poverty and destitution.

Migrant families often become aware that they are subject to the NRPF policy when they encounter a crisis situation, such as family breakdown, unemployment, health issues or housing problems. At that point, they approach social services for support only to learn that, due to this policy, they are not able to access support such as social housing or social security.

As a consequence, they often find themselves pushed to the margins of society as a result of poverty and racism. Many of these migrant families include young children, who are among the most vulnerable people affected by this policy. While the policy foresees some exceptional support to families with children – those without children are excluded from any public support – local authorities and social services providers often make it extremely difficult for these migrant families to substantively claim these rights (Flynn et al., 2018; NELMA).

These precarious circumstances can make it very difficult for migrants to participate in reflection and critique of this policy, because all of their energies are focused on day-to-day survival. In our research project, we used the arts-based participatory methods to work with a group of migrant mothers affected by the NRPF policy to enable their collective voice to be heard. These methods were important as they allowed the women to share their experiences with each other and the research team, to develop collective knowledge, overcome stigma, and articulate a critique of the policy's detrimental effects. Together we developed short theatre scenes shared at a workshop with policy makers and practitioners. The theatre methods allowed the women to be actors, directors and story tellers, who could imagine and try out social interventions, rather than simply showcasing their vulnerabilities as a result of this dehumanising policy.

We developed a short theatre scene, which gave rise to discussion with workshop participants from public and voluntary sector organizations and activists, which is documented in a short video (Performance by the Mothers with No Recourse to Public Funds Group, http://fass.open.ac.uk/research/projects/pasar/videos/policy-day). The theatre scene is based on Elaine's experience, but was further elaborated to articulate the collective experiences of participants. Elaine had been working for many years for a large supermarket. As the Home Office required her to sign into the Immigration Reporting Centre, she needed to take time off every two weeks to do so. Her manager used his knowledge of her vulnerability to bully her and change her onto an unfavourable shift work pattern: from midnight to four o'clock in the morning, even though she had just had a baby. When she approached her union representative, they were not supportive, but instead, told her she should be glad to have a job at all as an immigrant! Her fellow workers also stigmatised her as a supposedly 'illegal immigrant' and she eventually lost her job. As her husband was unable to work for health reasons, she was not able to pay rent and subsequently the family, including her six-year-old son, had to live in houses of friends and acquaintances, surviving on their monetary support for four years. Elaine's experience shows how racism, anti-immigration policies and austerity exacerbate the effects of racialized migration policies to render it increasingly difficult for migrant families to bring up their children in dignity (Erel, 2018).

Theresa, another of the mothers who shared her experiences of this policy, has lived and worked in the UK for 20 years and, like all the women in our project who were either born in the Caribbean or West African nations, she expressed strong links with UK because of colonial ties. Theresa's landlord increased her rent to a level she could not afford to pay on her low income as a care worker on a zero-hours contracts. When she was consequently evicted, she approached the council for accommodation only to learn she was subject to NRPF. The council therefore refused to help her, instead sending her on a circuitous route to a range of other organizations. When finally she approached our partner organization, Praxis, she was able to successfully claim her right to temporary accommodation because, despite its claims to the contrary, the local authority has a duty under Section 17 of the Children's Act to prevent children from becoming destitute. However, this did not address Theresa's needs, as the accommodation was unsuitable. Along with her three children she was housed in a one bedroom flat, where she had to sleep in the kitchen due to lack of space. Furthermore, this accommodation was located in a different London borough from where Theresa had previously lived. As we learned, it is an increasingly common practice for local authorities to house families affected by NRPF out of borough (Flynn et al., 2018). For Theresa, this meant she had to travel for over an hour to her youngest son's school.

Despite the increasing number of families affected by the NRPF policy, there is little awareness of it in wider society. Thus, when we organized the policy day in February 2017, we encountered interest from a wide range of organizations. One of the pernicious effects of this policy, we found, was that it increased the social isolation of families affected by it. Being subject to NRPF was seen as stigmatizing the family as being potentially 'illegal' migrants, and also opened those affected by it to economic and sexual exploitation, as many participants had found it difficult to talk about their status. Within a broader discursive climate, where migrants are seen as outsiders to the nation, it was furthermore made difficult to claim 'the right to claim rights' (Isin, 2017, p. 506). By using arts based participatory methods, the PASAR project was able to bring these migrant mothers into dialogue with practitioners, activists and policy makers. This happened using a range of formats, including keynote talks by Ruth Lister, a member of the House of Lords, and Colin Yeo, an immigration barrister; talks by the research team; the performance and discussion of the short theatre scene; breakout small group discussions between research participants and workshop attendees; and a closing roundtable.

The range of different interactions fostered by these different formats encouraged and permitted a range of ways for research participants to engage. Beyond simply showcasing their difficult situations, they were also part of discussions and exchanges. As a consequence of this event we were invited by the All Party Parliamentary Group on Migration to show a short play we developed together about their experience of NRPF at the House of Commons, and further took this short play to a range of events to highlight this problematic policy, including to migrant community organizations, statutory organizations, activist events and arts venues. We also developed a longer play performed at a theatre (https://richmix.org.uk/events/me-i-just-put-british/) and produced, with Counterpoints Arts and film maker Marcia Chandra, a short film 'Black Women Act!' (http://fass.open.ac.uk/research/projects/pasar/videos) which we were able to present at a range of community, arts and activist events and conferences.

While each of these occasions presented opportunities for different forms of engagement with different types of audiences and spect-actors, throughout these different engagements the research participants became increasingly articulate on the detrimental effects of the NRPF policy, but also about their own position in society as people with the right to claim rights. By claiming the right to claim rights, participants struggle against the injustice of this policy, which excludes them from taking part in the welfare state to which they themselves have contributed, as individual migrants, but also, they argue, through their colonial history.

Conclusion

The PASAR project explored the uses of participatory arts-based methods for creating understandings and representations of migrant families that can make visible their experiences and subjugated knowledges. We worked together as researchers, arts practitioners, participants and with our partner organizations to explore and challenge the marginalized positioning of migrant families in current debates on migration, characterised by a hostile climate to migrants.

While we recognize that such challenges have their limits, the processes where both participants and researchers work together to reflect on their experiences and construct new understandings that challenge the racist logic of these policies of constructing them as undeserving outsiders are important for engaging with activists, practitioners and policy makers, as well as communities of other migrant families. By claiming centre stage to initiate and enter such debates about a policy designed to marginalize and silence migrant families, participants directly challenged these racist practices and claimed the right to equal participation.

Note

1. This policy deprives many migrants from the right to access benefits and housing support, driving them into poverty, will be discussed in more detail below.

References

Ahmed, S. (2013). *The cultural politics of emotion.* London: Routledge.

Bacal, A. (2018). The promise and challenges of transformative participatory action-research in the 21st century–the legacy of Paulo Freire and Orlando Fals-Borda. In A. M. Bilfeldt Sogaard Jorgensen, J. Andersen, & K. A. Perry (Eds.), *Aktions for skningens potentialer og ud for dringer.* Copenhagen: Aalborg University Denmark.

Bhambra, G. (2014). *Connected sociologies.* London: Bloomsbury.

Boal, A. (1998). *Legislative theatre. Using theatre to make politics.* London: Routledge.

Boal, A. (2000). *Theatre of the oppressed.* London: Routledge.

Clark, A., & Emmel, N. (2010). Using walking interviews. Morgan Centre. Manchester University. Retrieved from https://eprints.ncrm.ac.uk/id/eprint/1323/. Accessed on October 21, 2021.

Collins, P. H. (2009). *Black feminist thought: Knowledge, consciousness, and the politics of empowerment.* London: Routledge.

Erel, U. (2016). *Migrant women transforming citizenship: Life-stories from Britain and Germany.* London: Routledge.

Erel, U. (2018, May). Saving and reproducing the nation: Struggles around right-wing politics of social reproduction, gender and race in austerity Europe. In *Women's studies international forum* (Vol. 68, pp. 173–182). Oxford; New York, NY: Pergamon.

Erel, U., Reynolds, T., & Kaptani, E. (2017). Participatory theatre for transformative social research. *Qualitative Research, 17*(3), 302–312. doi:10.1177/1468794117696029

Erel, U., Reynolds, T., & Kaptani, E. (2018). Migrant mothers' creative interventions into racialized citizenship. *Ethnic and Racial Studies, 41*(1), 55–72. doi:10.1080/01419870.2017.1317825

Flynn, D., Erel, U., O'Neill, M., & Reynolds, T. (2018). *Tracey the 'no recourse to public funds' policy in UK immigration law–a source of injustice, inequality and destitution.* Retrieved from http://fass.open.ac.uk/sites/fass.open.ac.uk/files/files/PASAR/NRPF%20Report%20Jan20.pdf

Foucault, M. (1980). *Power/knowledge: Selected interviews and other writings, 1972–1977.* New York, NY: Vintage.

Ganguly, S., & Jana, S. (2010). *Forum theatre and democracy in India.* London: Routledge.

Ingold, T., & Vergunst, J. L. (Eds.). (2008). *Ways of walking: Ethnography and practice on foot.* Aldershot: Ashgate Publishing, Ltd.

Isin, E. (2017). Performative citizenship. In A. Shachar, R. Baubock, I. Bloemraad, & M. Vink (Eds.), *The Oxford handbook of citizenship.* Oxford: Oxford University Press.

Jeffery, L., Palladino, M., Rotter, R., & Woolley, A. (2019). Creative engagement with migration. *Crossings: Journal of Migration & Culture, 10*(1), 3–17.

Kaptani, E., Erel, U., O'Neill, M., & Reynolds, T. (2021). Methodological innovation in research: Participatory theatre with migrant families on conflicts and transformations over the politics of belonging. *Journal of Immigrant & Refugee Studies, 19*(1), 68–81. doi:10.1080/15562948.2020.1843748

Kaptani, E., & Yuval-Davis, N. (2008). Participatory theatre as a research methodology: Identity, performance and social action among refugees. *Sociological Research Online, 13*(5), 1–12.

Kara, H. (2015). *Creative research methods in the social sciences: A practical guide.* Bristol: Policy Press.

Lentin, R. (2003). Pregnant silence: (En) gendering Ireland's asylum space. *Patterns of Prejudice, 37*(3), 301–322.

Liberty. (2018). *A guide to the hostile environment.* London: Liberty.

Mignolo, W. (2012). *Local histories/global designs: Coloniality, subaltern knowledges, and border thinking.* Princeton, NJ: Princeton University Press.

Minkler, M. (2005). Community-based research partnerships: Challenges and opportunities. *Journal of Urban Health, 82*(2), ii3–ii12.

NELMA. NRPF is state violence! Retrieved from https://nelmacampaigns.wordpress.com/nrpf-is-state-violence-2/. Accessed on November 19, 2019.

O'Neill, M. (2008). Transnational refugees: The transformative role of art? *Forum Qualitative Sozialforschung/Forum: Qualitative Social Research, 9*(2).

O'Neill, M. (2014). Participatory biographies: Walking, sensing, belonging. In *Advances in biographical methods* (pp. 93–109). London: Routledge.

O'Neill, M. (2017). Walking, well-being and community: Racialized mothers building cultural citizenship using participatory arts and participatory action research. *Ethnic and Racial Studies, 41*(1), 73–97. doi:10.1080/01419870.2017.1313439

O'Neill, M., Erel, U., Kaptani, E., & Reynolds, T. (2018). Participatory theatre and walking as social research methods-A toolkit. Accessed on November 4, 2019.

O'Neill, M., Erel, U., Kaptani, E., & Reynolds, T. (2019). Borders, risk and belonging: Challenges for arts-based research in understanding the lives of women asylum seekers and migrants' at the borders of humanity. *Crossings: Journal of Migration & Culture, 10*(1), 129–147.

O'Neill, M., & Hubbard, P. (2010). Walking, sensing, belonging: Ethno-mimesis as performative praxis. *Visual Studies, 25*(1), 46–58.

O'Neill, M., & Roberts, B. (2019). *Walking methods: Research on the move.* London: Routledge.

O'Neill, M., & Webster, M. (2005). Creativity, community and change: Creative approaches to community consultation. In P. Henzler, B. Skrzypczak, & B. Warsaw (Eds.), *The social animator: Role or profession.* Warszawa: Centrum Wsperiana.

Reynolds, T. (2003). Black to the community: An analysis of 'black' community parenting in Britain. *Community, Work & Family, 6*(1), 29–45.

Reynolds, T. (2005). *Caribbean mothers: Identity and experience in the UK.* London: Tufnell Press.

Reynolds, T., Erel, U., & Kaptani, E. (2018). Migrant mothers: Performing kin work and belonging across private and public boundaries. *Families, Relationships and Societies, 7*(3), 365–382.

Reynolds, T., Erel, U., Kaptani, E., & O'Neill, M. (2017). Practice policy briefing: Participatory action research-engaging marginalised communities in policy and practice. Retrieved from https://www.open.ac.uk/ikd/sites/www.open.ac.uk.ikd/files/files/working-papers/PASAR%20briefing%202017_Engaging%20marginalised%20communities%20in%20policy%20and%20practice.pdf. Accessed on October 21, 2021.

Reynolds, T., & Zontini, E. (2014). Bringing transnational families from the margins to the centre of family studies in Britain. *Families, Relationships and Societies, 3*(2), 251–268.

Ryan, L., & Vacchelli, E. (2013). 'Mothering through Islam': Narratives of religious identity in London. *Religion and Gender, 3*(1), 90–107.

Smith, L. T. (2013). *Decolonizing methodologies: Research and indigenous peoples.* London: Zed Books Ltd.

Tilley, L. (2017). Resisting piratic method by doing research otherwise. *Sociology, 51*(1), 27–42.

Tyler, I. (2010). Designed to fail: A biopolitics of British citizenship. *Citizenship Studies, 14*(1), 61–74.

Vacchelli, E. (2018). *Embodied research in migration studies: Using creative and participatory approaches.* Bristol: Policy Press.

Yuval-Davis, N., Wemyss, G., & Cassidy, K. (2019). *Bordering.* Hoboken, NJ: John Wiley & Sons.

Chapter 5

The Movement toward Knowledge Democracy in Participatory and Action Research

Erik Lindhult

Abstract

One common feature of different variants of participatory and action research is rejection of technocratic, undemocratic elements in science and inquiry, aiming to break the dominance of traditional academic views of science. These variants open up broader participation of people, and emancipate knowledge creation for the production of actionable knowledge with transformative potentials. The purpose of this chapter is to recognize and clarify a striving for knowledge democracy in these explicit or implicit democratizing ambitions and tendencies in the sense of broadening the participation of concerned parties in research and development work on open and equal terms. This recent concept, still in the process of formulation, has been proposed as a global mobilizing and unifying thinking for distributed networks and movements for participatory oriented research. The concept and movement had an initial embedding in the First Global Assembly for Knowledge Democracy in June 2017, Cartagena, Columbia. The purpose of the chapter is to elaborate on the meaning of knowledge democracy as a vision for the participatory and action research community. Particularly I will distinguish between different orientation to knowledge democracy, and the character of the logic of a more, open, democratic and coproductive science that can be a carrier of it.

Keywords: Knowledge democracy; action research; participatory research; participatory action research; co-production; democratic science

Transformative Research and Higher Education, 107–128
Copyright © 2022 Erik Lindhult
Published under exclusive licence by Emerald Publishing Limited
doi:10.1108/978-1-80117-694-120221006

Introduction – The Road toward Democratization of Research and Knowledge Democracy

Knowledge democracy as a concept was first emerging around 1990. An important impetus was the participatory turn in the second wave of the action research tradition developed into PR and PAR – Participatory Research and Participatory Action Research. Gaventa (1991) saw PAR as the most promising vehicle for 'knowledge democracy.' The concept did not develop further in use until nearly 20 years later. Budd Hall and Rajesh Tandon brought it up as a name for a movement in research and transformation for giving voice to and empower popular and indigenous knowledges (Hall, 2011; Hall, 2018; Hall, Escrigas, Tandon, & Sanchez, 2014; Hall & Tandon, 2017; Tandon, 2013, 2014a, 2014b; Tandon, Singh, Clover, & Hall, 2016). In the last decade, more attention on the concept has developed in the action research community, e.g., through special issues (Action Research Journal and Educational Research Journal, see Openjuru, Jaitli, Tandon, & Hall, 2015; Rowell & Feldman, 2019), and well as several journal and book chapter contributions (Coghlan & Brydon-Miller, 2014; Feldman & Bradley, 2019; Hong & Rowell, 2019; Rowell, 2019; Rowell & Hong, 2017; Wood, McAteer, & Whitehead, 2019). In 2017, the first global assembly of knowledge democracy was arranged by Action Research Network of the Americas (ARNA) (Hall & Tandon, 2018; Seeley, McAteer, Sánchez, & Kenfielde, 2019). This meeting was a way to bring together disparate communities and networks of action research globally, building on the tradition from the two earlier Cartagena conferences 1977 and 1997, in memory of the leading Columbian action researcher and social scientist Orlando Fals-Borda. The impetus for the renewed interest is as a potential common strategic orientation for the disparate global AR community. The discussion continues beyond this first assembly concerning the concept and its meaning, strategic work and the furthering of a movement (https://knowledgedemocracy.org/).[1] The purpose of the chapter is to elaborate on the meaning of knowledge democracy as a vision for the participatory and action research community. Particularly I will distinguish between different orientation to knowledge democracy, and the character of the logic of a more, open, democratic, and co-productive science that can be a carrier of it.

The structure of the chapter is as follows; First, I locate the striving of democratizing research in the action research tradition as the main carrier of the movement. Second, I describe the meaning and rationale of knowledge democracy and its link to democratizing science and knowledge production. Third, I identify three different orientations and strategies in the movement toward knowledge democracy where the understanding and role of science and scientific inquiry and its relation to distributed knowledge and research capacity in society is a core feature. Fourth, I identify assumptions and logic of more co-production oriented approaches in comparison with 'normal' scientific approaches and its significance for knowledge democratization.

---

[1] I grately appreciate and have learned a lot through the work by the Knowledge Democracy Group: Lonnie Rowell, Olav Eikeland, Ruth Balogh, Jane Springett, and the author.

Democratizing Research in the Action Research Tradition

I will particularly focus on the field and research traditions of participatory and action research that has been since its origin in the 1940s at the forefront of democratizing efforts, generally under the heading of Action Research (AR), after the participatory turn in the 1970s also named Participatory Action Research (PAR) and Participatory Research (PR). The traditions of participatory and action research have been leading the development in transformative research, where transformative education is part of the core processes, e.g., as in ALAR integrated as action learning. This evolving field has pushed for knowledge democratization both in involving different groups in society and focus on their knowledge interests and needs for problem solving and social transformation and in influencing academia and scientific community to shift its perspectives, theories and practices on research and science to be more conducive and supportive of more participatory ways of understanding and doing it.

One common feature of different variants of participatory and action research is rejection of technocratic, undemocratic streaks in science and inquiry, aiming to break the dominance of traditional academic views of science, opening up for broader participation of people, and emancipating knowledge creation for the production of actionable knowledge with transformative potentials. Already in the inception of AR in the group around Kurt Lewin there were initial steps in knowledge democratization in the striving for more relevant and useful knowledge for solving social problems, directing knowledge production toward resolving important social problems and thus making the emerging social science relevant for a broader group of people. Action-research was written with a hyphen indicating the close connection between action and research, change efforts and problem solving and at the same time developing and testing scientific hypothesis and theories. It was seen as research on and for action (Lewin, 1946) where the production of books does not suffice. Lewin and his colleagues innovated problem oriented, experimental and participatory approaches to research and change. Action-research was seen as 'the experimental use of social sciences to advance the democratic process' (Marrow, 1977, p. 128). Lewin was a strong defender of democracy, something which he saw his research on group dynamics, leadership and group decisions as corroborating. The role of forming group norms, through group discussion, leadership and group decision was key for changing behavior, something that expert advice could not accomplish. Action-research in line with lessons from group dynamics supported more informed citizens, and producing knowledge to support democratic processes. His experimental studies on group leadership showed for Lewin that autocracy is imposed on people, but democracy is not the same as laissez-faire but is practices that have to be learnt. This popular competence challenge echoes Aristotelian and Rousseauan views on the good polity (Eikeland, 2008).

Already Lewin and colleagues developed 'participant' action-research opening up for involving concerned people in doing research, e.g., in community or organizational self-surveys, with researchers providing methodological expertise and managing the process. Participation was important in order for individuals to accept the information from research and overcome resistance to applying research findings and to effect changes for improving problem situations. But it was experimental action-research that was the most advanced, but also the most difficult form where both theory testing and use as well as change could be incorporated in the research design.

While the first generation focused on developing the emerging social sciences into a force for solving social problems it did not question the largely positivist and empiricist scientific models. Knowledge democracy was in making available the epistemic force of science where action-research was a way to committing people to accept the results of science by participating in the research and change processes. It was a forerunner to today's ideology of open science, as well as citizen science; the involvement of people in fact finding and analysis. It can be linked to an informational or integrational view of knowledge democracy where access to the fruits and practices of science is central.

Self-education is the main goal for participation. Supporting the democratic process by informed, educated citizen, and at the same time accepting the assumed beneficial force of science and its expertise embedded in academic system. As moderate view of knowledge democracy, it was a movement toward democratization of research, but not yet knowledge democracy. The participating non-academics was not recognized as having expertise a par with academic researchers, and theory was in the hands of them. Furthermore, the models of research and science was not questioned. Knowledge was something coming out of the research process based on competent use of scientific methods rather than through distributed processes in society.

During the 1970s more participatory and more engaged research developed. It is revealing to compare the two anthologies on PAR published around 1990 (Fals-Borda & Rahman, 1991; Whyte, 1991), on the whole representing the ideologies of the north and the south (Brown & Tandon, 1983; Johansson & Lindhult, 2008). Whyte (1991) on the whole focused on PAR as 'applied research' where 'some of the members of the organization we study are actively engaged in the quest for information and ideas to guide their future action' (Whyte, p. 20), in spaces that adapted to existing system. Fals-Borda and Rahman (1991) had stronger claim for participation as creating power equalization among people in popular movements and research as a way to upset the elitist conditions in academia and society at large. It was in the context of the southern anthology that 'knowledge democracy' was first put in use. It represented reformative and transformative views on research e.g., inspired by Marxist views of recognizing and developing popular sciences, critique of dominant, elitist academic ideologies (de Sousa Santos, 2007; Hall, 1978) as well as immanent critique of prevailing praxis of science (Eikeland, 2006, 2007, Feyerabend, 2010). A more value and interest sensitive, ecologically and socially more sustainable as well as democratic and politically inclusive science was envisioned. It also inspired some scholars, Fals-Borda was one of them, to leave the academic community in order to develop science and research in the interest of people epistemologically neglected and marginalized.

In the 1990s, a third generation is recognizeable with a focus on institutionalization and successive integration in academic system. The focus was here more on making space for action and participatory research in prevailing scientific community, sometimes taking the form of guerilla warfare on dominant ideologies of science and its embodiment in academic system. E.g., Herr and Anderson (2015) sees the ultimate academic integration as the possibility of writing action research dissertations. While Fals-Borda argued for the development of popular science with its own verification criteria, Herr and Anderson instead used the tactic of widening the discussion of validity also to include democratic and dialogic validity in a broader bandwith of validity. The relation between traditional academic science and different forms of knowledge and knowledge production system in society is a core issue in conceptualizing and strategic development of knowledge democratization.

Knowledge Democracy and Democratizing Science and Knowledge Production – Meaning and Rationale

Knowledge democracy is not obviously understandable. It is nearly a contradiction in terms. Knowledge is based on truth while democracy is based on the will, decision and governance of the people as constituency and concerned public in a certain domain. An agreement or decision of concerned people is not the same as true knowledge. While the first Lewinian inspired generation was limited in terms of democracy, the second generation might be accused of going native and too much adopting the views of people in the domain of inquiry, and loosing scientific perspectives and objectives. Going democratic seems to be also a risk. Good knowledge cannot be based on voting procedures, as what is democratic is more of people having power of voice and influence rather. It may need some knowledge on own interests and needs, but science cannot be the same as the account that best support different interests. Can the two concepts go together? Are there risks of merging them? On the other hand, there are alternative views on both science and democracy where they go together, and that's something we will focus on.

A movement toward knowledge democracy as knowledge democratization is an ongoing, never-ending process and striving. In the first use of the concept, Gaventa states that 'PAR methodology appears to be the most effective way of building "knowledge democracy" today' (Gaventa, 1991, p. 158). Knowledge democracy for Gaventa and Fals-Borda means to recognize and enable wider sources of knowledge of people and communities in society beyond traditional academic science, in order to transform conditions for marginalized people. 'The sum of knowledge from both types of agents…makes it possible to acquire a much more accurate and correct picture of the reality that is being transformed. Therefore academic knowledge combined with popular knowledge and wisdom may result in total scientific knowledge of a revolutionary nature which destroys the previous unjust class monopoly. This dialectical tension in commitment-and praxis leads to a rejection of the asymmetry implicit in the subject/object relationship that characterizes traditional academic research and most tasks of daily life. According to participatory theory, such a relationship must be transformed into subject/subject rather than subject/object. Indeed, the destruction of the asymmetric binomial is the kernel of the concept of participation as understood in the present context (researcher - researched) and in other aspects of the daily routine (family, health, education, politics and so forth). Thus to participate means to break up voluntarily and through experience the asymmetrical relationship of submission and dependence implicit in the subject/object binomial. This is the essence of participation. The general concept of authentic participation as defined here is rooted in cultural traditions of the common people and in their real history (not the elitist version), which are resplendent with feelings and attitudes of an altruistic, cooperative and communal nature and which are genuinely democratic' (Fals-Borda, 1991, p. 4f).

According to Rahman; 'at issue for PAR now and in the future is increasing the input and control of enlightened common people – the subordinate classes, the poor, the peripheral, the voiceless, the untrained, the exploited grassroots in general over the process of production of knowledge and its storage and its use. One purpose is to breakup and/or transform the present power monopoly of science and culture exercised by elitist, oppressive groups' (Rahman & Fals-Borda, 1991, p.30; see also Hall, 1978; Rahman, 1985). Thus 'knowledge democracy' was put to use in a more radical stance in the AR community. As we will see later there are also more moderate and reformist stances.

Knowledge democracy means that different forms of knowledge, expertise and inquiry, as well as the people and systems carrying these resources and capacities, is recognized on equal terms. It also refers to the character of democratic institutions, systems and practices that are enabling open and fair treatment of expertise and its recreation and cross-fertilization in societies. Professional, experiential, spiritual, and practitioner knowledges are recognized and treated equally in line with an extended epistemology (Heron, 1996).

Knowledge is the precious good with which humans can develop ever more value enhancing, powerful and humane ways of life. AR is according to the definition of Reason and Bradbury (2001) aimed at the flourishing of people and their communities. Knowledge is or can bring enlightenment and emancipation (Habermas, 1974); freedom to be enlightened from dominating prejudices and powers in tradition as well as freedom as ability to envision alternatives and struggle and innovation of better conditions of living. Knowledge is also power to improve circumstances and transform situations to improve living conditions.

Science is the best available ways of inquiry and research for development of knowledge in different fields of learning and practice. It is a name for competent inquiry (Dewey, 1939a), itself developed successively through experience, learning, and inquiry process in different communities of practice and inquiry. The overall goal and vision of knowledge democracy is building a knowledge society of educated people and systems that have the best capacity to realize a sustainable and good community. Knowledge democracy as a vision is itself integrated as an important dimension in deepening democracy and making it more participatory, more able to realize basic human values, and more efficient in problem solving and innovation (Gaventa, 1991; Hall, 2011). An important challenge, and a core reason to focus on knowledge democracy, is that knowledges and capacities for reason and inquiry go unheeded or is discriminated. The freedom of education and inquiry through science and different form of knowledge production, reproduction, and co-creation are in different ways restricted. Academic institutions as the embodiment of prevailing models of science may often represent these restrictions today. Hall and Tandon (2017) (see also Hall, 2021) sees knowledge democracy as a striving for decolonialization of knowledge combatting the unequal production and distribution of knowledge with a source in the historic silencing of knowledge created by those outside of Eurocentric dominated academia (see de Sousa Santos, 2014). Emanating from and partly still upheld by walled universities differentiating those inside the wall as knowers and experts and those outside it as non-knowers. Hall (2021) outlines a number of principles of knowledge democracy which are in his view fundamental for epistemic justice (as well as consequently social justice); (1) Recognition of multiple epistemologies, (2) Be attentive to social, creative and arts-based ways of creating knowledge, (3) Recognition of lived experience, social movements and community organization as sources of knowledge, (4) The centrality of people's knowledge to political and cultural change, (5) Respect of the ownership rights of Indigenous Peoples of their own cultural and linguistic knowledge, and (6) Support for free open access sharing of knowledge as a principle of open science. At the same time, there is also plurality and openness in different academic domains today, e.g., indicated by expansion in the legitimacy and use of participatory and action research approaches and methodologies. Academic is sometimes seen as impractical, ivory tower research divorced from practice. But academia may on the positive side, partly as a vision for the future, be seen as taking the role as guardian of high quality knowledge and inquiry in all its many-sided forms and practices.

Political and social institutions can be a threat to knowledge democracy in the sense that the quality of knowledge is not available or is eroded through skewed facts, fake news, and story inventions for demagogic purposes. Quality checks and control on social media publishing is often wanting. Is freedom of speech, including bending the truth and propagating lies, threatening freedom of education and inquiry? Knowledge democracy can support critical literacy and the force of valid knowledge in public discourse in face of demagogy, internet trolls, and propagation of unsubstantiated rumors.

Democratization of knowledge production is the never-ending movement, processes, and efforts to realize and take advantage of knowledge and inquiry capacities in society on the road toward knowledge democracy. Democratization means that knowledge production is governed, conducted, and utilized to a larger extent with influence and involvement of concerned stakeholders and expertise, thus on more equal terms among implicated parties. Democratization may involve different areas, made to a certain degree, and in a particular way. Action research, PAR and participatory research can support democratic knowledge production and scientific activity for achieving better practical outcomes and enhanced quality of knowledge production. But it is important how it is conceived and conducted in order to achieve both good practical and theoretical results (Wood et al., 2019).

The movement toward knowledge democracy is an intellectual one in the sense of critique of prevailing more restricted, often elitist, and developing understandings, reasons and experience of viable more democratized knowledge production. It is also fundamentally a practical one in reconstructing research and education practices and their conditions so that more effective and efficient participatory organization and methods are realized. It is also a normative-political effort in transforming institutions and organizations for research and education so that it is good soil for different forms of inquiry and knowledge and is enabling for participation of all scholars of learning.

Knowledge democracy is also ideal and utopian providing orientation and direction for efforts of improving conditions. Like in all conceptions, there are idealizing dimensions concerning the true, good and beautiful social life. Platonism has it place in development of viable utopias. Alternative construction is important in breaking the monopoly of academic knowledge. But also improving and deepening democracy through enabling access and influence.

There are different views on what is the best ways ahead; Fals-Borda and de Sousa Santos see the epistemic ideology of western science as something to critique. Gaventa points to new ways of understanding science and its role in and relation to society that can empower epistemically subjugated expertise and actors (Gaventa, 2008). Hall, Tandon, Tremblay, and Singh (2015) see university-society partnerships development and working with inclusion of indigenous knowledge systems. From my own Scandinavian context with a deep tradition of democratizing strivings in science and research a rich tapestry of strategic orientations can be recognized (Gunnarsson, Hansen, Nielsen, & Sriskandarajah, 2015). There is a long tradition of popular education through study circles and folk high schools in democratic, self-educational forms with similarities to Freirean pedagogy, also inspiring the development of a methodology of 'research circles' in the 1970s (Holmstrand, Härnsten, & Löwstedt, 2008). Further steps were taken around 2010 in building a national PhD/research education programme in 'Democratic knowledge and change processes' initiated by Swedish Participatory Action Research Community (SPARC) open for all citizens as a way to disseminate PAR research norms and methodology. From broad national strivings of democratizing working life, a dialogic tradition of doing action research based on broad participation of all concerned with dialogue on equal terms – democratic dialogue – as spearhead was developed (Eikeland, 2008; Gustavsen, 1992; Lindhult, 2021; Pålshaugen, 2014) in line with the principle of participation described by Fals-Borda and Rahman (1991). From a tradition of participatory community development a critical utopian approach to action research e.g. through citizens engaging in future workshops, was developed (Egmose et al., 2020) with similarities with community PR approaches of Hall and Tandon. In addition, there are fairly strong and plural traditions of practice-based research, e.g. in the form of interactive research (Svensson, Ellström, & Brulin, 2007), action oriented research in school and care settings (i.e. Rönnerman, 2004) as well as ongoing evaluation research (Brulin & Svensson, 2012). These strivings enrich the movement towards knowledge democracy.

Movement toward Knowledge Democracy – Different Orientations and Strategies

Knowledge democracy is still rather open and vague as a concept and as shifts in thinking and practice. As a step in clarification, I will distinguish and typify different orientations and positions. The Table 5.1 typifies three orientations that can be recognized in literature from more moderate to more transformative.

The typification is made to distinguish different orientations and positions in the landscape of actors engaged in the movement toward knowledge democracy. It also is the point of departure for different strategic orientations on the democratization road. The typification is in Weber's sense 'ideal types'; idea-constructs, thought pictures, that help put the seeming chaos of social reality in order, and is helpful for making distinctions and comparisons. But as Weber pointed out, systematic thought distorts the inexhaustible variety of reality (Weber, 1975, p. 9f).

Weber was aware of the fictional nature of the 'ideal type' and did not claim its validity in terms of a reproduction of or correspondence with social reality. A solution often proposed to attain a degree of objectivity by those sharing Weber's kind of methodological perspectivism is weighing the various evaluations against one another and making a 'statesman-like' compromise among them. Such a practice, which Weber calls 'syncretism' is according to him not only impossible but also unethical, for it avoids 'the practical duty to stand up for our own ideals' (Weber 1904/1949, p. 58[3]). Weber recognizes the unavoidable value orientation and necessity of engagement also in science. Scientific activism is not only necessary for the norms of science (Dewey, 2008; Lindhult, 2015) but also for the vision and ideals of knowledge production, its outcomes and beneficiaries. This is explicitly recognized and inherent as research design parameter in action research (Lindhult & Axelsson, 2021). It is according to Reason and Bradbury (2001) generally focused on human flourishing. It is based on the Kantian enlightenment motto *Sapere aude!*, think for yourself, dare to be wise, i.e. knowledge mobilization and generation where naming the world as Freire (1971) say is a core research activity, as a spring for autonomy, responsibility (*Mündigkeit*) and empowerment. The typification outlined is linked to positions that also is based on visions, ideals and assumptions for how forms of knowledge and knowledge systems, and the people engaged in them, are treated in society, and the way it in its turn can enable and deepen democratic practices, systems and way of life. It is an expression of different possible ethical ideals and visions to stand up for as Weber say. I believe it is also open for statesman-like compromises, Aristotelian phronesis if you will, in the situated movement toward knowledge democracy as a step to make democracies and science more participatory. The movement may be the core problematique in line with Macpherson's (1977, pp. 94, 98) view; 'the main problem about participatory democracy is not how to run it but how to reach it'. It is a Freirian problem of conceptualizing and naming knowledge democracy in order to clarify orientation, aspects, and direction of it a dialogic praxis.

A moderate view on knowledge democracy can be called an informational position. It is informational in the sense that openness and access to scientific

Table 5.1. Orientations to Knowledge Democracy.

	Informative	**Reformative**	**Transformative**
Focus in knowledge democratization	Openness of and access to science, stakeholder participation for information gathering, learning and commitment	Interaction and collaboration for co-producing/co-creating knowledge among distributed forms of expertise	Emancipation, empowerment of subjugated knowledges and inquiry
Main philosophical point of departure	Empiricist (interpretative)	Pragmatic (constructivist)	Critical (radical), epistemic colonialism, neo-marxist
Strategic orientation	Education (bildung), competence development, informed, literate citizens, citizen science (mostly)	Participation in action/experiential inquiry, learning and change work to solve problem and improve situations	Mutual commitment to empower popular, indigenous knowledge, and democratize science
Science, academia and participation	Acknowledgement and participation in the norms of science, open, supportive academia	More need/use focused, practical/constructive science with broader bandwith, reformed, interactive, collaborating academia	Popular science, indigenous knowledge systems, transformed, more democratic science. Popular academia
Reference in AR tradition	Lewinian tradition, organization development	Collaborative AR (i.e. Coghlan, Gustavsen etc.), interactive research	Participatory/ critical AR, Fals Borda, Freire, Gaventa, Hall & Tandon, McTaggart, Rowell
General reference	Open science, transdisciplinary science (mostly), RRI, Mode 2	Dewey, Schön, Mode 2(/3)	de Sousa Santos

knowledge and to valid information is a core dimension of knowledge democratization. Thus science is a force in enlightenment in the sense that people are enabled to be informed and educated. Participation of different forms of expertise and stakeholders can be done through transdisciplinary research and responsible research and innovation (RRI). The informational orientation understands science as although plural in disciplines and methodology having some common ground of understandings and norms. Generally there is an empiricist and positivist leaning; ontologically there is a given empirical reality, and epistemologically reality is the arbiter of truth in line with a mirroring or correspondence theory (Rorty, 1979).

It can be linked to an interpretative orientation where the meaning of information can vary based on e.g., contextual, cultural, or political frames of reference, but still the point is that there are more or less correct views albeit often uncertain and not fully known, i.e., objectivist hermeneutics as Alvesson and Sköldberg (2018) calls it. Strategically the movement and efforts toward knowledge democracy is focused on education (*bildung*), competence development, informed, literate citizens, that can be engaged in research through citizen science. Knowledge democracy in this moderate sense was already evident in the Lewinian origin of action research in the 1940s. Its limits are in maintaining scientific theory and methodology as an academic expertise.

A reformist orientation to knowledge democracy sees a need to modify and transform science, academia and its interaction in society in order to move toward knowledge democracy. The theory monopoly of science and academic researchers is questioned and the distributed experience, knowledge, and expertise of people in society are acknowledged, opening up for interaction and collaboration for co-producing/co-creating knowledge among distributed forms of expertise. A reformist view is based on the assumption that knowledge and knowledge production is distributed in society, and that people have experience, expertise and capacities of reasoning and inquiry frequently not acknowledged in science and academia. Its reformist point of departure in knowledge democratization show itself in the belief that academia and the prevailing theories, norms, and practices of science can be influenced and developed in order to accommodate, mobilize and integrate distributed forms knowledge and inquiry of people. So that the academic community can at least tolerate and harbor excluded or denigrated forms of knowledge, practical forms of knowledge, and engaged scholarship.

Participatory and action research struggles to implement different tactics to carve out spaces in scientific community and university system for more democratized knowledge mobilization and production and influence understanding of science to be more open to and supportive of knowledge of citizens and professionals in its theory and practice of research. It is a long-term guerilla war against more restrictive epistemic ideologies and practices.

A transformational or more radical view on knowledge democracy raises a stronger critique of prevailing and dominant scientific institutions and sees science as governed by those in power, which also are the core beneficiaries. There are democratic deficits in elitist system of knowledge production to the extent that knowledge and inquiry capacity of citizens and in society at large is not fairly taken into account. Particularly there are lacks in knowledge production in the interest of underprivileged groups. Popular sciences and indigenous ecologies of knowledges beyond academic and traditional scientific systems need to be defended and mobilized. Epistemic colonialization of knowledge production through Western science is according to de Sousa Santos (2007, 2014), Grosfoguel (2013) and Hall & Tandon (2017) setting up cultural barriers between academic expertise and assumed lesser knowledge of people in society. It has resulted in epistemicide, i.e. the denigration and outright killing off of indigenous knowledge systems. A more radical view also has drawn inspirations from neo-Marxist critique of bourgeois science and the need for development of a science of the proletariat, e.g. from Gramsci's view of the common sense of people that can be developed into good sense in interaction with organic intellectuals (Gramsci, 1971). Elitism and inequality in knowledge production are often seen as strengthened by market and capitalist as well as by authoritarian or less democratic political systems. A transformative orientation challenges the unequal condition for actors to participate in dialogue and the risk of cooptation to dominant views and powerful actors. Participatory oriented research need to support development of critical consciousness of power, subjugation as well individual and collective empowerment through popular communities and learning systems.

A common movement in knowledge democratization is the striving for a more dialogic, subject-subject, co-learning relation among actors, assuming all have something to contribute and something to learn. This is a common streak in different positions. In a democratic dialogue, all parties must be open for reasoning. How build a democratic infrastructure that enable subject-subject relations and dialogue on equal terms? (Fals-Borda & Rahman, 1991; Gustavsen, 1992). A problem is limited knowledge of more democratic alternatives and ways to understanding and conducting science and research activities. Modified or new, more democratic and engaged science understanding is needed.

Conceptualizing a More Democratic Logic of Research

A core dimension of the different orientations is the understanding of science and its knowledge democratizing character and potentials. A fruitful point of departure is the way science and academic institutions can collaborate and support knowledge production in society in more inclusive and democratic sense. One movement in science and research is that knowledge is recognized as co-produced among different parties, not just produced one-sidedly by academic actors with domains of reality and society as research sites and data sources (Lindhult & Axelsson, 2021). A co-production point of departure implies a shift in understanding of knowledge production. Knowledge is seen as coproduced between different academic and non-academic actors, with a view of knowledge and knowledge production as distributed, varied and mutual. Thus, 'in order for co-production to occur, academics and practitioners must adopt an alternative outlook on knowledge in which both academic and practitioner knowledge is viewed as distinct, yet complementary' (McCabe, Parker, & Cox, 2015, p. 3).

It leads to research approaches focused on pooling of expertise and research/learning capacities and resources of involved parties. McCabe et al. (2015) finds a ceiling in co-production to the extent that this alternative co-production outlook on knowledge is not present or developed through questioning traditional views. Co-production has the potential of producing more relevant and valid knowledge as well as enhanced value for partners, stakeholders, and society. However, the collaborative and active elements add complexity, and need some other competences, methods and resources than more 'solitary' (ivory-towerish) research. It is in line with the movement from mode 1 to mode 2 form of knowledge production in the institutions and practices of science described by Gibbons et al. (1994). In recent years, research councils and academics have moved toward increasingly utility oriented and more transformative view of research, emphasizing the need for academic research to deliver demonstrable benefits to the economy, society, public policy, and the communities within which research takes place (Beebeejaun, Durose, Rees, Richardson, & Richardson, 2014; Beebeejaun et al., 2015; Martin, 2010). This requirement for greater 'accountability' and more 'engaged' scholarship has increased attention on the interactive ways of producing knowledge (Svensson et al., 2007). It is a collaborative and interactive process involving academic and non-academic participants in the production of knowledge (Pohl et al., 2010). Co-production means working together and building relationships between different groups of people to generate knowledge that coherently incorporates the different viewpoints (Van de Ven, 2007). Co-production in research assumes that the best research practice lies in a synthesis of academic research, practitioner knowledge and research participant 'expertise by experience' (Beebeejaun et al., 2015). In co-productive research project, the different stakeholder parties are actively involved in the organizing learning and knowledge production processes as equals and, as a result, the boundaries between the roles of academic and non-academic actors may become blurred. Pohl et al. (2010) describes an example of an action research project where co-production of knowledge was used to reach a mutually acceptable outcome. It a Bolivian context, it aimed to resolve a conflict between indigenous peasants who inhabited the Tunari National Park area, and the central government who wished to promote conservation in the area by placing severe restrictions on the land use. By discussing the issues with both of the parties, systematically analyzing the results, and utilizing their own disciplinary knowledge, the researcher was able to demonstrate that the peasants' traditional land use practices were in fact very effective in maintaining ecosystem diversity. When the government officials became aware of this, their objections to the peasants' presence were dissipated.

The characterization of co-production as research methodology concept indicates that is has some unusual features compared to 'normal' research. Co-production understood as research approach shifts the logic of understanding science and doing research. In comparison to 'normal' scientific approaches, co-productive research approaches has five special features related to research understanding, purpose, relation to stakeholders and affected, position of research and researchers, and how knowledge development about research objects is done. Fig. 5.1 describe these dimensions as well as their significance for knowledge democratization.

	"Normal" scientific approach	Co-productive approach	Significance for knowledge democracy
Research understanding	Data gathering and analysis to find patterns in reality synthesized in theory (empiricist)	Combining knowledges and mobilizing research capacities in practice (experiential, practical)	Widened, inclusive view on knowledge, expertise and scientific inquiry
Purpose	New, valid knowledge as contribution in a scientific field	In addition, useful knowledge for practice, improvement and transformation	Different knowledge needs and interests fairly taken into account
Relation to stakeholders/ affected	Research *on* Subjects as study objects/data source ("respondents")	Research *with* or *by*, Subjects as participants/actors in research	More equal relations among parties with democratic dialogue as co-active mechanism
Position of research(-ers)	Detached, passive (outside research context)	Engaged, (inter-)active Researchers, can have various positions and roles	Contextual and value(s) driven, scientific activism for shared values/general interests
Knowledge development about research object	Depicting them as they "are" (spectator research), partly conceptually constructed by researcher	Also co-constructing/creating research object (interactive and practice based research)	Opening up and democratizing reality/object construction through cooperative inquiry

Fig. 5.1.   Logic of Coproductive Research Approaches and Its Significance for Knowledge Democracy.

Although there is a broad spectrum of understanding of research today, I believe it is fair to say that an empiricist orientation is 'normal' emphasizing data gathering and analysis to find patterns in reality synthesized in theory. Co-production means a shift toward a more experiential and practical understanding focusing on combining knowledges and mobilizing research capacities embedded in practice and different forms of expertise. While the purpose in 'normal' research is to seek new, valid knowledge as contribution in a scientific field, co-productive research in addition seek useful knowledge for improvement and transformation. In addition to academic goals also practical goal is included, typically to resolve problems, alter the prevalent social conditions or to resolve a conflict. Purpose is embedded in problem context, its stakeholders and their knowledge needs and interests, and challenges of transformation. People in the research domain are commonly study objects and data sources, e.g., as 'respondents,' in 'normal' research. Co-productive approaches also conduct research *with* people as well *by* people themselves thus emphasizing a more equal relationship between researchers, practitioners, and communities. While the position in 'normal' research tend to be detached and passive outside the context of research, in co-production positionality tend to be more engaged and (inter-) active opening up for a multitude of positions and roles of researchers (e.g. evaluator, advisor, designer, etc.). People related to research domain is taking the role as research participants, partner and co-researchers. The participants becomes more of co-learners, and the process one of mutual learning and interaction to understand issues and create knowledge in multiple, overlapping roles. In 'normal' research, research objects are often seen as given to be faithfully depicted through research, in less positivist research, allowing for conceptual construction of objects by researchers. In coproductive approaches knowledge creation process is more organized to allow genuine participation at all stages, combining different forms of knowledge and research/learning, including both spectator/observational and practical/constructive knowing. This coproductive research opens up for co-creating and co-constructing research objects, not only depicting them, like in design science and professional practice (Frisina, 2002; Schön, 1983; Simon, 1996).

The shift in logic of knowledge production is in different ways significant for moving toward knowledge democracy. Dominant research understanding tends to limit the understanding of high quality knowledge and its production to what is generated by an educated elite of academic scholars in university institutions. Co-production orientations supports widened, inclusive views on knowledge, expertise and scientific inquiry where transdisciplinary, professional, indigenous and popular inquiry, and knowledge systems are recognized (Bunders-Aelen et al., 2010). Knowledge democratization is deconstructing the linear model of knowledge production (Schön, 1983) where basic research is divorced from interests in application and use, instead different knowledge needs and interests fairly taken into account in the contextual organizing of inquiry in relation to concerns and issues of stakeholders. It means a shift toward more equal relations among concerned and knowledgeable parties with democratic dialogue as co-active mechanism in collaborative and mutual knowledge production (Fals-Borda & Rahman, 1991; Gustavsen, 1992; Lindhult, 2015). As knowledge production like all human practices is driven by purposes, values, and norms of excellence in certain situated communities, research requires engagement and scientific activism for shared values and general/mutual interests ideally agreed on by parties involved (Lindhult, 2019). These values include norms for truth seeking and validation of epistemic claims as well as valuation of purposes and consequences of research and knowledge uses. These values, norms and assumptions need to be sufficiently open to be able to recognize and assess the relative validity of different claims to knowledge and practices of inquiry but at the same time avoid epistemic relativism. E.g., modern medicine has in many areas advanced significantly beyond traditional medical knowledge systems, like ability to develop and produce quite efficient vaccines. At the same time modern medical practices can learn from traditional medicine and combine knowledge elements from it with existing methods, like in the case of acupuncture or in how to achieve a more balanced relation between body, nature, and mind. What is striven for is knowing as Aristotelian phronesis (practical wisdom); 'a true and reasoned state of capacity to act with regard to the things that are good or bad for man' (Aristotle, 1980).

It means integrated and balanced judgement based on various available forms of knowledge on how to act in the situation at hand. This is closely related to Dewey's understanding of scientific inquiry as the transformation of problematic situations to situations where problem dimensions are resolved (Dewey, 1939a), e.g., a patient is recovering from illness or illness is avoided through preventive measures like vaccination or healthy lifestyle. There are here ancient (e.g., Aristotle) as well as more modern (e.g., Condorcet) and recent views on democracy (Cohen, 1986) arguing that citizens tend on average to have sufficient knowledge and judgmental competence (i.e., phronesis) to collaboratively discern the common good through discussion and majority decision, implying that knowledge democracy in this wider sense is viable. Thus, combined knowledge and 'science' of people, with academia, free media, free speech and free association as enabling institutions, can lead to reasonable outcomes and common advantage under favorable circumstances. It is also used in participatory innovation procedures where mobilization of the wisdom of people are striven for.

Last but not least, options for knowledge and inquiry democratization are opened up when scientific knowledge production is expanded from an empiricist view of science and research, where research is seen as mirroring reality as given through our senses and data generating equipment in theories (Rorty, 1979), into engaging in reality in collaboration with stakeholders in order to transform it (e.g., see Freire, 1971; Dewey, 1939a; Fals-Borda, 1979). The purpose of knowledge production and science is shifted toward democratic co-creation of conditions, objects, and solutions that can enhance human value and flourishing. It is in line with Freire's understanding of praxis as well as Dewey's vision of creative democracy to be approached through social intelligence and cooperative inquiry (Dewey, 1939b).

I believe the movement toward knowledge democracy requires working on a broad front with interrelated issues and ways for democratizing knowledge production. Knowledge democracy means that knowledge dissemination, production, and use in society are on equal terms between forms of knowledge, inquiry, and expertise and among stakeholders. AR and PR has been in the forefront of development, but there are a numerous areas contributing more or less significantly to this movement, e.g., design sciences, design thinking, user involvement, service science, collaborative and interactive research, indigenous research, action learning, systems thinking, responsible research and innovation, project management, feminist studies, co-production, arts based research. Just to mention a few of the multiple allies participatory and action research has in the further movement towards knowledge democracy.

Concluding Remarks

The concerns and strivings for knowledge democracy is related to the role of knowledge and science in society. It provides a direction for dealing with the dominance and perceived elitism of particularly positivist and western models of science and the organization of academia and scientific community reproducing the denigration of other forms of knowledge, scholarship and knowledge system. Specific forms and understanding of knowledge and science, and the experts seen as possessing it, is given too much authority and power at the expense of democratic processes. In the AR community with its focus on equalizing the epistemic status of actors the issue of conceptual and model dominance is recognized as a risk. It implies concern for the often-limited respect for knowledge of people in our democratic institutions. The experience and expertise of people goes unheard or is outrightly suppressed. Citizen claims and arguments even when grounded in science are sometimes not acknowledged. Then democracy is deficient as knowledge democracy. The challenge is to combine the experience and expertise of all involved parties. The experiences of all are needed – in Follett's words: 'that is all that democracy means' (Follett, 1924, p. 19).

I have elaborated on the understanding of and movement toward knowledge democracy with the participatory and action research tradition as a central driver and carrier. More critical reflection and conceptual clarification on the concept of knowledge democracy is needed. Important issue are; What is knowledge, what is democracy, how do they go together, and how can it deepen democracy in knowledge societies? There is a need for openness and being humble, e.g., in considering that not all beliefs and commended practices of people and cultures can be qualified as knowledge. Knowledge democracy can be seen as carrying the enlightenment strivings to free people from prejudice both in thinking and in transformative practice. But no claims to knowledge is better than the trustworthiness of the validation practices it can mobilize to redeem the claims and convince others. Truth is often conceived as an abolute, but all claims to knowledge as based on human validation practices are fallible. The openness to be challenged is central where democratic dialogue is a basic norm for forms of knowledge and expertise to meet on equal terms. We need to understand cultural and institutional traditions and their trajectories of learning and inquiry, and sometimes agree to disagree but understand more of the cultural and historical basis for the competing claims (Janik, 1989). Claims to knowledge are also claims for ways of life where the knowledge is affirmed to work to produce cherished values for participants as truth for us in a certain communal and contextual setting. How relate to the knowledge of shamans in an equal way to western science? Knowledge democracy must be open to a diversity of forms of and claims to knowledge as well as a humbling view on the variety of claims to knowledge but it is not a licence for relativism.

References

Alvesson, M., & Sköldberg, K. (2018). *Reflexive methodology – New vistas for qualitative research* (3rd ed.). London: Sage Publishing.

Aristotle. (1980). *The Nicomachean ethics*. Oxford: Oxford University Press.

Beebeejaun, Y., Durose, C., Rees, J., Richardson, J., & Richardson, L. (2014). 'Beyond text': Exploring ethos and method in co-producing research with communities. *Community Development Journal, 49*, 37–53.

Beebeejaun, Y., Durose, C., Rees, J., Richardson, J., Richardson, L., Savini, F., & Salet, W. (2015). Public harm or public value? Towards coproduction in research with communities. *Environment and Planning C: Government and Policy, 33*(3), 552–565.

Biesta, G. (2007). Towards the knowledge democracy? Knowledge production and the civic role of the university. *Studies in Philosophy and Education, 26*(5), 467–479.

Brown, L., & Tandon, R. (1983). The ideology and political economy of inquiry: Action research and participatory research. *The Journal of Applied Behavioral Science, 19*, 277–294.

Brulin, G., & Svensson, L. (2012). *Managing sustainable development programmes. A learning approach to change.* Farnham, Surrey: Gower.

Bunders-Aelen, J. G. F., Broerse, J. E. W., Keil, F., Pohl, C., Scholz, R. W., & Zweekhorst, M. B. M. (2010). How can transdisciplinary research contribute to knowledge democracy? In R. In't Veld (Ed.), *Knowledge democracy–consequences for science, politics and media* (pp. 125–152). Heidelberg: Springer. doi:10.1007/978-3-642-11381-9_11

Coghlan, D., & Brydon-Miller, M. (Eds.). (2014). *Knowledge democracy. The Sage encyclopedia of action research.* Thousand Oaks, CA: Sage.

Cohen, J. (1986). An epistemic conception of democracy. *Ethics, 97*(1), 26–38.

Dewey, J. (1939a). *Logic: The theory of inquiry.* London: George Allen & Unwin Ltd.

Dewey, J. (1939b). Creative democracy: The task before us. In J. A. Boydston (Ed.), *John Dewey, the later works* (Vol. 14, pp. 224–230). Carbondale, IL: Southern Illinois University Press.

Dewey, J. (2008). *The later works, 1925 – 1953, Volume 13: 1938-1939. Experience and education, freedom and culture, theory of valuation, and essays.* Carbondale: Southern Illinois University Press.

Egmose, J., Gleerup, J., Nielsen, B. S., Brydon-Miller, M., Ortiz Aragón, A., & Kral, M. (2020). Critical Utopian action research: Methodological inspiration for democratization? *International Review of Qualitative Research, 13*(2), 233–246.

Eikeland, O. (2006). Validity of action research and validity in action research. In K. A. Nielsen & L. Svensson (Eds.), *Action and interactive research. Beyond practice and theory* (pp. 193–240). Maastricht: Shaker Publishing.

Eikeland, O. (2007). Why should mainstream social researchers be interested in action research? *International Journal of Action Research, 3*(1/2), 38–64.

Eikeland, O. (2008). *The ways of Aristotle–Aristotelian Phronesis, Aristotelian philosophy of dialogue, and action research.* Bern: Peter Lang Publishers.

Fals-Borda, O. (1979). Investigating reality in order to transform it: The Columbian experience. *Dialectical Anthropology, 4*(1), 33–56.

Fals-Borda, O. (1991). Some basic ingredients, In O. Fals-Borda & M. A. Rahman (Eds.), *Action and knowledge: Breaking the monopoly with participatory action-research* (pp. 3–12). New York, NY: Apex Press.

Fals Borda, O., & Rahman, M. (1991). *Action and knowledge: Breaking the monopoly with participatory action research.* New York, NY: Apex Press.

Feldman, A., & Bradley, F. (2019). Interrogating ourselves to promote the democratic production, distribution, and use of knowledge through action research. *Educational Action Research, 27*(1), 91–107.

Feyerabend, P. (2010). *Against method.* London: Verso.

Follett, M. P. (1924). *Creative experience.* London: Longmans, Green and Co.

Freire, P. (1971). *Pedagogy of the oppressed.* New York, NY: Herder & Herder.

Frisina, W. G. (2002). *The unity of knowledge and action: Toward a nonrepresentational theory of knowledge.* Albany, NY: State University of New York Press.

Gaventa, J. (1991). Toward a knowledge democracy: Viewpoints on participatory research in North America. In O. Fals-Borda & M. A. Rahman (Eds.), *Action and knowledge: Breaking the monopoly with participatory action-research* (pp. 121–133). New York, NY: Apex Press.

Gaventa, J., & Cornwall, A. (2008). Power and knowledge. In H. P. Reason & H. Bradbury (Eds.), *Handbook of action research: Participative inquiry and practice* (2nd ed.). (pp. 172–189). London: Sage Publications.

Gibbons, M., Limoges, C., Nowotony, H., Schwartzman, S., Scott, P., & Trow, M. (1994). *The new production of knowledge: The dynamics of science and research in contemporary societies.* London: Sage Publications.

Gramsci, A. (1971). *Selections from the prison notebooks of Antonio Gramsci.* London: Lawrence & Wishart.

Grosfoguel, R. (2013). The structure of knowledge in westernized universities: Epistemic racism/sexism and the four genocides/epistemicides of the long 16th century. *Human Architecture, 11*(1), 73–90. Retrieved from http://scholarworks. umb.edu/humanarchitecture/vol11/iss1/8/

Gunnarsson, E., Hansen, H. P., Nielsen, S. B., & Sriskandarajah, N. (Eds.). (2015). *Action research for democracy–intervening in the current crisis: New ideas and perspectives from Scandinavia.* London: Routledge.

Gustavsen, B. (1992). *Dialogue and development: Theory of communication, action research and the restructuring of working life.* Assen/Maastricht: Van Gorcum.

Habermas, J. (1974). *Theory and practice.* Boston: Beacon Press.

Hall, B. (1978). Breaking the monopoly of knowledge: Research methods, participation and development. In B. Hall and J. R. Kidd (Eds.), *Adult learning: A design for action: A comprehensive international survey* (pp. 155–168). Oxford: Pergamon Press.

Hall, B. (2011). *Toward a knowledge democracy movement: Contemporary trends in community university research partnerships.* Sao Paulo: Instituto Paulo Freire de Espana.

Hall, B. (2018). Beyond epistemicide: Knowledge democracy and higher education. In M. Spooner & J. McNinch (Ed.), *Dissident knowledge in higher education.* Regina, SK: University of Regina Press.

Hall, B. (2021). Knowledge democracy, and the decolonisation of knowledge. *Towards Knowledge Democracy,* Webinar 2021-05-25, Mälardalen University/ SPARC. Retrieved from https://play.mdh.se/media/t/0_kqdj82ts

Hall, B., Escrigas, C., Tandon, R., & Sanchez, J. G. (2014). Transformative knowledge to drive social change: Visions for the future. In GUNi (Ed.), *Knowledge, engagement and higher education: Contributing to social change* (pp. 301–310). New York, NY: Palgrave Macmillan.

Hall, B., & Tandon, R. (2017). Decolonization of knowledge, epistemicide, participatory research and higher education. *Research: Ideas for Today's Investors, 1*(1), 6–19. doi:10.18546/RFA.01.1.01

Hall, B., & Tandon, R. (2018). From action research to knowledge democracy Cartagena 1977–2017. *Revista Colombiana de Sociología, 41*(1), 227–236.

Hall, B., Tandon, R., Tremblay, C., & Singh, W. (2015). Challenges in the co-construction of knowledge: A global study for strengthening structures for community university research partnerships. Retrieved from http://unescochair-cbrsr.org/unesco/wp-content/uploads/2014/05/Hall.pdf. Accessed on September 30, 2016.

Heron, J. (1996). *Co-operative inquiry: Research into the human condition*. London: Sage.

Herr, K., & Anderson, G. L. (2015). *The action research dissertation: A guide for students and faculty*. Thousand Oaks, CA: Sage.

Holmstrand, L., Härnsten, G., & Löwstedt, J. (2008). The research circle approach: A democratic form for collaborative research in organizations. In A. B. Shani (Ed.), *Handbook of collaborative management research* (Chapter 9). SAGE Publication.

Hong, E., & Rowell, L. (2019). Challenging knowledge monopoly in education in the U.S. through democratizing knowledge production and dissemination. *Educational Action Research*, *27*(1), 125–143.

Janik, A. (1989). *Style, politics, and the future of philosophy*. Dordrecht: Kluwer Academic Publishers.

Johansson, A. W., & Lindhult, E. (2008). Emancipation or workability? Critical versus pragmatic scientific orientation in action research. *Action Research*, *6*(1), 95–115.

Lewin, K. (1946). Action research and minority problems. *Journal of Social Issues*, *2*(4), 34–46.

Lindhult, E. (2015). Towards democratic scientific inquiry? Participatory democracy, philosophy of science and the future of action research. In E. Gunnarsson, H. P. Hansen, & B. Steen Nielsen (Eds.), *Action research for democracy–intervening in the current crisis: New ideas and perspectives from Scandinavia*. London: Routledge.

Lindhult, E. (2019). Scientific excellence in participatory and action research: Part I. Rethinking research quality. *Technology Innovation Management Review*, *5*(9), 6–21.

Lindhult, E. (2021). Achieving scope and broad participation in participatory research. The 'dialogue democratic' network-based approach of Björn Gustavsen. In D. Burns, J. Howard, & S. Ospina (Eds.), *Handbook of participatory research and inquiry* (Vol. I). SAGE. (in publication).

Lindhult, E., & Axelsson, K. (2021). The logic and integration of coproductive research approaches. *International Journal of Managing Projects in Business*, *14*(1), 13–35.

Marrow, A. J. (1977). *The practical theorist: The life and work of Kurt Lewin*. New York, NY: Teachers College Press.

Martin, S. (2010). Co-production of social research: Strategies for engaged scholarship. *Public Money and Management*, *30*(4), 211–218.

McCabe, A., Parker, R., & Cox, S. (2015). The ceiling to coproduction in university–industry research collaboration. *Higher Education Research and Development*, *35*(3), 560–574.

Openjuru, G. L., Jaitli, N., Tandon, R., & Hall, B. (2015). Despite knowledge democracy and community-based participatory action research: Voices from the global south and excluded north still missing. *Action Research*, *13*(3), 219–229.

Pålshaugen, Ö. (2014). Action research for democracy - a Scandinavian approach. *International Journal of Action Research*, *10*(1), 98–115.

Pohl, C., Rist, S., Zimmermann, A., Fry, P., Gurung, G. S., Schneider, F., ... Wiesmann, U. (2010). Researchers' roles in knowledge co-production: Experience from sustainability research in Kenya, Switzerland, Bolivia and Nepal. *Science and Public Policy, 37*(4), 267–281.

Rahman, M. (1985). The theory and practice of participatory action-research, In O. Fals-Borda (Ed.), *The challenge of social change* (pp. 107–132). London: Sage Publications.

Rahman, M., & Fals-Borda, O. (1991). A self-review of PAR. In O. Fals-Borda & M. A. Rahman (Eds.), *Action and knowledge: Breaking the monopoly with participatory action-research* (pp. 24–34). New York, NY: Apex Press.

Reason, P., & Bradbury, H. (Eds.). (2001). *Handbook of action research. Participative inquiry and practice.* London: Sage.

Rönnerman, K. (2004). *Aktionsforskning i praktiken: erfarenheter och reflektioner.* Lund: Studentlitteratur.

Rorty, R. (1979). *Philosophy and the mirror of nature.* Princeton, NJ: Princeton University Press.

Rowell, L. L. (2019). Rigor in educational action research and the construction of knowledge democracies. In C. A. Mertler (Ed.), *The Wiley handbook of action research in education* (pp. 117–138). Hoboken, NJ: John Wiley & Sons.

Rowell, L. L., & Feldman, A. (2019). Knowledge democracy and action research. *Educational Action Research, 27*(1), 1–6.

Rowell, L. L., & Hong, E. (2017). Knowledge democracy and action research: Pathways for the twenty-first century. In L. L. Rowell, C. D. Bruce, J. M. Shosh, & M. M. Riel (Eds.), *The Palgrave international handbook of action research* (pp. 63–83). New York, NY: Nature America.

de Sousa Santos, B. (2007). Beyond abyssal thinking: From global lines to ecologies of knowledge. *Eurozine, 33*, 45–89.

de Sousa Santos, B. (2014). *Epistemologies of the south: Justice against epistemicide.* London: Routledge.

Schön, D. (1983). *The reflective practitioner: How professionals think in action.* Aldershot: Avebury.

Seeley, J., McAteer, M., Sánchez, C. O., & Kenfielde, Y. (2019). Creating a space for global dialogue on knowledge democracy: Experiences from the inaugural global assembly for knowledge democracy. *Educational Action Research, 27*(1), 22–39.

Simon, H. A. (1996). *The sciences of the artificial* (3rd ed.). Cambridge, MA: MIT Press.

Svensson, L., Ellström, P.-E., & Brulin, G. (2007). Introduction – on interactive research. *International Journal of Action Research, 3*(3), 233–249.

Tandon, R. (2013). Global democracy requires knowledge democracy. blog. Retrieved from http://unescochair-cbrsr.org/index.php/2013/09/15/globaldemocracy-requires-knowledge-democracy/. Accessed on October 1, 2016.

Tandon, R. (2014a). Knowledge democracy: Reclaiming voices for all. Retrieved from http://unescochair-cbrsr.org/unesco/pdf/Lecture_at_Univ_Cape_ Town-August% 20-2014.pdf. Accessed on September 30, 2016.

Tandon, R. (2014b). Global challenges. In GUNi (Ed.), *Knowledge, engagement and higher education: Contributing to social change, hampshire and.* New York, NY: Palgrave Macmillan.

Tandon, R., Singh, W., Clover, D., & Hall, B. (2016). Knowledge democracy and excellence in engagement. *IDS Bulletin*, *47*(6). December 2016: 'Engaged Excellence'.

Van de Ven, A. (2007). *Engaged scholarship: A guide for organizational and social research*. Oxford: Oxford University Press.

Weber, M. (1904/1949). Objectivity in social science and social policy. In E. A. Shils & H. A. Finch (Eds. and trans.), *The methodology of the social sciences*. New York, NY: Free Press.

Weber, M. (1975). *Roscher and Knies: The logical problems of historical economics*. New York, NY: The Free Press.

Wenger, E., & Snyder, W. (2000). Communities of practice: The organizational frontier. *Harvard Business Review*, Jan–Feb. 139–145.

Whyte, W. (Ed.) (1991). *Participatory action research*. Newbury Park: Sage.

Wood, L., McAteer, M., & Whitehead, J. (2019). How are action researchers contributing to knowledge democracy? A global perspective. *Educational Action Research*, *27*(1), 7–21.

Chapter 6

Transforming the University to Confront the Climate Crisis

John Foran

Abstract

Drawing on my own experiences at the University of California, Santa Barbara as a college professor of radical social change for 31 years who has been focused on the climate crisis for the past 10, I explore the crisis of higher education with respect to this most pressing existential challenge of the twenty-first century and propose various approaches, actions, activities, and projects for both classroom teachers and networks of educators.

These include the UC-CSU NXTerra Knowledge Action Network, the UCSB-developed nearly carbon neutral conference, and engaging students in designing and implementing systemic alternatives outside the classroom in their own communities such as Eco Vista in the 23,000-person community of Isla Vista just adjacent to UC Santa Barbara, among others.

The essay will end with a vision of a new type of university, exemplified in the world-spanning Ecoversities Alliance, and dreamed of in Transition U and Eco Vista U, two prototypes that I have been involved in co-creating with students, staff, faculty and community members in Santa Barbara, California, and in the Transition US movement.

Keywords: Climate crisis; alternative pedagogies; Ecoversities Alliance; Eco Vista; NXTerra; systemic alternatives

Introduction: Education in the ~~Triple Quadruple Quintuple~~ Sextuple Crisis

> Education should consist of a series of enchantments, each raising the individual to a higher level of awareness, understanding and kinship with all living things.
>
> –Unknown

Transformative Research and Higher Education, 129–144
Copyright © 2022 John Foran
Published under exclusive licence by Emerald Publishing Limited
doi:10.1108/978-1-80117-694-120221007

What is the pedagogy of justice in the current conjuncture where more and more of us recognize the future in the present?

–Manuel Callahan (2019)

The interlocked triple crises of capitalist globalization-driven inequality, bought- and paid-for democracies and pervasive cultures of violence – from our most intimate relationships to the militarism of the United States – have for a long time been bound up with the truly wicked fourth crisis of climate chaos. And now we have the wake-up moment of the coronavirus and the global rebellion for social justice of what might be called the George Floyd uprisings breaking upon these structural, systemic burdens (Foran, 2020).

So, how *do* we connect *this many* dots? Every movement, organization, systemic alternative and countless activists, theorists and intellectuals are asking this as the crisis unfolds.

The time has come to ask new questions of our own as teachers.

Such as, to take two:

What role does/can higher education – and colleges and universities in particular – play in addressing these crises?

How can we draw on our movements and systemic alternatives in humanity's decade of decision to create a different *kind* of university, more fit for our purposes?

Everywhere, there is evidence that people are re-thinking and imagining alternatives to our outmoded educational systems that pride themselves as the cutting edge of modernity (see the chapters on education in *Philosophy and Theory in Higher Education: Special Issue on the Anthropocene in the Study of Higher Education* (Gildersleeve & Kleinhesselink, 2019), particularly Ullmer (2019) and Maxwell (2019)). This re-thinking extends to our moribund traditionally defined academic 'disciplines' (for a look at my own, Sociology, see Foran, 2019). What systemic alternatives might offer economies and societies that work for all to meet real, basic needs; a new and better kind of politics and learning spaces to enable radical social transformation away from the corporate university constrained in its depoliticizing neoliberal straitjacket; shifts in culture and affect to design the whole ways of *non-violent* living we desire; and fair, ambitious and binding global approaches to the threat of climate chaos?

Sooner or later, climate change, of itself, will force systemic and radical social change on states and other elite institutions. As scholars, activists and teachers, we are compelled to ask in what ways we can assist at the birth of a pluriverse of possible paths for this journey.

This chapter hopes to open up and contribute to such conversations by touching on some actual on the ground practices and pedagogies. My audience is teachers and learners in high schools and in college or university settings.

The journey takes us first to a (hopefully) radically useful set of resources for teachers and students, and then to a classroom that is not a classroom, and finally to some visionary alternative universities who are already travelling the path. Let's go!

Part 1: NXTerra and the Nearly Carbon-Neutral Conference: Network Strategies of Providing Transformative Resources to Teacher-Activists of the Climate Crisis

> We tried to create an autonomous place, open to learn by doing rather than by studying, as it was suggested by Ivan Illich, as it were a joyful activity of free people.
>
> –Gustavo Esteva

NXTerra (https://www.nxterra.orfaleacenter.ucsb.edu/) is the name chosen for an innovative digital platform designed by a network of teachers in the University of California and California State University systems that was launched in late 2019 ('NXTerra' refers to both the platform/Website and to our actual knowledge action network/KAN). Its aim is to provide the materials for a 'transformative education for climate action' and it offers 18 'Topics' under the broad categories of the climate crisis, climate justice and critical sustainability.

Crossing the humanities, social sciences and natural sciences, topics range from climate change and religion to systems thinking, from climate fiction to climate governance and from oceans and wildfires to community-engaged research, indigenous leadership, consumerism and inclusive environmental identities. Here students and teachers who want to find videos, readings, syllabi, classroom activities and more can draw freely from the resources we have archived and curated for this purpose. If, for example, a teacher of climate science wants to consider the importance of movements for climate justice by global youth in order to offer their students an outlet if they want to take action after learning the disturbing facts of our predicament, those materials and links can be found on the site.

Indeed, any teacher's eyes open to the distress and anxiety that students increasingly feel today and who wants to be able to help them work through and with those feelings can find help at the 'Climate Emotions' page, put together by Sarah Ray, author of *A Field Guide to Climate Anxiety: How to Keep Your Cool on a Warming Planet* (2020).

If one teaches sustainability studies and wants to go beyond the discourse of small 's' sustainability that promises a renewable energy future sometime around 2050, or even the UN's more comprehensive Sustainable Development Goals, then they can look for materials under what we call 'Critical Sustainability Studies' and topics such as 'Deep Adaptation', 'Systemic Alternatives' or 'Infrastructure: Past, Present and Future'.

A humanities teacher of language, the arts or the philosophy of environmental and climate issues can find a primer on climate science in the 'Bending the Curve' page developed by Veerabhadran Ramanthan, professor of atmospheric and climate sciences at the Scripps Institution of Oceanography, one of the world's great climate scientists who is engaging with the urgency of politics and the empowerment of young people inside and beyond the classroom. Ken Hiltner, a professor of English and Environmental Humanities offers all the materials he has developed for what might be called 'Climate Crisis 101' for advanced high school students and college first-years, including the course Website and YouTube channel videos.

My own topics on the site are 'Climate Justice Movements' and 'Systemic Alternatives', my two best hopes for confronting the climate crisis. Both offer learners practical hope and ideas for engagement outside the classroom. Under the heading of systemic alternatives are materials on Transition Towns, *buen vivir*, de-growth and ecosocialism, among others. And the one on climate justice movements offers an introduction to the quickly growing and inspiring global network of movements led by young people, frontline and fenceline communities of color, indigenous peoples, inhabitants of small island states and people who are doing the work of climate justice in all of these settings.

These are not just theories about radical transformation or stories about far-away struggles but instead invitations and maps for teachers and students who want to learn and connect with them in the real world.

The Nearly Carbon-Neutral Conference Is Here

Readers should also know about the 'nearly carbon-neutral conference' model developed over the past five or so years by UCSB Professor Ken Hiltner. In the following excerpt from the White Paper/Practical Guide he elaborates on how and why academics must consider and amend their habits of flying to conferences [this was before the Corona Crisis, of course, but one fears that we will return to this practice as soon as it seems feasible]:

> [T]raveling by air is a privilege that few share globally.... Even among Americans, half do not annually fly and just a quarter do so three or more times a year. Unfortunately, academics often find themselves in this last, rarified group because of conference travel....
>
> What's worse, the traditional conference has more than just environmental shortcomings. The cost of airfare from anywhere in the developing world to anywhere in North America or Europe is often greater than the per capita annual income in these countries. Consequently, scholars from most of the world's countries, and nearly the entire Hemispheric South, have long been quietly, summarily excluded from international conferences....
>
> What's to be done? While attending fewer or only local conferences is an option, at UCSB we have been developing and

experimenting with an online, nearly carbon-neutral (NCN) approach for conferences. This model was first implemented in May of 2016. A second NCN conference, which featured Bill McKibben as one of its keynote speakers, took place at UCSB in Oct/Nov of 2016....

When asked if this NCN conference approach was successful, 87% of the speakers from the first event responded 'yes', 13% 'not sure', and 0% 'no....'

In a nutshell, here is how this NCN approach works:

Speakers record their own talks....

Talks are viewed on the conference website.... Talks are organized into panels (i.e. individual webpages – just like a traditional conference....

Participants contribute to an online Q&A session. During ... two or three weeks, participants can take part in the Q&A sessions for the panels, which are similar to online forums, by posing and responding to written questions and comments. Because comments can be made at any time in any time zone, participants from across the globe can equally take part in the conference....

While this NCN model is just one of many possible, because this approach has advantages that go beyond helping to mitigate climate change, it makes clear that a range of new technologies have opened up exciting possibilities for reimagining the traditional conference:

Without the requirement of travel, scholars can participate from nearly anywhere on the globe....

Similar to open-access journals, the archive created by NCN conferences (both recorded talks and Q&A transcripts) gives nearly anyone anywhere on the globe, as long as Internet access is available, instant and lasting access to all the cutting-edge material introduced at the event. In contrast, traditional conferences are often closed-door affairs open to only a privileged few...

On average, the pilot conferences' Q&A sessions generated three times more discussion than takes place at a traditional Q&A....

Because the cost of an NCN conference is considerably less than its traditional counterparts, a range of groups and institutions, such as schools in the developing world currently lacking the significant financial resources required to coordinate international conferences, are now able to do so. Our pilot conferences were cobbled together largely using free, open-source software...

Such events can result in far more efficient use of a conference goer's time, as one can quickly scan through the text of a talk or a Q&A session for material of interest....

[G]iven the horrific environmental costs and inherently exclusionary nature of traditional conferences, the time has come to radically rethink this cornerstone practice of our profession. This NCN conference experiment is an attempt to do just that.

(Hiltner, 2020)

I find it humbling and powerful that a simple professor of English has found a solution to what was previously considered nearly impossible (and thus outside the scope of the effort) by the otherwise ambitious Carbon Neutrality Initiative of the University of California, a ten-year project to reduce the greenhouse gas emissions of the 10 campuses of the system to zero by the year 2025.

This suggests what we already know: that humanity's challenge to confront the climate crisis is not going to be led by governments, university-based climate scientists, corporations and other market actors, but from the bottom-up, and relying in part on the full spectrum of approaches currently existing in the world's schools.

Part 2: 'Eco Vista' and 'The World in 2025': Taking the Classroom into the Community

There is something frightening about facing new systemic pressures alone, be that challenges with pandemics, conflict, dislocation, trauma, family, mental health, financial meltdown, work, tragedy or a deeper crisis of meaning. For some of us, the old institutions, the old communities, might be a factor in mitigating systemic pressures of making a life in an increasingly complex world work. But for too many people, they are all too alone in their struggle to survive. In this context, what should a young person do? What is the best strategy for equipping yourself for life on a precarious and complex planet? And how best to contribute?

–Hassan (2020)

My educational philosophy and pedagogical approach grace the syllabi of all my courses and reads in part:

We are called now to get our hands, hearts, and heads aligned for action in the real world.

Learning and teaching are complex, endlessly fascinating collaborations. I soak up enormous amounts from the students and teaching assistants in my classes, whom I view as colleagues and companions on an intellectual, sometimes life-changing journey. My goals for my classes include the development of critical thinking skills, acquiring the ability to work collaboratively, honing the art of applying theoretical concepts to actual historical, contemporary and even future situations and making connections between what we study and how we live.

I consider the educational encounter a *radical* process, because it contains the potential to change all involved in it and thereby to contribute, however indirectly, to social change in the world beyond the classroom.

Two of the courses I teach every year now are Sociology/Environmental Studies 130SD: 'The World in ~~2050~~ 2025: Systemic Alternatives' (the strike through of 2050 was found to be necessary a year or so ago due to the rapidly accelerating pace of the climate crisis) and Sociology 130EV: 'Eco Vista: Creating Systemic Alternatives'. I taught the first of these in the spring of 2020, entirely on-line, as the corona crisis shut down face-to-face teaching about 10 days before the start of the ten-week spring quarter.

They go hand in hand because in the first we explore the pluriverse of systemic alternatives [indeed, we rely heavily on the path-breaking 2019 compendium of systemic alternatives found in *Pluriverse: A Post-Development Dictionary*, edited in 2019 by Alberto Acosta, Federico Demaria, Arturo Escobar, Ashish Kothari, & Ariel Salleh], with an eye to thinking through our collective crises to glimpse the values and practices of the various types of worlds we might want to live in as this crucial decade unfolds. Doing this in the midst of the corona crisis took us out of any comfort zones we might have enjoyed and reinforced the necessity of collective reflection and work to take the first difficult steps towards those worlds.

The second course is more hands-on. 'Eco Vista' was the name chosen in 2017 by a group of students at the University of California, Santa Barbara, acting together with long-time community members to describe their vision of turning their rather unusual community of Isla Vista into an eco-village in the next eight to 10 years. 23,000 people live together in an area of 0.54 square miles, 80% of them between the ages of 18 and 24.

After a forty-year battle again landlords, college administrators, and the county of Santa Barbara, Isla Vista elected its first local government in late 2016 – the Isla Vista Community Services District. Two years later another referendum empowered this new government to tax utilities, drawing revenue to a $1 million annual budget by 2020. This would soon be followed by an even more surprising development as community interest in carbon-neutrality, just transition, critical ecological post-sustainability and systems change from below has grown deep roots (Lodise, 2019).

The community of Isla Vista presents many opportunities for active engagement with some of the most critical issues facing US society – food insecurity and injustice, landlord rip-offs, houselessness and tenant struggles, mental and now physical health epidemics, sexual violence and the lawlessness of police-community interactions. This is not to mention the too many to list 'non-human-oriented examples: ocean pollution/trashing, tree removal instead of tree planting and proper care to reduce ambient temperatures and sequester carbon, encourage avian wildlife, produce food and shelter other beneficial plant-life and especially pollinator insects, etc' (Maia, personal communication, 7 July 2020).

There are now more than 300 people on the Eco Vista e-list, with bi-monthly General Assemblies that have continued to meet on-line during the corona crisis. There are on-going working groups involved in projects including an urban food forest and community gardens, creating a circular economy and a community 'development' plan, spiritual activism, an Eco Vista club at the University and more. As we imagine the future, we also have the precious legacy and ideas of the late resident scholar and activist Michael Bean, who just before his untimely death in February 2022 created an *Eco Vista Sourcebook* of imaginative ideas and detailed proposals for bringing about Eco Vista (Bean, 2020; see also the beautiful film *Eco Vista: Imagine If* (Emrick, 2019)).

In the fall of 2019, the Environmental Studies/Sociology 134EC class 'Earth in Crisis' engaged in a two-week exercise to produce the beginnings of an 'Eco Vista Green New Deal' that resulted in a 27-page list of proposals for aligning Isla Vista's next community development planning process with the most progressive versions of the concept, such as the Red Deal, the US Green Party's plans, the feminist GND, Bernie Sanders's detailed platform and ecosocialist ideas (Eco Vista Green New Deal, 2021). In March 2020, the Eco Vista Transition Initiative became the 169th member and the newest link in the Transition US network.

Conceptually our efforts are grounded in the latest thinking about Transition Towns, de-growth, *buen vivir*, just transition, radical climate justice and the many worlds to be found in the compendium of systemic alternatives *Pluriverse: A Post-Development Dictionary* (2019). Another approach that guides our thinking and practice is adrienne maree brown's *Emergent Strategy* (2017), which counsels working from the bottom up in an inclusive and un-predetermined way to generate collective analyses enabling members to articulate their desires and most sought after outcomes.

Some of this finds expression in the community values Eco Vista has embraced and our invitation for participation, open to all who agree with them:

Community values and principles

We are inclusive.
We are democratic.
We are non-violent.

We work collectively whenever possible, and all are free to organize their own activities and projects.

We are open to all points of view that are aligned with these values and supportive of the Eco Vista Mission.

We act and live out of love for the dignity of all living beings, and base this love on social and climate justice, and on radical hope.
(www.ecovistacommunity.com)

Eco Vista's purpose is to inspire and instigate the foundation of a community with renewable energy, a flourishing and regenerative agro-ecology of public urban gardens, cooperative, affordable eco-housing, a circular eco-economy based on solidarity and meeting the real needs of the inhabitants, radical self-governance and community priorities determined by all who reside here, and to do so within a vibrant web of visionary cultural creativity.

We are aiming high: to assist in laying the foundations for the establishment of an ongoing, multigenerational, student-community initiative for an equitable and just transition in Isla Vista, California, and to put the result, Eco Vista, forward as an experiential model that other small towns with college students might want to freely adapt for their communities. We consider what we are trying to do skill-building experiments in sustainable, resilient, participatory development, in a place we call Eco Vista, a very real place and also a timeless, cosmic community of radical visionaries and seekers.

We know that to achieve this aspirational aim will require significant political organization, social movement building and visionary policy proposals – including the design of and strategy for achieving a systemic alternative – and perhaps even the invention of a new kind of party (Foran, 2020)!

Our mission statement suggests that

In the end, Eco Vista is … a promise, a pledge, a dream, a future.

The promise of Eco Vista is that together we might create a place that is life-affirming for all its inhabitants and that might inspire others elsewhere – particularly young people in their own communities – to use their imaginations to create the innovative future communities we all want to live in, right now!

Our pledge to each other is to co-create, imagine, dream, and transform our community into a place that matches the name of Eco Vista. We want to dream and make manifest this vision together with you!

The Eco Vista dream is a communal, shared, joyful adventure – may it transport us to a place worthy of the love we feel for it.

The future of Eco Vista is … well, that's what we hope and aim to find out!

Coda: Building More Real-World Skills in the Classroom

In the fall of 2020, with colleagues Ken Hiltner and David Pellow I helped establish a new Professional Certificate program at UC Santa Barbara called 'Environmental and Climate Advocacy, Leadership and Activism' [or ECALA, for short]. It is open to people all over the world (though it is expensive for non-UCSB students).

The program begins with an Introduction to the broad field of Environmental and Climate Advocacy, Leadership and Activism which will feature the chance to learn from and interact with a range of invited guests, most of them from outside the university. By the end of the class, students develop an original, self-chosen project in consultation with a faculty advisor. Along the way students also take three relevant UCSB courses from a list of electives which you can see on the Website (https://professional.ucsb.edu/certificate-environmental-climate-advocacy).

The process culminates in a Capstone course, where students share their new knowledge with their peers and we all reflect on the entire journey we have made together. Some of the first cohort's projects include:

> Localized Isla Vista, *Daphne Prodis and Isabella Binger*
>
> An Oily Future or a Just Transition for Santa Barbara County's Petroleum Industry? *Wesley Martinez*
>
> Growing Solutions, *Cambria Wilson and Candela Goni*
>
> Applying Black Feminism to Isla Vista: a plan for coalition building and intersectional activism, *Julia Samuel*
>
> Art is a Right Zine, *Elena Salinas*
>
> Environmental Imagination, *Tiara Triplett*
>
> Latinx Leaders Paving the Way for Environmental Justice, *Liz Melena*
>
> Free Box, *Ash Valenti*

In the end, what is possible depends on the student's own vision and imagination!

Part 3: Towards a Pluriverse of Climate Justice Universities

> The crisis we are in indicates that we are brushing up against the limits of human reason. It is time we re-activate our diverse perceptions, senses, intuitions and entanglement with the non-human world.
>
> –From the Ecoversities website, https://ecoversities.org/about/

I would like to close this chapter with a look at a few of the exciting visions of a new *type* of university, some of which I have encountered in my pedagogical wanders across the web, many of them gathered in the *Ecoversities Alliance* – as well as others which exist only in my mind's eye, such as *Transition U* and *Eco Vista U.*

One of the most generative of pedagogical projects is Ecoversities, which was founded in 2015 with a gathering of 55 people from 23 countries at the Tamara Eco-village in southern Portugal. This was followed by a second gathering at EARTH University in Costa Rica two years later and a third in 2018 at Swaraj University in Udaipur, India. It's worth observing that I have only recently discovered them, a delay which signals the importance of knowing about each other's efforts so we can learn from and work with each other, especially given the ecological and public health limits posed by the pandemic and the technological advances that make it possible to work together despite them.

Noting that the name itself draws on 'the meanings of "home" as locality and as an "economy",' Ecoversities opens its website with these observations:

> ecoversities: learners and communities reclaiming diverse knowledges, relationships and imaginations to design new approaches to higher education.
>
> What might the university look like if it were at the service of our diverse ecologies, cultures, economies, spiritualities and Life within our planetary home?
>
> Here you will find an ecosystem of communities and organizations that are re-imagining the idea of the university and the purpose of higher education....
>
> The Ecoversities Alliance is committed to radically re-imagining higher education to cultivate human and ecological flourishing. Ecoversities seek to transform the unsustainable and unjust economic, political and social systems/mindsets that dominate the planet.
>
> (https://ecoversities.org/about/)

One might think of the whole as a sort of World Social Forum of alternative education and pedagogy produced at diverse gatherings which have met to collectively analyse common problems and co-create alternatives based on a network model after the initial gathering has forged relationships. With more than a hundred schools and projects of all kinds taking part, the Ecoversities Alliance does not take itself as a formal organization but rather 'a process of trust and mutuality, a growing web of relationships that have been nurtured through our gatherings and beyond. *We are committed to learning from/within/beyond diversity*' (Ecoversities Alliance, emphasis in the original). Readers may be familiar with some of the learning spaces involved, such as Findhorn College in Scotland,

Deer Park Institute Center for Indian Wisdom Traditions in India, Kufunda Village in Zimbabwe, the School of Engaged Art Chto Delat in Russia, Swaraj University in Rajasthan, Universtatea Alternativa in Bucharest, Schumacher College in England, Gaia University in Colorado, Universidad de la Tierra or Unitierra in Oaxaca, Mexico and its California counterpart, the Convivial Research and Insurgent Learning set of tools.

Hoping to nurture 'an ecology of knowledges, radical pedagogies and learning commons which expands human consciousness and cultural and ecological regeneration', the Alliance sets out the following values and orientations (this list is taken verbatim from the website):

Emergence
An invitation to the unknown, allowing diverse ways of being, knowing, doing, relating to emerge.

Inquiry in Solidarity
An invitation to be authentic and critically engaged with co-learners, whilst invoking self-reflection, kindness and compassion to support others in their own inquiries and discoveries.

Experiential Learning
Learning with our senses, stories, spirits, hearts, hands, heads and homes in order to find ways we are interconnected and entangled in each other's struggles and dreams.

Emplacement
An invitation to reconnect with and learn from the land, the place and the non-human. To engage in and promote deep localization.

De-colonising
An invitation to address, explore and unlearn the dimensions of oppression, power and privilege that are part of our own lives, relations, tools, structures, histories and beliefs.

Inter(trans)cultural Dialogue
An invitation to learn in-between cultures, epistemologies, cosmologies and to learning ways we might not recognize or have experienced before. To learn from/within/beyond diversity.

One of the significant outcomes of their collaboration is the *Pedagogy, Otherwise Reader*, edited by Alessandra Pomarico (2018), containing essays, testimonies, poems and images by many members of the Ecoversities Alliance. Pomarico herself, writes intriguingly of a 'third pedagogy' to be found (or imagined) somewhere between the business-as-usual university setting and the 'de-schooled, unlearning, creative' setting, inviting us to enter that space with no roadmap or boundaries where the real magic of 'a radical tenderness can appear, that commitment and support develop, friendships blossom, alliances form, people fall in love, heal, build and weave their paths together. It is in those intimate contexts that a revolutionary, radical love made of a thirst for justice, militant gentleness and subversive soulfulness can form' (Pomarico, 2018, pp. 157–158).

In another essay, Manuel 'Manolo' Callahan describes the work at the Universidad de la Tierra Califas, situated around the San Francisco, San Jose and Oakland Bay Area in California:

> UT Califas is not confined to any buildings, nor does a cumbersome bureaucracy constrict it. Its 'architecture' does not require a physical space much less shelter a bureaucratic apparatus.... As a prefigurative, convivial, and networked pedagogy UT Califas embodies a praxis of inquiry that claims the future in the present, hosting spaces that refuse to wait for a day when we can dismantle the dominant educational system.
> (Callahan, 2018, p. 95)

He concludes, and rightly so: 'We must, as the Zapatistas recommend, learn how to learn. The global north must learn to learn from the global south and we must learn to learn from each other or we will consume our planet to extinction' (Callahan, 2018, p. 105).

A question that arises for all systemic alternatives of all kinds is how to thrive in a malfunctioning global economy and in nation-states whose primary raison d'être is to support that economy to the detriment of their own inhabitants and life itself. One inventive and highly intriguing model is that of the 'distributed open cooperative organization', or DisCO, laid out in the document, *If I Only Had a Heart: A DisCO Manifesto* (Troncoso & Utratel, 2019). The Guerrilla Media Commons and Guerrilla Translation Collective in Andalusia, Spain, are organized in this fashion, melding technologies like blockchain but going beyond them in a radical direction by repurposing them for cooperatives run on principles that draw from feminist economics (such as fair compensation for the care work performed by members/partners in the coop), the commons movement and Peer to Peer practices and 'open-value accounting' of the ecological consequences of production.

What if this sophisticated model for alliances and networks of organizations that do climate justice work for free in movements, paid labor gigs for some of its members and shares for doing the care work that makes everything run was applied to alternative education to address the perennial issue of how its participants survive/thrive/live while doing the work. This model – and others like it that are emergent – certainly bears study and further discussion.

I will conclude with mention of two fledgling initiatives I am deeply involved with and that are only emergent for now, one of which no longer exists. The latter was a project called Transition U that sought to co-create with students, teachers and community members in the Transition US movement. Convened in the pages of *Resilience.org*, the e-journal of the Post-Carbon Institute and from among the membership of the Transition US movement in the fall of 2019, a group of educators from pre-kindergarten to adult education began to meet to discuss how we might work with students outside of the classroom and engage community members in the process of building systemic alternatives (Foran, 2019a). We ultimately re-constituted two working groups, one for ages from zero (!) to middle school (eighth grade in the United States where students are typically 12–14 years old) and one for high-school and college-age students. Thus the project was renamed 'Transition Schools' and the two groups within it adopted the names 'Educare' and 'Transition U' respectively.

In January 2021, we held our first public event, a meeting of a high school class on alternative economics taught by Alison Malisa in the Bay Area of California and some of the college students of UC Santa Barbara involved in the Eco Vista project. Alison facilitated a fascinating dialogue following the script of '100 Days of Conversation', a US-wide set of conversations with high school and college students about their experiences and visions of education during and after the pandemic (100 Days of Conversations).

Nevertheless, in early 2021, when we re-assessed our work, we came to the conclusion that our numbers were too small to constitute an ongoing working group within Transition. In the end, I found too few college teachers in the US Transition network to try the Eco Vista model in other settings. One hopeful development was the proposal that Transition US consider forming a working group centered on youth in general going forward.

I still believe that if fully realized, the potential of such a broader intergenerational network of educators might be game-changing, as it would bring young, creative people into the Transition Movement and its many like-minded initiatives flying under their own banner anywhere. At the same time, it could seed innovative Transition living laboratories inside and outside college and university (and younger) communities, generate new knowledge, practices and experiences of Transition; contribute to knowledge for Transition work by spreading awareness of such work in our schools; scale up our efforts to new locations, demographic groups and communities; and ultimately help chart their way into the challenges of addressing the sextuple crisis (Foran, 2019a).

The second initiative is the 2021 launch of 'Eco Vista U' as a teaching/learning/ resource space of our Eco Vista community project adjacent – and now we come full circle – to the University of California, Santa Barbara in the town of Isla Vista. So far, we have founded the Eco Vista Climate Justice Press and published a series of e-books, including *The Whole Eco Vista Catalogue* (Foran 2021a, 2021b, 2021c).

The title of our first e-book, a work of climate fiction called *See You in Our Dreams* (Maía, 2020), may be the most fitting conclusion to this chapter!

References

Bean, M. (2020). Eco Vista Sourcebook. Retrieved from https://ecovistacommunity. com/eco-vista-project-sourcebook/

Brown, A. M. (2017). *Emergent strategy: Shaping change, changing worlds*. Oakland, CA: AK Press.

Callahan, M. (2018). Insurgent learning and convivial research: Universidad de la Tierra, Califas. In A. Pomarico (Ed.), *Pedagogy, otherwise: The reader* (pp. 92–119). Musagetes, ON: artseverywhere. Retrieved from https://ecoversities.org/ wp-content/uploads/2018/11/Pedagogy-Otherwise-Reader.pdf

Eco Vista Climate Justice Press. Retrieved from https://ecovistacommunity.com/climate-justice-press/

Eco Vista Green New Deal. (2021). Retrieved from https://ecovistacommunity.com/eco-vista-green-new-deal/

Eco Vista U. Retrieved from https://ecovistacommunity.com/eco-vista-university/

Emrick, S. (2019). Eco Vista: Imagine if. Film. Salty Sie Productions. Retrieved from https://www.amazon.com/Isla-Vista-Citizens-History-Second/dp/1799247864/ref=sr_1_2?dchild=1&keywords=Isla+Vista+Citizen%27s+History&qid=1587335273&s=books&sr=1-2

Environmental and Climate Advocacy, Leadership, and Activism. Certificate Program, University of California, Santa Barbara. Retrieved from https://professional.ucsb.edu/certificate-environmental-climate-advocacy

Foran, J. (2019). Sleepwalking is a death sentence for humanity: Manifesto for a sociology of the climate crisis and of climate justice. In K.-K. Bhavnani, J. Foran, P. Kurian, & D. Munshi (Eds.), *Climate futures: Re-imagining global climate justice* (pp. 105–113). London: Zed Press. Retrieved from http://www.resilience.org/stories/2017-10-02/sleepwalking-is-a-death-sentence-for-humanity/

Foran, J. (2019a, September 9). Transition U: An invitation to join a global knowledge action network of educators. Retrieved from https://www.resilience.org/stories/2019-09-09/transition-u-an-invitation-to-join-a-global-knowledge-action-network-of-educators/

Foran, J. (2020, July). Eco Vista in the quintuple crisis. *Interface: A Journal for and about Social Movements*, *12*(1), 284–291. Retrieved from https://www.interfacejournal.net/wp-content/uploads/2020/05/Foran.pdf

Foran, J. (2021a). The world in 2050 2025: Systemic alternatives. Class, University of California, Santa Barbara. Retrieved from https://nxterra.orfaleacenter.ucsb.edu/wp-content/uploads/2020/05/Foran.Syllabus.SOC-130SD.-The-World-in-2050-Sustainable-Development-and-its-Alternatives-UCSB-2020.docx

Foran, J. (2021b). Eco Vista: Creating systemic alternatives. Class, University of California, Santa Barbara. Retrieved from https://nxterra.orfaleacenter.ucsb.edu/wp-content/uploads/2021/03/SYLLABUS-Systemic-Alternatives-Eco-Vists-Creating-Systemic-Alternatives-John-Foran-SOC-130EV-UC-Santa-Barbara-Winter-2021.pdf

Foran, J. (Ed.). (2021c). *The whole Eco Vista catalogue*. Retrieved from https://ecovistacommunity.files.wordpress.com/2021/02/final-3.pdf

Gildersleeve, R. E., & Kleinhesselink, K. (Eds.). (2019, April). *Philosophy and theory in higher education: Special issue on the Anthropocene in the study of higher education* (Vol. 1). Retrieved from https://www.peterlang.com/fileasset/Journals/PTIHE012019e_book.pdf

Hassan, Z. (2020, May 4). The university of full catastrophe learning. Retrieved from https://ecoversities.org/the-university-of-full-catastrophe-learning/

Hiltner, K. (2020). A nearly carbon-neutral conference model white paper/practical guide. Retrieved from http://hiltner.english.ucsb.edu/index.php/ncnc-guide/#opening

Kothari, A., Salleh, A., Escobar, A., Demaria, F., & Acosta, A. (Eds.). (2019). *Pluriverse: A post-development dictionary*. New York, NY: Columbia University Press. New Delhi: Tulika/AuthorsUpFront. Retrieved from file:///C:/Users/User/Downloads/Pluriverse_A_Post-Development_Dictionar%20(1).pdf

Lodise, C. (2019). *Isla Vista: A citizen's history* (2nd ed.). Independently Published. Retrieved from https://www.amazon.com/Isla-Vista-Citizens-History-Second/dp/ 1799247864/ref=sr_1_2?dchild=1&keywords=Isla+Vista+Citizen%27s+History &qid=1587335273&s=books&sr=1-2

Maía. (2020). *See you in our dreams*. Isla Vista: Eco Vista Climate Justice Press. Retrieved from https://ecovistacommunity.files.wordpress.com/2020/05/syiodreams. pdf

Maxwell, N. (2019, April). The scandal of the irrationality of academia. In R. E. Gildersleeve & K. Kleinhesselink (Eds.), *Philosophy and theory in higher education. Special issue on the Anthropocene in the study of higher education* (Vol. 1(1), pp. 105–128). Retrieved from https://www.peterlang.com/fileasset/Journals/ PTIHE012019e_book.pdf

Pomarico, A. (Eds.). (2018). *Pedagogy, otherwise: The reader*. Musagetes, ON: art-severywhere. Retrieved from https://ecoversities.org/wp-content/uploads/2018/11/ Pedagogy-Otherwise-Reader.pdf

Ray, S. (2020). *A field guide to climate anxiety: How to keep your cool on a warming planet*. Berkeley, CA: University of California Press.

Troncoso, S., & Utratel, A. M. (Eds.). (2019). If I only had a heart: A DisCO Manifesto – Value sovereignty, care work, commons and distributed cooperative organizations. Jointly published by DisCO.coop, the Transnational Institute, and Guerrilla Media Collective. Retrieved from https://www.tni.org/files/profiles-downloads/disco_manifesto_v.1.pdf

Ullmer, J. B. (2019, April). The Anthropocene is a question, not a strategic plan. In R. E. Gildersleeve & K. Kleinhesselink (Eds.), *Philosophy and theory in higher education. Special issue on the Anthropocene in the study of higher education* (Vol. 1, pp. 65–84). Retrieved from https://www.peterlang.com/fileasset/Journals/PTIHE012019e_book. pdf

Chapter 7

Transformative and Social Learning – In the Tradition of Freire

Frans Lenglet

Abstract

It is argued that social learning, transformative learning, collaborative learning and transgressive learning are branches and offshoots of the same 'learning tree'. This chapter examines the sources and evolution of theories of education and learning focused on transforming the learners' self-understanding and transforming the structures and social arrangements in which they and their educational and learning processes are embedded. The 'transformative learning' theories reviewed here span the last 50 years. They critique and go beyond the functionalist understanding that education and learning are meant to socialize learners within existing or dominant cultural and societal structures and/or in function of the transmission of knowledge, skills and attitudes from generation to generation. The first part of this article covers transformative learning and learning for transformation in the tradition of Freire, Habermas, Mezirow, and others. The second part concentrates on more recent ideas of collaborative learning, social learning and deliberative social learning evolving into transformative, and transgressive learning. By highlighting the warp and weft of the conceptual traditions and pedagogical practice within a variety of contexts and conditions, a colourful tapestry of transformative education and learning emerges. It is shown that, over time, the pertinence of transformative learning has only increased. The evolution of transformative learning presents itself as a virtual cycle, starting from marginalized and excluded people and communities via individual persons engaged in adult education and environmental education, to (groups of) people participating in collaborative and transgressive social learning, thereby becoming capable and empowered actors in processes of societal change and transformation.

Keywords: Transformative learning; social learning; collaborative learning; deliberative learning; transgressive learning; meaning making; agency; empowerment

Transformative Research and Higher Education, 145–160

Copyright © 2022 Frans Lenglet

Published under exclusive licence by Emerald Publishing Limited

doi:10.1108/978-1-80117-694-120221008

Introduction

Around the world, people are seeking and applying innovative forms of learning, organisation, cooperation and decision making, at the local, regional, national, international, and global level when addressing the complex and 'wicked' nature of such global and local challenges as climate change and environmental destruction, biodiversity loss and water scarcity, inequality and exclusion, poverty and social injustice, cultural marginalization and political non-representation in their different manifestations and at different scales – challenges that are being highlighted and exacerbated by the Covid-19 pandemic and the measures taken in its wake. School-based education, either in the guise of 'quality education' called for by the fourth Sustainable Development Goal (see Wulff (2020) for a critical assessment thereof) or in the guise of OECD's 'twenty-first Century Skills' (Schleicher, 2018), is not enough or appropriate enough for acquiring and exercising the aptitudes, knowledge, skills, values and dispositions for dealing with these intertwined challenges. In fact, the ubiquitous school-based education systems are one of the main ways through which these challenges and their underlying structures, paradigms and ideologies are being nurtured, perpetuated and reinforced (e.g., Carnoy, 1972; Piketty, 2020).

It is almost a truism that mainstream educational content and pedagogical methods are mirroring society's mainstream behavioural patterns, cultural and conceptual frameworks, and power and authority structures. By socializing the youth, education replicates these patterns, structures and associated mind sets. In contrast and simultaneously, it can also be observed that much educational content, methods and practices are implicitly nursing emancipatory assumptions that, taken at face value, encourage teachers and learners to question and deviate from mainstream patterns, frameworks and structures. As such, education does not automatically replicate society but can harbour the seeds for societal emancipation, change and transformation (Eribon, 2018). A contemporary example thereof is how Hong Kong's 'liberal education' curriculum may have fuelled the student protests of the last couple of years. According to May and Qin (2019), many of the protesting students credited this curriculum for gaining insight and understanding in the ways the Chinese government is undermining Hong Kong's democratic traditions and conditions. At the same time, leading Hong Kong politicians backed by the Chinese government tried to replace 'liberal education' with 'patriotic education'.

A less recent example is education in the Soviet Union. Having been influenced by Dewey's 'progressive education' and simultaneously being aligned with the original ideals of the Russian Revolution, it may have contributed to 'glasnost' and 'perestroika', just before the country's demise. According to one observer, 'Soviet schools and other educational establishments of 60s and 70s were incredibly ambivalent institutions.' To call a typical Soviet school a democratic institution would be an oxymoron. Nevertheless, it 'included elements of democratic decision making and social activism. Children were constantly challenged to organize themselves, to go out into larger world and make a difference. (....) In most schools (....) democracy and authoritarianism coexisted, despite [the] widely held belief, that it is impossible' (Sidorkin, 1988, p. 5).

In contrast, the reverse may also occur, namely when explicit governmental education policy has an emancipatory ethos, while hidden or not so hidden official instructions and incentives reward conformity. In several Asian countries, for example, contrasting and even contradictory signals about educational policy and practice are being observed: one for international and another for domestic consumption. In its Rethinking Schooling study, the Mahatma Gandhi Institute of Education for Peace and Sustainable Development (MGIEP, 2017) describes and discusses the observed discrepancy: On the one hand, some governments have embraced Education for Sustainable Development (ESD) as part of their official educational policy. Therefore, they can be expected to encourage public education to adopt content and practices that '(....) empower[s] learners to take informed decisions and responsible actions for environmental integrity, economic viability and a just society, for present and future generations, while respecting cultural diversity' (UNESCO, 2021). On the other hand, the same governments, implicitly and explicitly, provide teacher training as well as curriculum and syllabus instructions and guidelines that promote and legitimize perspectives, practices and behaviour associated with populist, nationalist and anti- or fake-science notions that run counter to the principles of open, inquiry-based, culturally sensitive and participatory education and learning.

Since the arrival of mass public schooling, there have always been parents, teachers, students, researchers, activists, education practitioners and 'common citizens' who believe that it is not enough to rely on education's internal contradictions or implicit emancipatory or transformational assumptions for timely and effectively addressing small-scale, large-scale, local and global challenges and dilemmas of daily survival and long-term sustainability. Therefore, they have used and are using other forms of education and learning that avoid the restricting traps of standard pedagogical methods and standard curricula while actively engaging learners in learning that brings about the social and individual change and transformation that the 'wicked' issues require. Such 'alternative' forms of education and learning appear under a wide variety of labels: transformative learning (Mezirow, 1991), learning as transformation (Mezirow, 2000), social learning (Wals, 2007), learning for change (Mehlmann, 2013), collaborative and disruptive learning (Wals & Lenglet, 2016), or a combination of two or even three of these labels together, such as transformative, transgressive social learning (Lotz-Sisitka, Wals, Kronlid, & McGarry, 2015).

The purpose of this article is to briefly examine the evolution and intellectual sources of theories of education and learning – not merely in function of socializing the learners within existing or dominant cultural and societal structures or in function of the transmission of knowledge, skills and attitudes from generation to generation, but rather in function of transforming the learners self-understanding as well as the structures, arrangements and configurations in which they and their educational and learning processes are embedded.

The idea of transformative learning or learning for transformation, as conceived by Mezirow, will be central to the first part of this article. The article's second part will concentrate on the ideas of collaborative and social learning evolving into disruptive and transgressive learning.

As will be shown below, the different transformative learning traditions and approaches have three central characteristics in common: critical reflexion, social learning and action, albeit in different degrees. Critical reflexion, the first characteristic, refers to when learners are confronted by situations that challenge them in their taken-for-granted, day-to-day realities at the personal, collective, and systemic level. The second characteristic, social learning, is learning in a context and learning within social relations. Learning does not take place in a vacuum. What is learned and how is influenced by a multiple of contextual variables, which the learners as members of different groups, classes and cultures bring with them. The economic, political, legal, cultural and ideological forces that impinge on these social formations confine and shape the actual learning process and determine where, when and how it occurs. At the same time, learning always occurs in interaction with other people: those involved as co-learners, teachers and facilitators, and those in the learners' living, working, cultural and political environments, either closer or farther away in time and space, including the family, the workplace, the political, sports and cultural associations, the region, the country and the world. As for the third characteristic, transformative learning is action-oriented; often it is action-driven learning. In the process of transformative learning, the learners who are challenged to examine the status quo are invited or compelled to act by changing and modifying the psychological and structural conditions and determinants of their personal and collective behaviour. This last characteristic is associated with (participatory) action research, as presented and illustrated in the other book chapters.

Part I Transformative Learning

Standing in the American 'progressive education' tradition and building on notions of emancipatory education, as proposed by Paolo Freire and Jürgen Habermas (see below), Mezirow (1991), formulated his theory of transformative learning based on research among a group of US women returning to post-secondary study after an extended time out of education or paid work. He attempted to determine how their learning, organized around their own experience, would influence their beliefs, values, perspectives and aspirations. His research suggested that the learner's interpretation of the learning experience creates meaning. This in turn leads to a change in behaviour, mindset and beliefs. In other words, learning occurs when an individual encounters an alternative perspective, and, consequently, prior habits of mind are called into question. Thus, for Mezirow, transformative learning became the process by which previously uncritically assimilated assumptions, beliefs, values and perspectives are 'discovered', questioned and reassessed (similarly to Andersen's and Frandsen's chapter in this book). Being challenged in their beliefs, assumptions and perspectives leads active learners to question themselves. The resulting 'paradigm shift' has a transformational effect on their future experience including self-awareness, behaviour and belief systems. In the same line of reasoning,

Cranton (2006) argues that transformative learning is learning that transforms problematic frames of reference to make them more inclusive, discriminating, open, reflective, and emotionally able to change. Only by problematizing these 'prior' or 'given' frames of reference transformative learning does take place. Problematization or active reflection of unexamined frames of reference and personal and societal belief systems is, therefore, central to the learning process.

Six Approaches

Over time, a variety of approaches to such problematization, the subsequent 'unveiling' and the resulting transformation have coalesced. As cited by Plastow (2008), Taylor (2008) distinguishes six such approaches or traditions:

(1) The psychoanalytic approach, which goes back to Carl Jung. It sees transformative learning 'as a process of individuation, a lifelong journey of coming to understand oneself through reflecting on the psychic structures (....) that make up an individual's identity' (Taylor, 2008, p. 7).

(2) Central to the psychodevelopmental approach is the idea that individual psychological development and learning over time involve movement through progressively more complex ways of knowing and meaning making.

(3) The social-emancipatory approach, most strongly associated with Paolo Freire, promotes 'a theory of existence that views people as subjects, not objects, who are constantly reflecting and acting on the transformation of their world so it can become a more equitable place for all to live' (Taylor, 2008, p. 8). In this sense, transformative learning is ideology critique. Its goal is social or societal transformation, not just individual transformation.

(4) The neurobiological approach sees 'learning as 'volitional, curiosity-based, discovery-driven, and mentor-assisted' and is most effective at higher cognitive levels' (Janik, 2005, p. 144). It suggests that 'transformative learning (1) requires discomfort prior to discovery; (2) is rooted in students' experiences, needs, and interests; (3) is strengthened by emotive, sensory, and kinaesthetic experiences; (4) appreciates differences in learning between males and females and (5) demands that educators acquire an understanding of a unique discourse and knowledge base of neurobiological systems' (Taylor, 2008, p. 8).

(5) The cultural-spiritual approach of, for example, Dirkx (2001) goes beyond Mezirow's 'rational' approach. 'It stresses the importance of incorporating imagination, intuition, soul and affect in the process of transformative learning' (Cranton, 2006, cited in Plastow, 2008, pp. 4–5).

(6) In the planetary approach, the purpose of transformative learning is the reorganization of the whole political, social, educational system within a planetary context. It emphasises the existential context of human development within a larger narrative of the development of the universe, influenced by environmental and sustainability thinking.

In summary, the first two approaches, exemplified by Bandura (1977). among others, consider transformative learning as a central component of the psychosocial development of individuals as they grow older. The third approach, associated with Freire, focuses on self-empowering individuals as acting on their conditions and relationships in the context of their groups, communities, class and society. The fourth and the fifth approach expand the rational orientation, strongly present in Mezirow, by explicitly including psychological and spiritual dimensions. The sixth approach stresses that truly transformative learning, of individuals and society at large, must explicitly refer to the ecological and planetary dimensions of the human condition.

Phases of Transformative Learning

The expected or desired transformation that is common and central to these six approaches is the outcome of a process. The central components of this transformative learning process (according to Mezirow) include perspective transformation, frame of reference, meaning perspective, habit of mind, disorienting dilemma, critical self-reflection, in addition to learning processes, meaning schemes, and meaning perspective. Kitchenham (2008) contends that these central notions borrow from, reflect and correspond with: Kuhn's 'paradigm', Freire's 'conscientization', and Habermas' (1971, 1984) 'domains of learning'. The notion of 'frame of reference' (formed by historical and familial and social context) comprises habits of mind (non-examined reasoning) and meaning perspectives (coherent interpretation schemes). This could be considered a specification of Kuhn's (1962) paradigm concept as applied to society in general beyond the immediate domain of scientific development. The notions of 'disorienting dilemma' (experiential confrontation with other or conflicting realities), 'critical reflection', 'critical self-reflection about underlying assumptions', and 'critical discourse' corresponds to Freire's (1970) conscientization, defined as 'learning to perceive social, political, and economic contradictions – developing a critical awareness – so that individuals can take actions against the oppressive elements of reality.' Finally, the learning process and meaning schemes find their source of inspiration in Habermas's (1971) proposed three domains of learning: (1) technical (task specific and rote learning), (2) practical (mastering of social norms), and (3) emancipatory (introspective and self-reflective).

Mezirow, Freire and Habermas

In a video interview with three of his graduate students (Bloom, Chang, & Duca, 2015), Mezirow himself explicitly acknowledges the influence of Marx, Freud, Freire, Habermas and Socrates as well as Lindeman (1926). The link between these thinkers is obvious, especially as far as critical reflection is concerned. Morrow and Torres (2002, p. 64), for example, suggest that Habermas and Freire 'share crucial views on science, society, critical social psychology, and educational praxis that are mutually illuminating and offer a new point of departure for a critical theory of education'. Similarly, Fleming (2014), who has expanded Mezirow's understanding of transformative learning, recognizes Habermas' critical theory as one of transformative learning's foundations, next to the humanistic tradition, which, of course, is also strongly represented in Freirean thought.

Despite transformative learning's 'critical theory' connections, critics of Mezirow's ideas, such as Morrow and Torres (2002), have remarked that his transformative learning has a strong or almost exclusive focus on the psychological dimensions of the learners' transformation to the detriment of structural or systemic transformation. In their view, Mezirow's conception ignores or downplays this transformation's inevitable articulation with the context of the learner and the learning process – a context that has restraining and facilitating aspects (see below). They may have a point, given the great difference between the issues and groups of people with which Freire worked ('the oppressed' in the title of his 1970 book) and those with which Mezirow carried out his research (US middle class women). But it can be equally argued that Mezirow's formal analysis of this context is rather complete and therefore allows for elucidating what transformative learning does with learners, their immediate and wider (structural) environments, and their perceptions thereof, however different these may be in their sociological structure and political orientations.

Freire, Habermas and Mezirow explicitly recognize the restraining and facilitating aspects present in the learners' background and context, and in the interaction with other learners. On the restraining side are the learners' social, economic and cultural history of their familial and social group or class, and the associated meaning perspectives, self-understanding, frames of reference and habits of mind. They form the boundaries or obstacles to the learners' disposition and ability to learn and transform; they are the forces that both challenge and channel non-reflection, critical reflection and learning. The disorienting dilemma, with which the learner is confronted, poses a challenge to these boundaries. On the facilitating side of the context is the immediate learning environment where the learners meet and interact with other learners, and where they may be exposed or may expose themselves to new (learning and reflecting) experiences. Thus, the disorienting dilemma creates opportunities, perspectives and encouragement for transformation to take place, at both the individual and collective level (In his 'Retour à Reims', Eribon (2018) illustrates the interplay between these restraining and facilitating forces by giving a fascinating sociologically formulated rendition of his own transformative evolution: from a 'private' working-class closeted gay boy in a 1970s French provincial town to a 'public' cultured intellectual in an early twenty-first century Paris).

Transformative learning happens in interaction with oneself and with others. It places a premium on reflection and reflexivity vis à vis assumptions and experiences underlying one's own behaviour and the behaviour of others. It results in transformation: the active opening to and the embracing of new perspectives and inputs, and therefore new behaviour(s). Transformative learning and transformation, thus conceptualized, gain in significance against the background of the current ecological, health and social justice crises.

Transformative learning happens in connection with others. The others are part of the learner's history, background and reference groups. The others are also co-learners, whether as members of a community or social movement, or as participants in (in)formal learning settings, such as classrooms, courses, training programs, research projects, community development initiatives or a combination thereof.

Part II Social Learning

In view of the above, it can be argued that all transformative learning is social learning, or as Wals concludes

> (...) all meaningful learning is inter-relational (with others, including other species, with place, and indeed with oneself) and requires some level of reflexivity by mirroring the significance of one's encounters with the inner sediments (frames, values, perspectives and worldviews) of prior experiences. The result tends to be a process of further solidification (freezing) or a loosening (unfreezing) or a modification (re-framing) or even the parallel occurrence of all three.
>
> (Wals, 2012, p. 8)

Frandsén's and Andersen's chapter in this book addresses the same notions in relationship to action research.

Two Distinctive Traditions

All learning, in any context, is social or interrelational. But social learning, as a theoretical concept and not a mere descriptor, is more specific. Social learning proper is central to at least two distinct traditions: (1) the tradition of learning theory and developmental psychology, and (2) the tradition of natural resource management and environmental or sustainability education.

(1) *The developmental psychology tradition*
    In developmental psychology, it is understood that a growing child is continuously learning about its surrounding material, social and cultural world, using all its senses. For the child or learner, social learning is the reciprocal interaction between cognitive, behavioural and environmental influences. According to Bandura (1977), social learning happens through active appropriation of what is being observed. This includes assimilation, resistance, adaptation and modification. Social learning does not happen as the mere response to reinforcing stimuli, as the behaviourists such as Skinner (1965) theorized.

The notions of social learning and transformative learning conceptualize what happens during the learning process and as the result thereof. While 'active modelling' by learners is central to Bandura's concept of social learning, Mezirow's theory focuses on the transformative learning moment experienced by (women adult) learners, when challenged to examine assumptions about their own behaviour and expectations. In both instances, the resulting transformed behaviour emanates from an active process of observation and reflection.

There is also a chronological connection between the two concepts: in the life of a learner, transformative learning may occur after much social learning has occurred already. Mezirow's adults were challenged to take a critical look at their behaviour that to a large extent was shaped by the social or active modelling learning of their younger years. A third connection between the two concepts is the emphasis placed on the agency of the learners, i.e., their capability of making choices. Learners are likely to differ in the nature and scope of their agency, and therefore in the extent to which they can identify pathways for further (personal) development that deviate from or even transgress established patterns of behaviour and thinking.

(2) *The natural resource management and environmental education tradition*

In the last decades of the 20th century, theories in the domain of environment and ecology started to conceptualize social learning as a process of social change in which people learn from each other in ways that can benefit wider social-ecological systems. Originating from concepts of organizational learning, as proposed by among others Argyris and Schön (1978) and Senge (1990), this school of thought is informed by social theories of learning, which define learning as active social participation in the practices of a community (Wenger, 1998). They emphasize the dynamic interaction between people and the environment in the construction of meaning and identity (Muro & Jeffrey, 2008).

In line with this tradition, environmental education and education for sustainable development (ESD) have adopted social learning both as a tool and as an outcome of a process of learning. Wals, van der Hoeven, and Blanken (2009) describe social learning as

> ...bringing together people of various backgrounds and with different values, perspectives, knowledge and experiences, both from inside and outside the group or organisation, in order to engage in a creative quest for answers to questions for which no ready-made solutions are available.
>
> (Wals et al., 2009, p. 11)

The absence of ready-made solutions is particularly obvious in the case of 'sustainability' issues such as climate change, resource depletion, and social and economic injustice. Echoing the essence of Mezirow's transformative learning it is suggested that 'social learning is a process in which people are stimulated to reflect upon implicit assumptions and frames of reference, in order to create room for new perspectives and actions' (Wals et al., 2009, p. 9).

The commonality of social learning and transformative learning is also seen in the overlap or similarity between their respective learning approaches. This is illustrated by the list of social learning's most important characteristics as drawn up by Wals et al. (2009, p. 9):

- It is about learning from each other, together.
- It is assumed that we can learn more from each other if we do not all think alike or act alike, in other words: we learn more in heterogeneous groups than we do in homogenous groups.
- It is about creating trust and social cohesion, precisely in order to become more accepting and to make use of the different ways in which people view the world.
- It is about creating 'ownership' with respect to both the learning process and the solutions that are found, which increases the chance that consequential actions will take place.
- It is about collective meaning making and sense making.

Collaborative Learning or Deliberative Social Learning

When faced with complex or 'wicked' social, economic and environmental issues, collaborative learning or deliberative social learning

> ...allow(s) the various parties and stakeholders involved to recognize the facts of a complex situation, to appreciate the sense and meaning that the different parties attach to these facts in their complexity, and, to allow commonalities and, therefore, potentially common approaches and possible solutions to the issues at hand emerge.
>
> (Wals & Lenglet, 2016, p. 59)

Collaborative learning extends social and experiential learning into the realm of societal organization. By explicitly bringing together a diversity of stakeholders, often with opposing interests and agendas, the learning is immediately linked to socio-political structures, behavioural patterns and social and cultural dynamics on the ground. By examining and questioning assumptions underlying the behaviour and opinions of the different groups, it is likely to disrupt the status quo. Collaborative learning allows 'new' knowledge and understanding to emerge and to become actionable in and through actual interaction, competition, struggle and collaboration. In this sense, collaborative learning fits in with the traditions and perspectives of 'pedagogy of the oppressed' (Freire, 1970) and 'deliberative dialogue' (Habermas, 1984).

For collaborative learning to be successful, some of the following conditions need to be met:

- All participating stakeholders are ready and willing to engage in a conversation about an issue, problem or *problématique* that is of common concern, to explore what it is and what it means, and how it can be addressed.
- It is valued by the participants. They expect their investment in the process – in terms of time, money, effort, political capital, etc. – to produce beneficial experiences and outcomes, especially in the longer term. They recognize the legitimacy of the convenor and facilitator.
- It is structured in such a way that it offers a safe space, both physically and socially: participants can express themselves without attribution or retribution, and learn to do so in a non-adversarial and non-confrontational manner.
- It encourages participants to actively learn about, listen, explore and understand the diversity of their opinions, interests and concerns. They range widely outside their own familiar territory and frameworks.

In the last 30 years, another strand of collaborative and deliberative learning and decision making has emerged. Its basic tenet is that that decisions that are reached through a process of collective reasoning will produce more legitimate and publicly oriented outcomes as a result (Hendriks, 2009). An early manifestation of this strand, in 1990s USA, is the Consensus Council, 'facilitating conversations and building agreements that empower people, transform communities, and advance the public good' (The Consensus Council, Inc., 2020). A more recent manifestation is the citizens' council or citizen's assembly. Its purpose is to encourage active citizens' participation in deliberating major societal issues in preparation of governmental policies and programs. The Irish citizen assembly of 2016–2018 around the issues of abortion, aging population, referenda and climate change is one example out of many (Forsberg, 2020).

A Note on 'Dissension', 'Conflict' and 'Consensus'

The literature on social and deliberative social learning around complex or wicked issues places strong emphasis on the heterogeneity of the learners and groups of learners. It is assumed that a complex issue cannot be addressed or resolved by a solution-oriented or problem-solving approach, applying a mere technical or technological analysis. Precisely because of the complexity and non-determinedness of the issue, because of its differential repercussions on distinctly different social, economic and cultural formations and groups, and because of the differential effects of the eventual resolution of the issue, it is essential that the learners actively embrace this variety and diversity. Usually, therefore, groups of collaborative learners are socially, economically, politically and culturally heterogenous, not homogeneous. They consist of people with contrasting and even opposing mind sets, frames of mind and interests. The learning process itself is the place of meaning making and empowerment. Through the exchange of differing perspectives and opinions a common or shared definition of the issue at hand may emerge, as well as a shared understanding of the content and type of the desired transformative action. In this process, dissension and conflict occur. This is inevitable and necessary. As part of the process of conscientization, Freire (1970) presented and discussed several methods for making such conflicts visible and productive. Mehlmann (2013) and Westin, Calderon, and Hellquist (2014) are more recent examples of handbooks with methods and techniques for facilitating collaborative learning processes while resolving inevitable tensions and conflicts among the learners.

Transformative, Transgressive Social Learning

In the practice of much collaborative and deliberative learning, the learning process is facilitated in such a way that it leads to a consensual decision about possible actions for dealing with the issue under scrutiny: 'consensual' meaning that the final agreement is actively supported by all or a majority of participants or participating groups, while participants or groups that do not share the same opinion agree not oppose the concluded agreement. This perspective may lead to situations in which the social, economic, power and knowledge inequalities among the participants and their structural or systemic determinants are insufficiently addressed and reflected upon. In the absence of a critical assessment and understanding of the structural and systemic determinants of the inequalities among the participants as well as the inequalities within the issue around which the learning process is taking place, it is likely that the conclusions, agreements and actions resulting from the learning process will be inadequate. They may perpetuate and even entrench these inequalities. This concern is central to Freire's pedagogical analysis and to his methods. It is also central to the idea of transformative *cum* transgressive social learning, which is the most recent shoot on the transformative branch of the social learning tree. It combines the third and the last of the six approaches to transformative learning as identified by Taylor (2008), namely the social emancipatory approach and the planetary approach (see p. 153 above).

Originally the concept of transformative, transgressive social learning, coined by Lotz-Sisitka et al. (2015), was formulated for application in higher education. It can be equally well used in many other situations where people as citizens – and therefore as learners – face 'the indeterminate and boundary crossing nature of sustainability issues, coupled with the urgency to act [....]' (p. 73). The complexity, ambiguity, controversy and uncertainty surrounding these (wicked) issues compel higher education (or citizens in general) to rethink its very foundation. This 'suggests a paradigm shift and a transition towards doing better things differently (transformation) rather than doing what we do better (optimization)' (p. 73). There is, therefore, a need to adopt a transformative approach of 'thinking how the object of study itself is constituted, what tools are used to study it and what concepts are used to frame it' (p. 74). The authors argue that Mezirow's conceptualisation of transformative learning is incomplete: it does not fully theorise the relationship between cognitive transformation of individuals and social action or agency, especially when learners, in their daily lives or in formal schooling environments, are confronted by the need for social and collective transformation of human activity as demanded by the complexity of wicked problems. In order to enlarge and deepen the idea and practice of transformative learning, the authors elaborate the notion of transformative *cum* transgressive learning. For this notion they find support in four complementary conceptual traditions, spanning more than 100 years: (1) the reflexive social learning and capabilities theory nurtured by, among others, Nussbaum and Sen (1993) and O'Donoghue, Lotz-Sisitka, Asago-Adjei, Kota, and Hanisi (2007), (2) the phenomenology tradition nurtured by Dewey (1934) and Jickling (2009), among many others, (3) the social-cultural and cultural historical activity theory, nurtured by Vigotsky's (1978) idea of 'expansive learning', and (4) the new social movement, postcolonial and decolonisation theory, nurtured by, among others, Fanon (1952, 1961) and Freire (1970). This latter tradition is rapidly being updated, expanded and enriched by social, cultural and economic 'liberation' movements worldwide (e.g., Coates, 2018). In one form or another, all four approaches recognize that learning around existential issues cannot be done within the confines of cognition-focused, discipline-organized and institution-based education. For it to be transformative, it must disrupt and transgress the usual and systemically and culturally entrenched methods and ways of problem definition, knowledge construction, knowledge acquisition and knowledge application. It requires 'engaged forms of pedagogy that involve multi-voice engagement with multiple actors'. It emphasizes 'co-learning, cognitive justice, and the formation and development of individual and systemic agency' (Lotz-Sisitka et al., 2015, p. 78).

Conclusion

Social learning, transformative learning, collaborative learning and transgressive learning are branches and offshoots of the same 'learning tree'. In their own way, the four labels and their underlying assumptions and perspectives share the notion that individual and collective learning and associated behaviour happen in a context of time, place and interaction. They recognize that observation, experience, reflection of the self – as individual and as member of one or more groups and collectivities – and its environment are central to the learning process. Change and transformation in behaviour and action, whether by the individual or the collective or both, are embedded in the learning process and do emerge from it.

Structured social and collaborative learning allows stakeholders to identify pathways to decision-making about 'the commons' in situations of uncertainty, complexity, anxiety, ambiguity, ethics and moral dilemmas, thus arriving at actions and behaviours that open pathways for resolving them. Through systematic processes of observation, exploration, experimentation and reflection the learners actively examine the assumptions, mindsets and the mental and economic mechanisms that perpetuate or worsen unsustainable behavioural patterns and unsustainable societal arrangements underlying the existential issues. At the same time, the learning processes allow participants to create alternative or new behavioural patterns and societal arrangements that open perspectives to greater environmental, social and economic justice. Thus, social, collaborative and transgressive learning can be individually and collectively transformative. It can support learners to become capable and empowered actors in processes of societal change and transformation.

References

Argyris, C., & Schön, D. (1978). *Organizational learning: A theory of action perspective*. Reading, MA: Addison-Wesley.

Bandura, A. (1977). *Social learning theory*. Englewood Cliffs, NJ: Prentice-Hall.

Bloom, N., Chang, M., & Duca, D. (2015). Conversation at home with Jack Mezirow (video). Retrieved form https://www.youtube.com/watch?v=iEuctPHsre4

Carnoy, M. (Ed.). (1972). *Schooling in a corporate society. The political economy of education in America*. New York, NY: David McKay Company.

Coates, T-N. (2018). *We were eight years in power*. New York, NY: Penguin Random House UK.

Cranton, P. (2006). *Understanding and promoting transformative learning: A guide for educators of adults*. San Francisco, CA: Jossey-Bass.

Dewey, J. (1934). *Art as experience*. New York, NY: Minto, Balch & Company.

Dirkx, J. M. (2001). The power of feeling: Emotion, imagination, and the construction of meaning in adult learning. In S. B. Merriam (Ed.), *The new update on adult learning theory*. San Francisco, CA: Jossey-Bass.

Eribon, L. (2018). *Retour à Reims*. Paris: Flammarion.

Fanon, F. (1952). *Peau noire, masques blancs*. Paris: Editions du Seuil.

Fanon, F. (1961). *Les damnés de la terre*. Paris: François Maspéro.

Fleming, T. (2014). Axel Honneth and the struggle for recognition: Implications for transformative learning. In A. Nicolaides & D. Holt (Eds.), *Spaces of transformation and transformation of space. Proceedings of the XI international transformative learning conference* (pp. 318–324). New York, NY: Teachers College, Columbia University.

Forsberg, T. (2020). *Citizens' assemblies: A potential transformative method for addressing the wicked problem of climate change. A case study of the Irish citizens' assembly in 2016*. Uppsala: Uppsala University.

Freire, P. (1970). *Pedagogy of the oppressed*. New York, NY: Herter and Herter.

Habermas, J. (1971). *Knowledge of human interests*. Boston, MA: Beacon.

Habermas, J. (1984). *The theory of communicative action. Volume 1: Reason and the rationalization of society*. Boston, MA: Beacon.

Hendriks, C. M. (2009). Policy design without democracy? Making democratic sense of transition management. *Policy Sciences, 42*, 341–368. doi:10.1007/s11077-009-9095-1

Jickling, B. (2009). Sitting on an old grey stone: Meditations on emotional understanding. In M. Mckenzie, P. Hart, H. Bai, & B. Jickling (Eds.), *Fields of green. Restorying culture, environment and education*. Cresskill, NJ: Hampton Press.

Kitchenham, A. (2008). The evolution of John Mezirow's transformative learning theory. *Journal of Transformative Education, 6,* 104–123.

Kuhn, T. (1962). *The structure of scientific revolutions.* Chicago, IL: University of Chicago Press.

Lindeman, E. (1926). *The meaning of adult education.* New York, NY: New Republic Inc.

Lotz-Sisitka, H., Wals, A., Kronlid, D., & McGarry, D. (2015). Transformative, transgressive social learning: Rethinking higher education pedagogy in times of systemic global dysfunction. *Current Opinion in Environmental Sustainability, 16,* 73–80.

May, T., & Qin, A. (2019, September 1). The high school course Beijing accuses of radicalizing Hong Kong. *New York Times,* p. 7. Retrieved from https://www.nytimes.com/2019/09/01/world/asia/hong-kong-protests-education-china.html

Mehlmann, M. (2013). Learning for change. In search for patterns that bind us. Retrieved from https://books.apple.com/se/book/learning-for-change/id611746319

Mezirow, J. (1991). *Transformative dimensions of adult learning.* San Francisco, CA: Jossey-Bass.

Mezirow, J. (2000). *Learning as transformation: Critical perspectives on a theory in progress.* San Francisco, CA: Jossey-Bass.

MGIEP. (2017). *Rethinking schooling. The state of education for peace, sustainable development and global citizenship in Asia.* Delhi: Mahatma Gandhi Institute of Education for Peace and Sustainable Development. Retrieved from https://unesdoc.unesco.org/ark:/48223/pf0000260568

Morrow, R. A., & Torres, C. A. (2002). *Reading Freire and Habermas: Critical pedagogy and transformative social change.* New York, NY: Teachers College Press.

Muro, M., & Jeffrey, P. (2008). A critical review of the theory and application of social learning in participatory natural resource management processes. *Journal of Environmental Planning and Management, 51*(3), 325–344.

Nussbaum, N., & Sen, A. K. (Eds.). (1993). *The quality of life.* Oxford: Oxford University Press.

O'Donoghue, R., Lotz-Sisitka, H., Asago-Adjei, R., Kota, L., & Hanisi, N. (2007). Exploring learning interactions arising in school-in community contexts of socio-ecological risk. In A. Wals (Ed.), *Social learning towards a sustainable world* (pp. 435–449). Wageningen: Academic Publishers.

Piketty, T. (2020). *Capital and ideology.* Boston, MA: Harvard University Press.

Plastow, R. (2008). Fostering transformative learning in education for sustainable development (ESD): A review of the literature on transformative learning for practitioners of ESD. Retrieved from https://uec.academia.edu/RobPlastow

Schleicher, A. (2018). *World class: How to build a 21st-century school system, strong performers and successful reformers in education.* Paris: OECD Publishing. doi:10.1787/9789264300002-en

Senge, P. M. (1990). *The fifth discipline: The art and practice of the learning organization.* New York, NY: Currency Doubleday.

Sidorkin, A. M. (1988). *Authoritarianism and education in Soviet schools.* Paper 18. Faculty Publications. Retrieved from https://digitalcommons.ric.edu/facultypublications/18

Skinner, B. F. (1965). *Science and human behaviour.* New York, NY: Free Press.

Taylor, E. W. (2008). Transformative learning theory. *New Directions for Adult and Continuing Education, 119*(Fall), 5–15.

The Consensus Council Inc. (2020). Retrieved from https://agree.org/

UNESCO. (2021). *What is education for sustainable development?* Paris: United Nations Educational, Scientific and Cultural Organisation. Retrieved from https://en.unesco.org/themes/education-sustainable-development/what-is-esd

Vigotsky, L. S. (1978). *Mind in society.* Cambridge, MA: Harvard University Press.

Wals, A. (Ed.). (2007). *Social learning towards a sustainable world.* Wageningen: Wageningen Academic Publishers.

Wals, A. (2012). Foreword. In H. Lotz-Sisitka (Ed.), *(Re)views on social learning literature: A monograph for social learning researchers in natural resources management and environmental education* (pp. 5–7). Grahamstown and Howick: Environmental Learning Research Centre, Rhodes University/EEASA/SADC REEP.

Wals, A., & Lenglet, F. (2016). Sustainability citizens. Collaborative and disruptive social learning. In R. Horne, J. Fine, B. Beza, & A. Nelson (Eds.), *Sustainability citizenship in cities. Theory and practice* (pp. 52–66). Oxford: Routledge.

Wals, A., van der Hoeven, N., & Blanken, H. (2009). *The acoustics of social learning. Designing learning processes that contribute to a more sustainable world.* Wageningen: Wageningen Academic Publishers.

Wenger, E. (1998). *Communities of practice: Learning, meaning and identity.* Cambridge: Cambridge University Press.

Westin, M., Calderon, C., & Hellquist, A. (2014). *The inquiry based approach (IBA) - A facilitator's handbook.* Visby: Swedish International Centre of Education for Sustainable Development.

Wulff, A. (Ed.). (2020). *Grading goal four. Tensions, threats, and opportunities in the sustainable development goal on quality education.* Leiden: Koninklijke Brill.

Chapter 8

Finding Hope in an Absurd University*

Vicente Manzano-Arrondo

Abstract

It is unfortunately too easy to find examples of absurd functioning in the university. It has never been a perfect institution, because that is an impossibility. One observes in recent years that while its chronic problems have not disappeared, they have lost prominence in the face of a steamroller working at the planetary level. The university has plunged into an even greater absurdity. This institution that was created to be free and clearly work for human emancipation, through the expansion of knowledge, has chosen to submit itself as a slave to the dynamics of the current global model of society. By so doing, it further fosters slavery by strengthening this global hegemony. In the present contribution I choose three concrete examples of this absurdity. The first alludes to the recruitment and shaping of obedient teachers. In this sense, the university is not an exception to the banking system of education, but it raises the production of individual adaptation and obedience to its maximum exponential. The second example refers to the renunciation of the social usefulness of the knowledge that it produces. This is done by adopting operational models from the production of commodities, such as quality measurement and the like, which undermine the institutional mission of universities. The third great absurdity refers to the destruction of thought and language diversity, which are two sides of the same coin. While the aforementioned processes are readily noticed, there are alternatives to the absurd university that entail encouraging projects and realities under construction. My aim with this contribution is to present an analysis of the absurd university, and give visibility to these alternatives under way, linked to grassroots university movements and other hopeful socio-educational projects. This chapter has a particular focus on language, due to its complexity and relative neglect in academia.

*This unpublished text was translated by Azril Bacal Roij. The original Spanish version is available in http://viko.civiencia.io/dok/pdf/EsperanzaEnMedioDeUnaUniversidad Absurda.pdf.

Transformative Research and Higher Education, 161–179
Copyright © 2022 Vicente Manzano-Arrondo
Published under exclusive licence by Emerald Publishing Limited
doi:10.1108/978-1-80117-694-120221009

Keywords: Absurd university; useful knowledge; destruction of thought; human emancipation; language diversity; social engagement

Introduction

Spanish is my mother tongue and I reside in the periphery of power.

This is a confession needed in order to understand my contribution to what promises to become a thrilling book, at least in respect to the other chapters.

We usually talk about education and the university in an age, when the hegemony of market-oriented thought, culture, references, and use of English language, is found so much everywhere, that it is not visible anywhere. I needed many years of activism, in the entrails of the university, to realize the depth of the wound due to the commoditization of higher education. And it this experience which enables me to write with clarity about what it means to be surrounded by colleagues who regret not being born in New York.

The enclosed work is my answer to the invitation of Azril Bacal to write an article for a book, meant to be critical, descriptive and constructive, at the same time. He asked us to write texts that could raise the awareness of our potential readers, revealing what is going on, what are the causes behind it, and what are we doing about it. In order to be able to perform this demanding task, I am obliged to start with a merciless critique. Let me begin by describing the university as someone simultaneously located both as an insider and at the margins. I come from a very humble family background. I know from experience what it means to be hungry. Nobody in my family had completed secondary education. My experience of the university is thus charged with symbolism, as a reflection of this social background. From day one to this very moment of writing these lines, I have not stopped feeling that this institution is estranged from the immense majority of the population in every country of this planet. Most people, when waking up every morning, search for knowledge of use to them. That has not been accomplished by nightfall. My colleagues know how to answer questions not raised by the population. They write their answers or copy other answers provided by the current fashion. They shape their answers according to the explicit and implicit rules of the hegemonic model of higher education. They publish their writings in journals that have the green light from the multinational *Clarivate*. They write articles that nobody will read except others like them, more concerned with climbing their own private career ladder in the institution than listening to the questions raised on the street.

My research on what is happening in my university has accumulated and documented valuable information on this subject. This information however seldom reaches the hegemonic channels. I have lived daily the highest imaginable quotas of obedience at the institution that should in principle be free. Actually, it was conceived as the most free of all institutions, because society needs knowledge that is not for sale. At the same time I have met wonderful people, who are able to resist all pressures to conform. They continue to do at the university what a wise society expects from them, knowledge for the common good! It is a really simple matter. Everything begins with their personal courage to swim against the stream, and not expecting to be rewarded by the institution for their valuable contributions.

Let the above reflections summarize the *geist* of this chapter. What follows are details to illustrate my thoughts on the matter. These are organized as follows. The first section, entitled *three absurdities*, is conceived as a synthesis of what is happening in the institutions of higher learning at the planetary level. Next follows a theoretical proposal which helps me to understand what is going on in this institutions, also useful to guide actions in this respect. The last section describes some success stories of experiences under way that might be a source of inspiration.

Thank you for being there, wherever you are. I know that if you have opened this book and intend to read it, it shows that the university remains a continuing place of hope.

Three Absurdities

Recruitment and the Shaping of a Sheepish Teaching Corps

The educational system might be regarded as a process intended to shape and prize persons that adapt best to given circumstances. Our girls and boys enter the school system filled with diversity and creativity. The existing system is not only unprepared to recognize this wealth. This system is designed, on the contrary, to effectively shape all the individual persons subjected to this regime, and to clone them according to the same standardized student prototype. The expected outcome from this molding process is someone able to memorize, what he or she is told, to show discipline, and focus on one's own life project. In order to attain this end result, these individuals need to elaborate a successful strategy to perceive what is expected from them, and to deliver as expected (Manzano-Arrondo, 2017a). The educational system is constructed with a growing component of competitiveness. Therefore, the capacity to deliver what is expected is also translated in the speed of providing an answer: to be the first to announce the correct answer. This is a mild way or manner of speech to talk about an extremely obedient person. This is the way to reach the top of the mountain in higher education. Only the students who owning this capacity for conformity to the highest degree will succeed in their studies. Only these chosen ones will be able to nourish by later turning it into a university professor, maybe the most obedient animal that ever existed (Manzano-Arrondo, 2019).

A vast majority of the professorship are far from being revolutionaries. According to Balestena (2001), they are mostly centered on their own career success. As a result of this self-centered focus, Amigot and Martínez (2013) find evidence that institutions of higher learning are afraid of becoming lame ducks in the ranking systems and fashionable university brands. At the same time, they are able to criticize the stupidity and counter-productiveness of this kind of behavior. Hence, it's not just a case of sheer ignorance. The teacher's corps cannot pretend to lack knowledge in this respect. Well-grounded in empirical studies, Callahan,

Wears, and Weber (2002) and Cheng (2011) provide evidence that most professors are obedient without really believing in the norms they follow. They regard and justify this seeming contradiction as the way to survive in the system or, better stated, as the way to actually succeed in the field of higher education. Barnhizer (1993) and Derrida (2002) contend that obedience is the opposite antipode of what universities are supposed to be. What the majority of society needs is a free university. To be free in the university is not a luxury, but a responsibility.

This is the responsibility given by scientific knowledge and wisdom to guide the search for the best solutions to the problems afflicting society. An army of professors preoccupied with investigating what is most likely to succeed in the publication market constitutes an offense to society.

Refusal to the Social Utility of Knowledge

I recently published a defense of a university which favors knowledge (Manzano-Arrondo, 2019). In other words, a defense of a kind of university which values knowledge. This possible university is viewed as an institution made of persons who are not necessarily experts in any specific study field; an institution that is not estranged from the world. They are experts in another way, namely, in the way they know about the world. These 'barefoot' experts are found in the university, attentive to what happens in the lives of everyday people. They are humbly open to learn from them. Furthermore, they spread their expertise concerning the generation of knowledge pertinent to them. In a 1998 UNESCO meeting in Paris, a major effort to analyze and synthesize higher education appealed to the universities to guide the world with the knowledge produced in their midst. This institution asserted that the world needs more than ever a university that interprets what is happening around them and explains why it is the case.

The economization or commoditization of the planet, namely, the hegemony of a reductionist and simplistic way to understand economy, has been chosen as the number one priority of political governance (Fernández, 2009). It is understood in that frame of economic thought, that if a national territory reaches a sufficiently high level of the hegemonic economic indicators, then it is the time when the national population has reached the top level of happiness and can rest in peace. As a result of this view turned into policy, universities mutate from the ivory tower into factories producing merchandise (commodities). In the interim, according to Ellacuría (1999), the chronic problems of Humanity keep waiting for an answer. These problems refer to power inequities, wars, and ignorance disguised as overflow of information. This is why the university produces answers to question nobody raised or to questions asked by the centers of power. The majority population remains voiceless, it lacks channels to let their voices be heard in the institutions assumed to produce knowledge. This situation is even more complicated. Even if the voiceless could hold a microphone, it is likely that they would not know what to say.

The Destruction of Diversity

The third great absurdity refers to the destruction of the diversity of thought and language, two sides of the same coin.

The diversity of though naturally exists on multiple fronts. For instance, among students who might enter and remain in the university, or those excluded and denied this possibility.

As previously mentioned, not everyone has the same opportunity to gain access to the university.

Leaving aside the possibility of failures in the system, only the students most capable to adapt to the norm are able to succeed and enter the institutions of higher learning. Empirical studies by Espinoza and González (2012) and Malecki (2000) provide evidence showing that this sorting mechanism is a race filled with obstacles, which along the way expels the population with fewest economic resources. The expulsion of poor students, prior to and after entering the university experience, might be seen as a lost opportunity for the educational system and society. A loss of knowledge understood as the privation of a potential wealth of creativity, that persons who do not fit into the homogenous pattern which is defined a priori might potentially contribute to the university.

It is not only the diversity of thought, which severely suffers due to the process previously described but also thought itself that suffers. It suffers, for example, as a result of the process of evaluating scientific productivity. I have conducted a thorough review of most of the accumulated empirical studies, which convey a fundamental and definitive critique of this process of evaluation (Manzano-Arrondo, 2017b). This mode of evaluation is not only dubitably scientific, it is anti-scientific. The blind uncritical following of the wrongly named *impact factor* (it would actually be preferably called *simplified measure of citations*), as well as the related university rankings, has resulted as a consequence in the cruel loss of diversity at multiple levels. One of the main victims of this process is the pauperization of persons, teams, universities and disciplines, most concerned with being useful to their society.

The hegemonic process of evaluation of scientific productivity takes place, hand in hand, with another powerful component: the normalized discourse that only the English language is valid for science and, moreover, that every self-esteemed researcher must master this language (Manzano-Arrondo, 2018). One serious consequence of this screening process is that progressively the universities and scientific journals of the world express themselves in English, to the detriment of local languages, cultures and problems (Ammon, 2006; Hamel, 2007). Language is so present in everything that it is hardly visible. It is the vehicle for learning and thinking, for communicating, for succeeding or failing, for taking risks or for self-protection. It is most difficult for someone with English as mother language or who acquired it at an early age, to grasp what happens due to this linguistic hegemony. Namely, how it affects the daily life and future expectations of persons in other countries or regions of the world.

Hanafi (2011) and Majhanovich (2014), for example, describe how universities in their countries are categorized and evaluated according to the way they prioritize English, and according to how they play the publishing game conforming to the rules of citation. Lacey (2015) contends that English dominance in the academic domain goes hand in hand with military and economic domination, all of these features strongly intertwined. Koutny (2005) analyzes why language entails a peculiar way of being in the world which is reinforced in the universities.

The results of several empirical investigations conducted by me, currently on their way to be published in scientific journals, have unveiled a reality earlier unknown to me. These findings lead me to conclude that the global hegemony of the English language constitutes a problem of public health in general, and more particularly in the university world. This is why some liberation movements nowadays reclaim the scientific legitimacy of their native languages. This recognition entails a breaking away from the linguistic straightjacket inherent in the evaluation criteria of scientific activity.

A Biologist's Explanation

We often hear and listen that everything is changing, that the world is in permanent movement, and nothing is stable. This is one of the hegemonic myths. If everything changes, nobody should be content with continuing being as one is, stranded in the present situation.

The only recognizable demand is to dip into the *imaginaire* of permanent change, and everything else in the total picture (Grinberg, 2009). Moreover, change is not just any change. The implied meaning of the 'right' change is to adapt to the same direction towards which the world is seemingly moving. The assertion 'everything changes' does not help the sense of agency, namely, that the individual or group might consider changing the world. The implied meaning of the term change in the language of hegemony is that individuals and groups should adapt to the flow of changes that don't substantially change the world. Furthermore, this adaptive change must be done without attachment, without developing affective ties with any stage in the flow of change, since everything is unstable.

But that is not true. A calmer and reflexive look at the situation shows that it is not the case. What happens in reality is actually the opposite. In other words, life is seemingly 97% stable and 3% transformation. The quantitative aspect of these percentages is not pertinent per se. What is actually relevant is that inertia outweighs change. Nonetheless, our attention is focused on changes. It stands to reason. To focus on inertia nearly amounts to a waste of energy and attention. The available resources should be employed in what is bound to vary, in order to respond adequately and in due time. This is why contrasts attract our attention. A green worm crawling in a green leaf in a green forest goes unnoticed. It is precisely because woods are so green that 100% of our attention goes to a red butterfly, even though its mass is negligible in the surrounding background.

The human capacity to perceive change, along with the mind's incapacity to appreciate what is permanent, adds to a third element: fear of the unknown. Individual specimens of any and all species exhibit a tendency to preserve the familiar. This conservative pattern entails a fear of the unknown, which lies behind the attempt to maintain and protect what is known, as well as resistance to change. Let us call this pattern tendency C.

At the same time, individuals in all species exhibit a tendency towards adventure, a curiosity to go beyond the conventional limited boundaries. Let's call this attribute tendency V. My hypothesis is that tendency C must be the dominant norm in the aggregate sum of the community or group of individuals in every species. C must be dominant because the context is mostly stable. If the previous percentages were correct, these would also be perfectly reflected in every species: about 97% of C and 3% of V. A species with 100% C is doomed to disappear, because it would not be prepared to adequately respond to the few changes bound to occur, which though infrequent are bound to have vast consequences. In some individuals, tendency V is more accentuated. They are reckless, so they dare to enter the unknown. The majority of them are likely to perish. They are a sacrificial offering to statistics, playing however a key guarantee role in the total picture. Thanks to them, the community as a whole might be able to adequately respond to contextual challenges, and even improve their situation under conditions when their survival is not at risk.

This vision might be excessively daring. But in combination with human intelligence, it leads me to think that the tendency V is somewhat larger in our species than in other living species. But never superior to C which always prevails. This explains why it's easier to find adventurers among humans. However, their presence is never decisive. This biological and reductionist hypothesis enables me to understand and accept obedience as an expression of conservatism, fear to change, and inertia. Obedience, the tendency to conform, the fear of being different...are examples of C mechanisms. The university, which should be the V institution *par excellence* has decided to move in the opposite direction, i.e., to follow the censorship of change, and to obey even prior to the command. In other words, it begins to adapt to a change that is not yet in place, and yet it helps to trigger. This is why the university does not produce revolutions, except when students decide that it is time to revolutionize.

Hope under Construction

Universities are luckily populated by people. Most persons on Earth are habitually good persons, with a good heart. They wish themselves not to have problems in life, as well as wishing the same for other people. Most persons on this planet wake up every morning with the intention to solve all challenges in the way, to enjoy good moments, concerned with the wellbeing of their closest relatives and friends and thriving with life, if surrounded by peace.

One is likely to find persons in all universities who analyze what is happening in the world, and attempt to generate positive ways to deal with existing challenges and problems making use of the existing resources available in their universities. In addition to the classic research model and participatory action-research, we find the new practices of service-learning or learning while serving. This modality entails that the student actively learns the course assignment while providing a service to the community, often geared towards social change (Speck, 2001). There are a number of alternative or radical universities already in operation which are particularly courageous. In the sense that the theory and praxis of social transformation are located at the center of their hearts, minds, and curricula, making use of the material, structural and intellectual resources available in these institutions. Let us next examine some examples of these universities organically linked to social movements.

Unitierra: An Exemplary University

'Universidad de la Tierra' (*Unitierra*), located in Oaxaca, a region of Mexico, densely populated by Indigenous Peoples, was conceived by Gustavo Esteva (2014), a highly respected Mexican anthropologist. It is a learning institution without grades, courses, nor diplomas. It is organized as a university, in the sense that people enter this learning space to acquire knowledge at the level of higher education. They leave this place with knowledge equivalent to a university degree, with an expanded wisdom. With the kind of knowledge that is not reduced to theoretical features. The knowledge acquired at *Unitierra* is geared to a better understanding of the world where the students live. This understanding in turn leads to action in order to improve it. *Unitierra* emerged historically from the collective reflection of 16 Indigenous Peoples who inhabit the region of Oaxaca. This deliberation led them to conclude that an important explanatory cause of their problems lie in the domestication to which they are subjected all the way from grade school. They realized that only one indigenous person per 1,000 attained a university degree, which in turn was of little help in getting a job. In this way, numerous voices and wills of peoples got together to create something special.

Esteva (2014, p. 44) wrote in this respect: 'We tried to create an autonomous place, open to learn by doing rather than by studying, as it was suggested by Ivan Illich, as it were a joyful activity of free people.' The choice of the curricula and study fields was reached by consensus among students, activists, and teachers, working together to analyze, understand, share, and act upon. *Unitierra* has managed to construct a non-hierarchical institution, based on the innate longing to learn. It functions like assemblies intertwined with the community, and fused with various movements asserting the dignity of all its constituents. It does not only teach in their physical plants but also teaches as an open university through its editorial activity, websites, radio programs, and it works together with social movements beyond the geographic space.

University and Social Engagement: A Grassroots Academic Movement

In 1990, the Spanish government started a harsh university reform. It was similar to what was implemented in other countries, beginning with the Chilean experiment in the 1980s (Spinoza, 2008). This early start, in the shadow of the neoliberal shock, was followed in countries as diverse as Australia (Worthington & Higgs, 2011), Indonesia (Susanti, 2011), Sweden (Musial, 2010), Greece (Venieris & Cohen, 2004), Japan (Yamamoto, 2004), Turkey (Kennedy, Senses, & Ayan, 2011), and Kenya (Johnson & Hirt, 2011), just to mention a few national samples of such hegemonic reforms.

These 'reforms' comprised a number of changes such as: (1) To apply a model of academic accounting that entails a vision of the university as a factory that produces things, such as scientific articles, patents, and number of graduates who have to submit their work to a continuous set of quantitative measures, (2) to shape students prepared to be available in variable times, places and tasks, according to the demand of the markets, and (3) to apply the knowledge produced in this reformed academic frame to the current demands of business enterprises. Paradoxically, it is in the universities located in the central countries, already familiar with this model of university, where one finds more liberty to promote some exceptions to the rule, such as to stimulate critical thought and international academic programs to aid other countries. These exceptions to the hegemonic norm don't entail any risk to the model just described.

In numerous universities, various movements rose against these reforms. It was a collective reaction to refute the new norm. These movements finally coalesced and agreed upon a structure to fight together against this reform. Some movements had as their aim to protect acquired rights. The movement gathered a notorious strength and engagement at the Universidad de Sevilla, in a process of collective reflection and action. This collective effort was centered on the vision and construction of a university for the common good. Having lost the normative battle, the collective 'University and Social Engagement' emerged as a network in 2001, with the participation of over 100 professionals from more than 20 different disciplines. This collective established the following lines of action:

(1) At the level of the engaged teachers, it entailed the organization of formal courses, seminars, and open courses to the public, designed to promote a transdisciplinary approach to the complexities of the nearby and distant worlds. This was done by making use of the diverse knowledge accumulated by the various disciplines present in this process. For example, one-day field studies were organized in every academic course to visit by bus surrounding areas of Sevilla, from nearby observation posts. At every stop, the members of the teachers' team interpreted the city from various study fields and per-spectives, such as: psychology, economics, urbanism, sociological, mathe-matics, agro-ecological, anthropological, etc.

(2) At the level of community, it meant to establish a bridge with the social movements in the city. In this way and in the course of time, various civil society organizations have approached us requesting university knowledge to help solve problems related to knowledge per se or action-related. In this front, we have written counter-reports, critical analysis in the realms of urbanism and agro-ecology, alternative proposals of interurban communi-cation, advisory support to marginal neighborhoods, etc. One of the

applications is the 'show-off' professor, someone who does not teach anything new, but shows up in the mass media, pretending to represent the citizen's movement, and trying to legitimize this pretense the prestige of their university.

(3) In reclaiming our academic rights, the network *Universidad y Compromiso Social* took different actions, such as democratic ways of designing projects, the distribution and diffusion of leaflets, campaigns, petitions and public activities, acting always together as a collective. At this very moment when writing these lines, the collective is firmly engaged in raising awareness of the climate emergency, making use of leaflets, courses, research, communicating with the administrations, collaborating with other movements sharing similar aims, etc.

(4) As a generative matrix, it gave birth to other social movements that germinated in Sevilla, as well as in other universities. Several academic activists in this social movement have helped to organize political parties, trade unions, neighborhood associations, and the like, and are often actively engaged in their activities.

The Citizen Barometer: A Bridge between University and Social Movements

For the past two decades, I have been teaching the course on data analysis in the department of psychology at *Universidad de Sevilla*. When I started, this subject was taught in an exclusively mathematical style, which required infinitesimal calculus, matrix algebra and similar contents. Together with my colleague Hassan Fazeli, we began to undress the mathematical format, with a focus on finding solutions to real practical situations and problems. In the end, I came to apply the service-learning approach to teaching/learning already mentioned. In this way, my students did not just learned abstract statistics. They became engaged in solving problems in close collaboration with neighborhood movements, and became acquainted and engaged with various neighborhoods in Sevilla. The typical situation might be portrayed as follows: (1) In the early organizational stage of the project, social movements need to know the neighborhoods where the students are involved. For instance, what is the reaction of the neighbors to the growing presence of immigrants and refugees, the degree of religious tolerance, or the rates of school failure of their offspring? (2) This process was continued by helping them define the objectives of their investigation. (3) The next task was to construct a questionnaire or instrument to measure the corresponding data at my office, which was discussed with the students on a consensual basis. All of this occurred prior to the beginning of the classwork as such. (4) Together with the students, we discussed the particular study in question, visited the neighborhood, conversed with the neighborhood representatives, and designed the fieldwork. (5) The students interviewed people in the streets and entered the data into the computer. We used the processed data to learn about statistics. (6) At the end of the classwork, already with the conclusions in hand, we organized an open meeting in the neighborhoods, where the students presented their results. After this first sharing of the findings with the community, these were further discussed in mixed groups of students and neighbors to deepen the comprehension of what was going on.

The above learning dynamics continues today in teaching subjects such as psychometrics and qualitative methodology. Similar innovative ways of teaching were explored in other study fields, which likewise resulted in particularly useful knowledge, grounded in accumulated contacts and previous experiences in the city. The gathered information revealed lots of shared concerns in different neighborhoods. This information was also useful for social movements not bound to specific zones. Against this background, we met with persons elected as representatives from a variety of social movements, such as neighborhood associations, human rights groups, energy justice committees, etc. These meetings took place until we first agreed upon common objectives, and later some specific ones. We elaborated together a questionnaire, which was enriched with the contributions from the collective of representatives.

Along this process, we enlisted the collaboration of colleagues from similar and different disciplines, whose diverse theoretical perspectives merged in the shared social practice. As a final result, hundreds of students learned the contents of their assigned courses making use of this dynamics of teaching/learning. In doing so, they shared the same questionnaire as the measurement instrument to do research in the whole city of Sevilla as their field of study and action.

This instrument was also used on different occasions. In this manner, the social movements and organizations had access to information on the issues that concerned them most, enabling them to calibrate the effectiveness of their activities. This explains why we named this praxis *The Citizen Barometer*. The effort to coordinate this load of work proved to be excessive for me. I did not manage to get a university team to support this program, forcing me to quit this project after various waves of applying this barometer. The gained experience was however very enriching and useful. Before leaving the project we were able to enlist local radios and other means of communication to keep citizens informed on what was going on matters important to them. A description of the method and the first round of application was published by Manzano-Arrondo (2014).

Units of Engaged Action (UEA): Immigration in Úbeda

Úbeda essentially is an agricultural city located in the Jaén province in Andalucía, Spain. Most of this province is dedicated to olive cultivation and olive oil production. The harvesting of olives takes place during the colder months in the year, towards the end of fall and the early winter. It is harsh manual labor which is mostly poorly paid. This situation explains why it is almost entirely done by labor immigrants, quite often undocumented workers from the Sub-Saharan region in Africa. They constitute highly mobile groups moving seasonally in the whole country, according to the harvest demands of different fruits and vegetables.

So it happened that I was invited to lead a workshop on the Units of Engaged Action (UAC) by a local university in 2015. They had read about these units in the book 'Universidad y Compromiso Social' (*University and Social Engagement*) from 2012. Shortly stated, they wanted to know more about this model of research and engaged action. I had described it at length and more detail in a publication from 2014 (Manzano-Arrondo & Suárez, 2015), which they did not know about. Groups of teachers applied the model during the workshop to real situations. One teacher among the participants designed a research project applied to the situation of immigrants related to the harvest of olives. I realized during this process that some immigrants who slept in the open had died due to exposure to the cold. I found out moreover that the institutional facilities were both insufficient and poorly utilized. A situation of lack of knowledge prevailed overall on what and how to operate in such conditions. I became involved in the process due to the active engagement of Beatriz Pedroza and José Luis Soto, the two teachers who decided to take advantage of the workshop to start a process of engaged research and action that made sense in this respect. Beatriz visited the people in the streets every night, taking along coffee, biscuits, and blankets, and thereby providing company to immigrants sleeping in the open air.

José Luis struggled meanwhile with the institutions, seeking help to improve this situation. He rarely succeeded in obtaining more than insufficient and inadequate institutional answers.

The Units of Engaged Action are organized in various stages. During the first stage a panel is organized with all the people included in this process: immigrants, solidarity organizations, local administration, police, university, students, administrative staff, and social services. At the same time, data are analyzed and common and sectorial objectives are defined.

Then follows the stage when the research methods and ways to gather data are agreed upon, thanks to the intervention of the university and its institutional support. The data are then analyzed. As a follow-up, ways to share and spread the findings are explored. Specific agreements and commitments are next established for each of the involved segments. There is a follow-up of the impact of the various activities as a way to close the circle, and return to the starting point based on data. There is no deadlines to these units (UEC). The ideal vision entails a natural transformation into a permanent feature of reality such as, for example, a platform of action. To facilitate the execution of the transformative project, the research methodology is centered on answers to questions raised by the participants during the design process, such as: What do we want to *learn*? What do we want to *communicate*? What do we want to *change*?

Jaén and Sevilla universities were involved in the UEC project through different courses and with members of their teaching staff. UECs benefitted from institutional economic support. The municipal council of Úbeda was involved, as well as the local police, religious groups, communication channels, citizen collectives, and immigrants themselves. It was tough work, not particularly in the gathering of data, nor due to linguistic problems; the main difficulty being the habitual ways institutions operate. One of the main problems we found was that the groups that were already working in the field wrongly assumed that they knew what to do, that what they were doing was appropriate, and there was no need to change or improve on anything; wrongly assuming that social problems inevitably remain invariable in place. This barrier was the hardest to overcome, but we succeeded in the end. The research findings revealed the numerous bumps in the road. They showed for instance, why immigrants do not use the institutional resources, even when badly needed. The results also unveiled the behavior of the plant owners, as well as the unconscious collaboration with this privileged segment of the population carried by many well-meant voluntary help organizations. It was also difficult to convince the institutions about the need to change their habitual ways of doing things. But they did accept the challenge to change and to modify their operative norms. The UEC approach additionally influenced the neighboring municipalities and remains active today, in spite of the drain of energy entailed in the attempt to maintain a fruitful dialogue with the administrations. A more extensive description of this experience has been written by Manzano-Arrondo, Pedrosa, and Soto (2017).

Esperanto and Liberation University Movements: Linguistic Emancipation

I have never been so surprised in my trajectory as researcher, educator and activist, as to discover the realm of linguistic oppression. This is illustrated with the following examples:

(1) In spite of the accumulated evidence showing that English is not as extended nor generally accepted, a myth has been constructed that everybody already speaks English, that it is indispensable and, last but not least, that it has nothing to do with cultural domination. I have found evidence of the prevalence of this myth among my colleagues, students and activists. The research I have conducted in this respect unveils the myth, and shows how deeply and perfectly entrenched in its established.
(2) My colleagues in university social movements close to me accept without doubts that we can change society, that we can exert influence in society, that transformation is possible. Yet when the subject of language comes to the fore, the reaction is that English is there, that it has to be acknowledged as a reality, without nothing more to be said. The prevalent feeling is that nothing can be done to change it.

Nonetheless, several alternatives of cultural and linguistic liberation are emerging in various corners of the world. Against the background of the vast landscape of emancipatory linguistics, even though not yet sufficiently strong, I will discuss the concrete reality of Esperanto. Assuming that knowledge about this language is not widely spread, it is important to introduce the reader to this language per se and its academic relevance. Several possibilities and realities concerning Esperanto are next entertained.

Esperanto[1]

Esperanto is a language constructed towards the end of the nineteenth century. Its fast diffusion slowed down in the aftermath of two world wars. Speakers of this language were widely persecuted by dictatorships of different political orientation. Nonetheless, the language is still alive in our days. In the year 2017, the 103rd World Congress of Esperanto was convened in Korea, followed in Portugal (2018), Finland (2019), and scheduled in Canada (2020).

This language operates with few rules, with no exceptions to the rule, and with a way to construct and use words easy to learn. It is empirically shown that to learn Esperanto facilitates the acquisition of other languages better than French, English or German. There is no official culture one is obliged to, no official language, nor a nation or state that controls or defends its ownership.

One is able to write poetry, novels and scientific articles in Esperanto. There are radio programs, music groups, magazines, etc. There are versions in Esperanto for computer programming, websites, Wikipedia, etc. Last but not least, one finds today all kinds of international associations related to Esperanto such as: stamp collectors, academic studies, youth and vegetarians, among other.

There are local Esperanto associations in many large and small cities, where one is able to study this language with no cost. Additionally, one finds a great number of courses on the web. For example, the version of *Duolingo* to learn Esperanto for English-speaking persons was launched in 2015, reaching an audience of half a million students by 2016. While the exact number of persons who speak Esperanto is not known, it is present in at least 150 countries.

Esperanto and the University

Infused with the same attitude maintained in the previous paragraphs, the next lines will describe concrete realities based in my direct experience. These lines do not represent the rich totality of what is happening in the world of Esperanto, yet they convey excerpts of its strength and utility.

Esperanto is taught at the university level. Particularly relevant is its presence in the Low Countries, Poland, Hungary, Brazil, China, South Korea and Japan. This language is taught at the University of Sevilla to students without credits. This task is carried by an academic collective with teachers from psychology, economics, tourism, philology and informatics. Additionally, we collaborate in this respect with the local Esperanto association, which is about 100 years old. At the same time, I am a graduate student in a three-year's course in inter-linguistics at the University Adam Mickievicz in Poland. Graduate students from Spain, France, Germany, Poland, Russia, South Korea, China, the USA and Brazil attend this course. All the classwork, printed materials, and websites are in Esperanto.

At this point in time, when writing these lines, I collaborate in the third academic and exchange cooperation project with seven African countries: Benin, Togo, Mali, Democratic Republic of the Congo, Rwanda, Madagascar and The Republic of South Africa. Esperanto is the language used to communicate between my university and the African counterparts. This project of academic cooperation aims at the construction of a network to dignify cultural and linguistic diversity in Africa. It begins with the design, written transcriptions and divulgation of stories that helps to reclaim the inclusive African culture heritage – against the legacy of French and British, but also Spanish, Portuguese, and recently Chinese colonial domination. These stories are registered in audio in the maximum number of African languages that the network is capable to sustaining.

I am also a member of an international collective of university teachers led by Angela Tellier, at the University of Essex (United Kingdom), which in turn is sponsored by two world organizations: the International League of Esperanto teachers (ILEI) in Switzerland, and the Esperantic Studies Foundation (ESF) in the USA. This collective conducts a follow-up of the ongoing studies, journals, publications and research on inter-linguistics in general, and Esperanto in particular. They register courses, list activities and supports similar university initiatives. The data base in our hands shows that this language is in good health at the institutions of higher learning and also that related activities are growing.

Esperanto as a Tool of University Liberation

As previously indicated, the current state of universities in the world at large leaves much to be desired. At the same time, however, it's hopeful that everywhere in the university world social movements erupt trying to bring some sense where nonsense prevails. These developments open the doors to hope, and the construction of better alternatives. These movements are often hardly noticeable, and frequently lack Institutional support. Such initiatives emerge thanks to the energy invested by activists on voluntary basis, often to the detriment of their individual advancement. In this climate, it's natural to conclude that to liberate universities in the world at large one needs to work on three parallel contested fields: (1) To focus on local contexts, where it is easy to realize to what extent the general knowledge generated by universities have actual use to benefit the majority of the people. In this respect, to gain awareness about whether or not such general knowledge responds to real needs. (2) To free our academic activities from the current hegemonic straightjacket, which is highly simplified, restricted and counter-productive. These latter features are part and parcel of the hegemonic quality measurement of scientific productivity, which distracts the attention, time, and efforts of the majority of the university teachers and researchers. An additional cost of this prevailing model is that it leads to the abandonment of the other key missions of the university, including the kind of research not directly related to the production of commercial goods. (3) To reclaim the dignity of the local languages as instruments of scientific work and communication and to protect them; thereby exploring and establishing new non-hegemonic strategies of international communication.

The previous reflections led me to the decision to study Esperanto as a way to seek and find solutions to the third contested terrain (point 3 above). At that time, I was already working intensely on the two previous points of contestation, along with a diversity of university colleagues from various disciplines. I took this decision in 2016. One year later, in June 2017, I had already given my first lecture conference in Esperanto on oppression at the university. By that time I had already established contact with various groups of Esperanto university teachers in various countries in the five continents. This activity enabled me to discover the long journey already advanced by the Esperanto movement in the protection of local languages and the proposal of a non-hegemonic model of communication.

A synthesis of the previous activities may be concretized in two points: (1) All persons have the right to make sufficient use of their mother tongue to attain the fundamental objectives of life, and (2) in situations of communication between persons with different languages, Could or should Esperanto be used as an auxiliary non-hegemonic language? 'Why non-hegemonic'? Because, (a) the use of Esperanto does not benefit one country in particular, (b) Esperanto-speakers have learned that language under equal conditions, given that native Esperanto speakers are unusual, and (c) the community of Esperanto-speakers share a fundamental preoccupation for cultural and linguistic equality. In this respect, I adapted the proposal of using Esperanto, presented above, for the purposes of academic communication as follows (Manzano-Arrondo, 2017a):

(1) To make use of local languages as dignified and useful for all university matters, such as teaching, research and extension.
(2) To emphasize the importance of research in the local environments, in order to answer to the real needs, problems, and challenges in these relevant contexts.
(3) To facilitate the use of Esperanto as a language of academic communication (research, teaching and social action), when required by the international situation.
(4) To provide effective solutions in situations in which university people need to communicate at the international level, but don't wish to make use of a standardized common language (automatic translations, mediations, systematization of scientific communications, etc.).

Final Reflections

All great social challenges have and continue to have serious difficulties to be accepted by many people and academics as having a solution a priori. This situation of hopelessness has happened and continues to happen with issues of gender inequalities, racist violence, labor rights, and respect for the environment. In spite of the extended inertia, millions of persons have accepted these challenges and are engaged in trying to solve them. By doing so, they are trying to change national and international academic norms. The battle for linguistic liberation is likewise difficult to recognize and accept at first. This process is accompanied with serious moments of institutional and individual inertia and difficult prognosis. Nonetheless, a growing number of activists has decided not to give up, thereby becoming contagious.

In all disciplines, one is able to obtain information about the origins of the authors of the main theories, as well as their contributions to scientific knowledge, according to place of origin. The result from this scanning systematically reveals the hegemony of English-speaking countries in the international academic world. If one discards the possibility of a more biologically evolved brain in these countries, the answer is found in its correspondence with other associated factors of political, economic, and military hegemony. The struggle for a more just world must directly address these challenges. The university has an opportunity to assume this task.

Notes

1. This text was written together with Professor Xavier Alcalde, during his stay at the University of Florence in 2018, related to the design of a questionnaire we constructed together, intended to measure the biased attribution held by university students about the actual use and spread of English.

References

Amigot, P., & Martínez, L. (2013). Gubernamentalidad neoliberal, subjetividad y transformación de la universidad. La evaluación del profesorado como técnica de normalización. *Athenea Digital*, *13*(1), 99–120.

Ammon, U. (2006). Language planning for international scientific communication: An overview of questions and potential solutions. *Current Issues in Language Planning*, *7*(1), 1–30.

Balestena, E. (2001). Ética del saber y de las instituciones. In E. N. Kisnerman (Ed.), *Ética, ¿Un discurso o una práctica social?* (pp. 45–62). Buenos Aires: Paidós.

Barnhizer, D. (1993). Freedom to do what? Institutional neutrality, academic freedom, and academic responsibility. *Journal of Legal Education*, *43*(3), 346–357.

Callaham, M., Wears, R. L., & Weber, E. (2002). Journal prestige, publication bias, and other characteristics associated with citation of published studies in peer-reviewed journals. *Journal of American Medical Association*, *287*(21), 2847–2850.

Cheng, M. (2011). The perceived impact of quality audit on the work of academics. *Higher Education Research and Development*, *30*, 179–191.

Derrida, J. (2002). *Universidad sin condición*. Madrid: Trotta.

Ellacuría, I. (1999). *Escritos universitarios*. San Salvador: UCA Editores.

Espinoza, O., & González, L. E. (2012). Estado actual del sistema de aseguramiento de la calidad y el régimen de acreditación en la educación superior en Chile. *Revista de la Educación Superior*, *41*(2), 87–109.

Esteva, G. (2014). La libertad de aprender. *Revista Interuniversitaria de Formación del Profesorado*, *28*(2), 39–50.

Fernández, A. (2009). Hacia una nueva conceptualización del homo-economicus. Aportes a la teoría del consumidor. *Visión de Futuro*, *12*(2), 1–20.

Grinberg, S. M. (2009). Tecnología del gobierno de sí en la era del gerenciamiento: La autoayuda entre el narcisismo y la abyección. *Psicoperspectivas*, *8*(2), 293–308.

Hamel, R. E. (2007). The dominance of English in the international scientific periodical literature and the future of language use in science. *AILA Review*, *20*, 53–71.

Hanafi, S. (2011). University systems in the Arab East: Publish globally and perish locally vs publish locally and perish globally. *Current Sociology*, *59*(3), 291–309.

Johnson, A. T., & Hirt, J. B. (2011). Reshaping academic capitalism to meet development priorities: The case of public universities in Kenya. *Higher Education, 61,* 483–499.

Kennedy, N. F., Senses, N., & Ayan, P. (2011). Grasping the social through movies. *Teaching in Higher Education, 16,* 1–14.

Koutny, I. (2005). Interkultura komunikado en Eŭropo: La angla kaj Esperanto kiel alternativaj komunikiloj. In E. C. Kinselman (Ed.), *Simpozio pri interkultura komunikado* (pp. 115–132). Dobrichovice: Kava-Pech.

Lacey, J. (2015). Considerations on English as a global Lingua Franca. *Political Studies Review, 13*(3), 363–372.

Majhanovich, S. (2014). Neo-liberalism, globalization, language policy and practice issues in the Asia-Pacific region. *Asia Pacific Journal of Education, 34*(2), 168–183.

Malecki, E. S. (2000). Teaching/power. Part II. *Radical Pedagogy, 2.*

Manzano-Arrondo, V. (2014). Il Barómetro Cittadino. La risposta dell'Universitá per unire didattica, ricerca, azione. *Rivista Internazionale di EDAFORUM, 9*(23). Retrieved from http://rivista.edaforum.it/numero23/monografico_Manzano.html

Manzano-Arrondo, V. (2017a). Lingva subpremata diskurso kaj nuntempa universitato. *Language Communication Information. Jesyk Komunikacja Informacja, 12,* 121–135.

Manzano-Arrondo, V. (2017b). Hacia un cambio paradigmático para la evaluación de la actividad científica en la Educación Superior. *Revista de la Educación Superior, 46,* 1–35.

Manzano-Arrondo, V. (2018). Aprendizaje, servicio y opresión. Liberando al opresor universitario. In V. Martínez, N. Melero, E. Ibañez, & M. C. Sánchez (Eds.), *El Aprendizaje-Servicio en la Universidad. Una metodología docente y de investigación al servicio de la justicia social y el desarrollo sostenible* (pp. 32–37). Salamanca: Comunicación Social.

Manzano-Arrondo, V. (2019). Qué estamos haciendo mal en la Universidad. En A. de la Herrán, J. M. Valle, & J. L. Villena (Eds.), *Qué estamos haciendo mal en la educación. Reflexiones pedagógicas para la investigación, la enseñanza y la formación* (pp. 157–182). Barcelona: Octaedro.

Manzano-Arrondo, V., Pedrosa, B., & Soto, J. L. (2017). Sinhogarismo inmigrante. Un caso de investigación-acción universitaria en el contexto de la recogida de aceituna en Úbeda. *Hábitat y Sociedad, 10,* 223–244.

Manzano-Arrondo, V., & Suárez Garcia, E. (2015). Unidad de Acción Comprometida: Una propuesta de solución ante el problema universitario del servicio a la sociedad. *Hábitat y Sociedad, 8,* 147–166.

Musial, K. (2010). Redefining external stakeholders in Nordic higher education. *Tertiary Education and Management, 16,* 45–60.

Speck, B. W. (2001). Why service-learning? *New Directions for Higher Education, 114,* 3–13.

Spinoza, O. (2008). Creating (in) equalities in access to higher education in the context of structural adjustement and post-adjustement policies: The case of chile. *Higher Education, 55,* 269–284.

Susanti, D. (2011). Privatisation and marketisation of higher education in Indonesia: The challenge for equal access and academic values. *Higher Education, 62,* 209–218.

UNESCO. (1998). *Conferencia Mundial sobre la Educación Superior. La educación superior en el siglo XXI. Visión y acción*. París: Ediciones de la UNESCO.

Venieris, G., & Cohen, S. (2004). Accounting reforms in Greek universities: A slow moving process. *Financial Accountability and Management, 20*, 183–204.

Worthington, A. C., & Higgs, H. (2011). Economies of scale scope in Australian higher education. *Higher Education, 62*, 387–414.

Yamamoto, K. (2004). Corporatization of national universities in Japan: Revolution for governance or rhetoric for downsizing? *Financial Accountability and Management, 20*, 153–181.

Index

—